Lucretius II

Lucretius II

An Ethics of Motion

Thomas Nail

EDINBURGH
University Press

Edinburgh University Press is one of the leading university presses in the UK. We publish academic books and journals in our selected subject areas across the humanities and social sciences, combining cutting-edge scholarship with high editorial and production values to produce academic works of lasting importance. For more information visit our website: edinburghuniversitypress.com

© Thomas Nail, 2020

Edinburgh University Press Ltd
The Tun – Holyrood Road, 12(2f) Jackson's Entry, Edinburgh EH8 8PJ

Typeset in 10.5/13pt Monotype Baskerville by
Servis Filmsetting Ltd, Stockport, Cheshire

A CIP record for this book is available from the British Library

ISBN 978 1 4744 6663 9 (hardback)
ISBN 978 1 4744 6665 3 (webready PDF)
ISBN 978 1 4744 6664 6 (paperback)
ISBN 978 1 4744 6666 0 (epub)

The right of Thomas Nail to be identified as the author of this work has been asserted in accordance with the Copyright, Designs and Patents Act 1988, and the Copyright and Related Rights Regulations 2003 (SI No. 2498).

Contents

A Note on the Translation and Text — vi
Acknowledgements — vii
Preface — viii

Introduction — 1

Book III
1. A Matter of Desire — 15
2. Kinophobia — 44
3. Critique of Kinetic Reason — 64
4. Dark Materialism — 85
5. The Ethics of Motion — 112

Book IV
6. Ethics of the Simulacrum — 147
7. All Perceptions are True — 169
8. The Material Unconscious — 191

Conclusion — 211

Index — 216

A Note on the Translation and Text

All quotations and citations from *De Rerum Natura* are cited from the Latin by book and line number. For English translations of the Latin I have followed Walter Englert's translation, *Lucretius: On the Nature of Things* (Newburyport, MA: Focus Publishing, 2003), sometimes modifying it slightly, and in some cases I have left the Latin words entirely untranslated. For example, in most places I keep the Latin word *corpora* instead of using the English translation 'atom'. For the Latin text I used the online edition at the Perseus Digital Library and the Loeb edition, Carus T. Lucretius, *De Rerum Natura* (Cambridge, MA: Harvard University Press, 1992).

In my own translations and commentary I have followed P. G. Glare, *Oxford Latin Dictionary* (Oxford: Clarendon Press, 1982), and Charlton T. Lewis and Charles Short, *A Latin Dictionary: Founded on Andrews' Edition of Freund's Latin Dictionary* (Oxford: Clarendon Press, 1879).

Acknowledgements

I am indebted to several places and people for their support and encouragement of this project. I am thankful to Harvard Gulch Park in Denver and my continually fruitful late-night strolls there with Josh Hanan and Chris Gamble (and Ryan Johnson who joined us there one beautiful moonlit winter night).

During the writing of this book St John's College offered me the rare invitation to present my work to a room full of students and faculty who had all read Lucretius – and I am thankful for all their feedback in this volume and to my hosts Raoni Padui and Maggie Evans McGuinness.

In the publication of this book I am grateful for the extremely detailed and generous feedback given to me by my anonymous reviewers. They helped make this book better than it was. I also greatly appreciated the editorial and proofing work of Dan Thomas and proofing work of Jacob Tucker. I thank Edinburgh University Press, and in particular Carol Macdonald, for her continued support and excitement about this three-volume project, as well as for her kindness, to which everyone who has worked with her can attest.

I would like to thank my family and especially my wife, Katie, for her continued support and feedback. They are the material conditions without which this work would not have been possible. I continue to be grateful, finally, to the South Carolina coast (and Kim and Lane Riddle) where I have returned to read Lucretius and watch the summer waves each time before writing.

Preface

A new Lucretius is coming into view today. Every great historical epoch returns to him like bees returning to their flower fields in search of nourishment. Each time, though, our return is different – like the expanding arc of a spiral. We bring new questions, find new answers, and make Lucretius speak to us again as if for the first time. We make Lucretius' epic poem *De Rerum Natura* into the mellifluous honey of a liquid antiquity that has always coursed through the veins of modernity like a spring of fresh meaning and inspiration.[1]

We thus return to Lucretius not as though he were an unchanging figure carved in stone but as if he were a rush of new life at the cutting edge of the twenty-first century. We stand in front of Lucretius' breathtaking and revolutionary poem not as passive students of unchanging relics in a museum but as active participants in a history of our present. Today, we are asking Lucretius again to tell us something about *nature*.[2]

I first returned to Lucretius in 2014, when I taught Book II of *De Rerum Natura* for a class on the philosophy of movement. I added Lucretius to the syllabus because he was an overlooked figure in the history of philosophy who wrote about motion. I was excited about the text, but I was also sceptical that anyone who believed in 'eternal unchanging atoms' could have *motion* as their philosophical starting point. What I encountered, however, absolutely shocked me.

There were no atoms. I scoured the whole Latin text. Lucretius never used the word 'atom' or a Latinised version of this word – not even once. Translators added the word 'atom'. Just as shockingly, I could not find the great isolated swerve in the rain of atoms, for which he is so well known. In Book II, Lucretius says instead that matter is *always* 'in the habit of swerving' [*declinare solerent*] (2.221) and *if it were not* [*nisi*], 'all would fall like raindrops' [*caderent*] (2.222). The solitary swerve and the rain of matter are *counterfactual claims*. Lucretius never said there was a rain and then one atom swerved. He says that matter is in the 'habit' [*solerent*] of swerving, meaning that swerving happens regularly. This, he says, is the only way to avoid the problem of assuming that something comes from nothing: matter must have always been swerving.

This small but significant discrepancy made me wonder what else had been left out of translations and interpretations. Could it be possible that there was a whole hidden Lucretius buried beneath the paving stones of Greek atomism? If there are no solid atoms and no solitary swerve in Lucretius, can we still make sense of the rest of the book? In 2016 I decided to find out. I dedicated a whole seminar just to Book I of *De Rerum Natura* read in Latin. To my delight a whole new view on this foundational text emerged that year. I published the results of this study in 2018 as *Lucretius I: An Ontology of Motion*.

Around this time I also began to notice an increasing number of major differences between Lucretius and Epicurus. One of the reasons I thought I would find atoms and isolated swerves in Lucretius was because of a long history of interpretation that conflated the two thinkers, just as earlier scholars had errantly done with Democritus and Epicurus.[3] There is no doubt that Lucretius studied and followed Epicurus, just as Epicurus had followed Democritus.[4] However, between the three thinkers there are worlds of difference that have not been sufficiently understood. Not all students *merely* imitate their masters. Sometimes imitation functions as a mask for a student to put forward her or his own ideas – which is what Lucretius did.[5] I thus began to unravel the 'Epicurean myth of Lucretius'.[6]

Lucretius did something very strange. He wrote Epicurean philosophy in the style and method of Homeric poetry and in doing so ended up completely changing the meaning of both.[7] Just like an ancient satyr play, Lucretius' poem has numerous invocations of bacchanalian intoxication,[8] sexual imagery, desire,[9] and deceptive invocations of gods he does not believe in (Venus and Mars), all affirmed joyfully alongside the destructive power of nature itself: death. This is in stark contrast with the contemplative, serious, pessimistic, and aloof style of Epicurus and his followers.

Epicurus had many Greek and Roman followers who wrote and promoted Epicurean doctrine,[10] but Lucretius did something no one had ever done before. He espoused a version of Epicurean philosophy in a book of Latin poetry written in Homeric hexameter. Why? For pleasure. He wanted to make something new by mixing the old traditions.

Lucretius performed a bewildering hybrid of two completely opposed figures and traditions (Homer and Epicurus) and made something novel: something uniquely Roman.

However, *De Rerum Natura* has largely been treated as a Homeric poem *about* Epicurean philosophy, but in this book I argue that there is also a hidden Epicurean philosophy of Homeric myth. In the end this is where the real brilliance and originality of Lucretius lies: not in Homer or Epicurus but in their perverse and twisted entanglement. There is thus a *becoming* Homer of Epicurus. It is a genuine injustice to reduce such a radical enterprise to *mere* Epicurean 'doctrine'.

The idea of philosophical *poetry* is a satyr's slap in the face to the entire Greek tradition of philosophy from Thales to Aristotle, *including Epicurus*.[11] With few exceptions, Greek philosophers systematically reduced Homeric poetry to irrational and sensuous mythology in order to define their new abstractions and idealisms against the straw man of the oral tradition. This was a founding moment of exclusion that has stayed with the Western tradition up to the present – contributing to a perceived inferiority of oral and indigenous knowledge. It is therefore completely unsurprising that today, when Lucretius is invoked as a philosopher, he is treated as completely reducible to the *real* Greek master: Epicurus. By doing so, the Western reception of Lucretius has reproduced the same Grecocentric and idealist tradition that vilified pre-Greek and Homeric poetry and archaic materialism. This is the same Western tradition that continues to devalorise oral knowledge and non-Western mythologies today.

Most Western philosophy, even in its most materialist moments, has in one way or another hated matter and the body.[12] Lucretius was the first from within this tradition to produce a true and radical materialism of sensation and the body. However, like Homer, Lucretius also paid the ultimate price for his materialist sins and was largely exiled from the discipline of philosophy. Either Lucretius was treated as a skilled poet of the Latin tongue *or* he was treated as a slavish imitator of the great master Epicurus. Never has Lucretius been read as an *original* philosophical poet of a radical materialism that goes far beyond anything Epicurus achieved. This book and its companion volumes are the first books to show precisely this.

Even more provocatively, Lucretius refused to use Epicurus' Greek terminology when many other Epicurean and Roman authors, such as Cicero, did so often and easily. The Romans are famous for renaming

Greek gods: the Greek Aphrodite becomes the Roman Venus, Zeus becomes Jove, and so on. However, it is also well known that there is no strict equivalence between the two deities. The translation was, as translations always are, a transformation that resulted in new stories and a shifting fluidity of roles among the gods. This, I argue, is what happened with Lucretius. *De Rerum Natura* was not written as Epicurean dogma.[13] It was an original work of philosophical poetry that translated Homeric mythology and Epicurean philosophy into the Latin vernacular and thus transformed them into an original philosophy of motion. A few scholars have noted the tension between Lucretius' poetic style and Epicurean doctrine, but none has suggested that it indicated anything philosophically original as a result.[14]

The unearthing of this 'hidden Lucretius' is the subject of the present work and its companion volumes. In the first volume, *Lucretius I: An Ontology of Motion*, I located a systematic ontology of motion and a new materialism beneath the atomist and Epicurean myth of Lucretius. In the present volume, I present the reader with a unique kinetic theory of *ethics*. This second volume builds on the ontological framework developed in the first and expands it explicitly to questions of life, death, knowledge, aesthetics, sex, ecology, and ethics – as they are discussed in Books III and IV of *De Rerum Natura*.

Each of the three volumes in this trilogy has been written so that it may be read either on its own or with the others. The themes of each of the volumes of the trilogy overlap with one another just as the content of the books in the poem do. However, each volume also focuses on distinct domains of philosophical inquiry: Volume I covers Lucretius' ontology and cosmology; Volume II covers his ethics, epistemology, and aesthetics; and Volume III, his theory of history. Together, these three volumes compose an original and nearly line-by-line reading of the entirety of *De Rerum Natura*.

Notes

1. Brooke Holmes, Dakis Joannou, and Karen Marta (eds), *Liquid Antiquity* (Cologne: König Books, 2017).
2. Pierre Vesperini, *Lucrèce: archéologie d'un classique européen* (Paris: Fayard, 2017), 13.
3. See Karl Marx, *The First Writings of Karl Marx*, trans. Paul M. Schafer (New York: Ig Publishing, 2006).

4. David Sedley, *Lucretius and the Transformation of Greek Wisdom* (Cambridge: Cambridge University Press, 2009).
5. See Vesperini, *Lucrèce*. Epicureanism was one of the most popular philosophical schools.
6. See Vesperini, *Lucrèce*, chs 12 and 13.
7. See Vesperini, *Lucrèce*.
8. See Thomas Nail, *Lucretius I: An Ontology of Motion* (Edinburgh: Edinburgh University Press, 2018), ch. 8.
9. Nail, *Lucretius I*, 43–50.
10. The most famous Roman Epicurean was Philodemus of Gadara (c. 110–c. 40 or 35 BCE).
11. Rare exceptions include the Greek philosophical poets Xenophanes, Parmenides, and Empedocles.
12. Carolyn Merchant, *The Death of Nature: Women, Ecology, and the Scientific Revolution* (San Francisco: HarperOne, 2008).
13. For an extremely well-argued defence of this point, see Vesperini, *Lucrèce*.
14. See Monica Gale, *Oxford Readings in Lucretius* (Oxford: Oxford University Press, 2007), 3; Vesperini, *Lucrèce*; Gale, 'Lucretius and Previous Poetic Traditions', in Stuart Gillespie and Philip Hardie (eds), *The Cambridge Companion to Lucretius* (Cambridge: Cambridge University Press, 2012), 59–75; James Warren, 'Lucretius and Greek Philosophy', in Gillespie and Hardie (eds), *Cambridge Companion to Lucretius*, 19–32.

Introduction

We are entering a century of motion. More than at any other time in history, people and things move longer distances, more frequently, more unequally, and more quickly than ever before. All that was solid has melted into air, and we are now all adrift like motes of dust on turbulent winds. In the world of the twenty-first century, movement and mobility increasingly define every major area of human activity, from society, science, and the arts to nature itself.

We know now, for example, that the entire universe is accelerating away from us in every direction, driven by a mysterious 'dark matter', and that all of reality consists of continuously fluctuating quantum fields. Digital images stream across the globe along these same fluctuating fields through mobile devices that connect the whole world in beautiful and precarious ways. These same flows also allow more people to move around the world than ever before in human history. We are living in an age of mass migration, when there are more than 1 billion migrants. As carbon dioxide levels and global temperatures rise, the Earth itself is now becoming more mobile. Even glaciers are on the move,[1] alongside half of all flora and fauna, migrating north at unprecedented rates.[2] Rising sea levels threaten to displace millions more people in the coming years.[3]

This *hyperkinetic modernity* poses new ethical questions that require new ethical frameworks and responses appropriate to our century. We need a new ethics that takes seriously the real historical primacy of motion and mobility that defines our age. If motion and mobility increasingly define our arts and sciences, why shouldn't ethics respond to this situation as well? We need an ethics that is responsive to our mobile lives and that takes human migration as a constitutive and foundational aspect of all social reality. As the entire biosphere changes, we need an ethics that is sensitive to the agency of matters both living and non-living.

It seems that everything is on the move today except our ethical theories and ways of thinking about the world. It is time for *new* ideas, even if those new ideas come from *old* books. The argument of this book is that we can find precisely such new ethical ideas in an unlikely source: an ancient volume of Roman poetry.

An Ethics of Motion

What new ethical idea can help us navigate the turbulent waters of the twenty-first century? I think Lucretius provides us with a least one answer to this question: an ethics *of motion*. What kind of ethics does this give us, and what problems does it solve in current ethical theory? I think it gives us four things:

1. It provides a strikingly contemporary and naturalistic foundation for all hitherto existing ethical theories. Ethics, like most of Western philosophy, has tended to locate its ground in human minds or human bodies, but has failed to explain how these so-called special ethical minds and bodies are the result of supposedly *unethical* natural processes in the first place. Lucretius' ethics of motion helps us better understand and reinterpret the material and naturalistic foundations of ethical practice.

2. It shows in detail several major errors in ethical thinking. For Lucretius, these errors all stem from the same source: the fear of death and the belief in transcendent sources of value. The purpose of the demystification of normative ethics is to help us to avoid falling prey to the unnecessary suffering that such sources produce, and instead direct us towards the realisation of our own immanent and collective desires within and alongside the natural world.

3. The materialist ethics of this book also provides us with a badly needed ethical theory that is *not centred* on human beings and biological life. Ethics, for Lucretius, is not something that originates with life or with the human intellect and is then applied to other types of beings. Lucretius argues, quite radically, that ethics is something that humans share with the rest of nature because we are all in motion. Lucretius thus offers us a non-chauvinistic ethics much better suited to responding to climate change and ecological crisis than our current anthropocentric models, including those that 'extend rights' to or find 'intrinsic values' in nature.

4. Finally, Lucretius' kinetic ethics provides us with a user's guide (rather than moral commandments) to managing our collective desires.

Ethical habits, for Lucretius, are not fixed in stone but require us to continuously reproduce them. Therefore we can, in principle, always produce something new. Lucretius also offers us several thermodynamic lessons about the energetic precarity of beings-in-motion and the material risks associated with energetic accumulation and expenditure.

This is, in short summary, an introduction to what I think Lucretius can offer us today.

Lucretian Ethics

But is there such a thing as a 'Lucretian ethics'? The almost universal answer to this question has historically been 'no': there is only an Epicurean ethics that Lucretius ventriloquised. One of the main arguments of this book is that there is a distinct Lucretian ethics – different from Epicurus and from other contemporary ethicists as well. The argument for this spans the length of this book and must be proven in textual detail. Below is only a brief introduction to some of the main differences.

Against Stasis, Against *ataraxia*

First of all, Lucretius' ethics is different from hedonism and asceticism – both attributed to Epicurus. Oddly enough, the most frequent interpretations of Epicurus' ethics seem completely opposed to one another. Epicurus sounds like a hedonist because he says pleasure is the highest good, but he is also sounds like an ascetic because he says that the maximum amount of pleasure one can obtain can be achieved only by detaching oneself from pleasure through self-discipline. More precisely, however, Epicurus called this highest ethical ideal ἀταραξία (*ataraxía*), meaning 'untroubled' or 'undisturbed', from the Greek word ταράσσω (*tarássō*, 'trouble, disturb'). The highest good, for Epicurus, is therefore to have no pain and no pleasure. This is achieved through a simple life of individual contemplation.

For Epicurus there are two kinds of pleasures: *katastematic* pleasures and kinetic pleasures. *Katastematic* pleasures are those that occur in the absence of pain [*aponia*] and in an undisturbed mind [*ataraxia*]. Kinetic pleasures, however, are those that occur through movement and action. The aim of Epicurean ethics is to attain the former and try one's best to steer clear of the latter. For Epicurus, only the gods exist in perfect *ataraxia*.

There are without doubt similarities between Lucretian and Epicurean ethics, but let's focus on two important differences. First and most important, for Lucretius there are only kinetic sensations because all of matter is in motion, including the mind. The interconnected, unceasing, and continuous movement of the mind, body, and soul is the main thesis of Book III. Lucretius is explicit in numerous places that there is nothing static in nature.[4] The mind cannot escape movement through egoistic contemplation. Thus one never will find Lucretius saying, as Epicurus does, that one should try and avoid all kinetic pleasures.

On the contrary, Lucretius' poem is filled with sensuous scenes of moving desire the like of which Epicurus would never have dreamed of writing, such as the erotic love scene between Venus and Mars (1.32–5), the poet's own intoxication and orgiastic penetration by the 'wand' of Bacchus (1.927–34), the auto-erotics of bodies along the riverbanks (2.29–33), and the ecstatic convulsions of reading philosophy (3.28–9). Lucretius even opens *De Rerum Natura* with a proem to Venus: the desire and pleasure of gods and men (1.1). There is perhaps no less Epicurean a way to open an Epicurean treatise than an invocation of a Venusian nature overflowing with desire, sex, war, and death, as Lucretius offers. However, Lucretius also never says that 'pleasure is the highest good'. He even explicitly warns against the dangers of romantic idealism (4.1121–40).

So Lucretius is neither a hedonist nor an ascetic, nor does he think there is any *ataraxia* in nature. This leads to a second difference with Epicurus: if there is no *ataraxia* in nature because matter is ceaselessly moving (2.97–9), then there can be no motionless and unperturbed Epicurean gods, either. Such gods are explicitly impossible for Lucretius, and so he invokes them only as ideas that 'sprung from [Epicurus'] mind' (3.14).

Against Transcendent Values

With the following simple philosophical statement, Lucretius opens up an entirely new ethical path: *everything moves*. If all of nature moves, there can be no unchanging, pregiven, or transcendent ethical values. Ethics is entirely immanent to action and sensuous practice. This means that there is no Platonic or metaphysical category of 'the good' for Lucretius. It also means that there are no Aristotelian virtues, either. Since virtues are by definition good things to do, the origin of this goodness that all virtues have in common only raises the metaphysical question of how such virtues became good in the first place. For Lucretius, there are no virtues or even any fixed definitions of virtues that precede or exceed the human movements that produce them materially, practically, and historically.

Furthermore, if everything is in motion, then hedonism, asceticism, and utilitarianism are unable to determine in advance what will produce pleasure and what will produce pain. This is especially problematic in the case of the creation of *new* unknown pleasures. Lucretius explicitly rejects any attempt to calculate the wildly different and changing pleasures and pains of different people and creatures (3.310–15). This does not mean that there are not situations of more or less pain for certain beings; it just means that the search for pleasure cannot be the *a priori* starting point of ethics. Pleasure-oriented theories all assume the existence of rational humans capable of the pleasure calculus, rather than showing how the value of pleasure itself emerged historically and practically in the first place. For Lucretius, pleasure and happiness have to be made through movement; they do not pre-exist the practical and sensuous conditions of movement.

Finally, and for similar reasons, for Lucretius there is no such thing as a static, universal, moral duty independent of the historical and sensuous actions that are affected by moral demands and actively reproduce them. Humans might perform various duties *as if* they were universal, ahistorical, and given from a god or human reason, but duty ethics offers no explanation of its own origin in nature.

In one way or another, all these ethical theories assume the existence of a transcendent value that simply exists without any explanation or theory of how such a theory could have emerged from nature in the first place. Ethics has largely abandoned nature. Instead, ethicists tend to posit the origin of such values in an unmoving human rationality, god, or other 'non-natural' form. Ethics has thus historically subordinated matter and motion to some other value as if this value did not *come from matter and motion itself.* For Lucretius, such ethical theories obscure the real desires of those performing them. The danger of this mystification, according to Lucretius, is that we become slaves to these ideas as if they had some kind of autonomy over our collective reproduction of them.

Lucretius' brilliant move was not to deny the existence of ethical practice but to provide a material, kinetic, and naturalist theory of its emergence. Lucretius thus gave us the first truly immanent ethical philosophy. He gave us an ethics that does not assume the existence of any transcendent value, but rather showed us how value itself emerges from nature and how new values and pleasures can be made.

Today the world is in motion, but our ethics are still based on ideas of *static* values. Something is wrong with this picture. One of the core arguments of this book and of Lucretius' philosophy more generally is that these static and unchanging moral theories stem from a fear of death. If there are transcendent and ahistorical values and we can think them, we believe this allows us to participate directly in their 'immortality' in some way. By participating in and contemplating such metaphysical values, including the *a priori* valorisation of sensuous pleasure or happiness, humans feel they have discovered something unchanging and fixed about nature. We have come to think of ethical abstraction and moral obedience as weapons against death.

Even contemporary neoliberal capitalism, for all its mobility, dynamism, adaptability, and responsiveness, remains obsessed with the static metaphysical belief in economic *value*: the belief in a quality-less *abstract quantity* of human labour time. Nothing could be more contrary to the vision of nature described by Lucretius than this.[5]

In direct contrast to nature's constantly changing and dissipating flow of matter, capitalist economics is also premised on the false notion of equality of exchange or equivalence. In nature, however, there is no such thing. Nature, for Lucretius, is neither identical to itself at any point nor identical between points. Matter always flows asymmetrically, entropically, and in metastable patterns of increasing non-equilibrium. Equivalence and equilibrium are, physically speaking, for Lucretius, violations of the historical tendency of the universe to kinetically dissipate and expend itself.

By acting *as if* equivalence, equilibrium, identity, and exchange are real aspects of nature, however, economics, and capitalist economics in particular, have increasingly damaged the Earth. When we act as if nature moves in one way when it really moves in another, huge disruptions in those motions occur. Capitalist constructivists have acted as if they could simply make up or construct a set of rules or values on top of nature and live in their own reality. They are like someone swimming upstream while insisting that it is the easiest and most natural way to move in the river.

Classical, neoclassical, and orthodox economic theory also acts as if economic exchange were a *reversible* process – when physically speaking, it is not. The philosophical assumption of economics since Hume has been that *scarcity* is the basis and starting point of economics – when, again, nothing of the sort exists in nature. The ideas of equivalence, equilibrium, reversibility, and scarcity are false – meaning that they have never been found in nature.

By acting *as if* a commodity were strictly identical to its exchange value (how much money it is exchanged for), capitalist economics have not considered the ecological impacts of deforestation, pollution, and climate change or the human impacts of social devalorisation (racism, sexism, classism) as integral and constitutive aspects of the economic process. These devalued flows of matter literally have 'no value'. As Marx rightly says, capitalists act *as if* the product is *abstracted* or independent from the process that produced it. As a counter-example, if we assigned even a modest monetary value to the energy expenditure of trees and plants, to women's domestic labour, or to migration and human displacement, profit would be impossible. In short, all economics, and capitalist economics in particular, requires the constitutive exclusion of the material kinetic conditions that support its abstract exchange process.

By privileging *life*, accumulation, conservation, and utility, capitalism devalorises and destroys everything it associates with death, expenditure, reciprocity, and non-useful waste. Hence, we have witnessed a long history of ecocide, indigenous genocide, slavery, patriarchy, forced migration, and biopolitics. Lucretius gave us the basic ontological and ethical diagnostic of this problem light-years ahead of his time.

The fear of death motivates all manner of metaphysical values and idealisms because we think death is a negativity or lack. We think that death and matter are inert and passive. The Western tradition fears nothing more than becoming 'nothing', and has invented all kinds of ideas to try and escape this fate (God, the soul, reason, and capitalism). This fear of death is also connected to the Western tradition's deep-seated hatred of matter and motion in all their manifestations (women, racial others, the poor, animals, nature, queer desires).[6] Hence, the increasing importance of recovering a new materialist and kinetic ethics today.

Even Epicurus' calm contemplation of eternal unchanging atoms falls prey to the same idealist fantasy found in Democritus' static atoms.[7] In contrast, however, I argue that Lucretius is a true materialist and an ethical naturalist. He alone embraced death because he alone believed in the active and creative power of continuously moving matter.

These are only the broad strokes of what Lucretian ethics is *not*.

But what *is* Lucretian ethics? Our answer begins in the next chapter. However, before turning to the details of Lucretius' ethical theory, a few methodological notes are in order to prepare the reader for how this book will proceed.

Method

This book is structured around four methodological axes.

Historical Ontology

We always come to a text-in-motion and from our own historical and geographical trajectories. Texts are not static things with fixed meanings determined by author or reception, but as material bodies they have their own agency and changing patterns. Every reading of a text is an event or process of collective creation between a variety of processes, including author, reader, text, geography, and history – like a story told by other stories. As historical processes the author, reader, and text are never fully present to themselves but enter into new combinations. Their being is *in motion*.[8]

However, this does not mean that rereadings of texts are arbitrary, or up to the free construction of human subjects who have nothing to do with the real being of the text. Each new reading is an iteration or rewriting of the real text inside the text, as a real dimension of the text. Accordingly, this book is not an attempt to fix an absolute meaning to Lucretius forever and all time, but rather to unfold another real dimension inside or beneath the old one. Each interpretation is like a simulacral membrane peeling off the text. It is not a copy but a real piece or aspect of the text.

Thus, the method of his book is *historical* in the sense that it is situated along specific geographical and temporal trajectories, but it is also *ontological* in the sense that its intersection with the text bears directly on the moving-reality of the text itself. This book is an intersection of paths or trajectories that, when looked at from a certain position, produce a real pattern or constellation.

Close Reading

This book is structured by a close reading of Books III and IV of *De Rerum Natura*, in which Lucretius puts forward his core ethical theory. Book III is about the mortality of the mind, body, and soul and argues against a static ethics of Epicurean contemplation. Since ethics has been largely idealist, Lucretius counters this first by providing a material and kinetic theory of the mind, body, and soul that produces such powerful abstractions in the first place. Here we get a fascinating new ethico-epistemology.

Book IV is about the powers of the mind, body, and soul. Here Lucretius argues against the existence of anything like an ideal or non-sensuous transcendent value. Lucretius gives us instead an ethics grounded in the sensuous movement of images. In other words he gives us a new ethico-aesthetics. The chapters and main headings of this book proceed sequentially, topic by topic, through the text. The purpose of this method is to show systematically and textually, not just argumentatively, that Lucretius had an ethics of motion and not an Epicurean theory of *ataraxia*.

Translation

The third methodological axis is translation. In this volume, I continue to leave untranslated the Latin word *corpora* to highlight the absence of any language of atoms, just as I did in *Lucretius I*. I also continue to stress the crucial difference between Lucretius' words for 'matter' [*corpora, semina, rerum primordia*] and his words for 'thing' [*rerum, rebus, res*], which are often conceptually and terminologically conflated in translation. Additionally, in this volume I have often translated the Latin term *primordia* as 'first-threads' in order to highlight its connection to the abundance of weaving and folding terminology used in Books III and IV: *textum, nexus, plexum, calathus, exordia*.

Perhaps more than any other books in *De Rerum Natura*, Books III and IV rely on weaving terminology and images to develop their core theories of mind, body, soul, perception, desire, and dreams. Therefore, I have also chosen to emphasise weaving terminology in order to show that instead of atoms, in Lucretius we find *flows* or *threads* of *woven matter*. If Lucretius is talking about discrete unchanging atoms then the consistent deployment of weaving images in the poem makes no sense whatsoever, because *atoms cannot fold or weave.*

Furthermore, the kinetic act of translation itself means that no one, especially not Epicurus, can be 'the last word' on the meaning of *De Rerum Natura*. Lucretius' act of translation actively makes something new and perhaps monstrous inside Epicurus that goes well beyond authorial intention and stems directly from a transfiguration particular to the

Latin language and culture. There is no translation that is not also a transformation. This is true both of Lucretius' reading of Epicurus and my reading of Lucretius, translating from Latin to English.

Lucretius says he is '*turning*' Epicurus' philosophy 'into my fatherly/native words' [*in patrias qui possim vertere voces*] (5.337). The Latin word *vertere*, to turn, takes on a crucial meaning here because it also refers to the unpredictable and unrepresentable 'swerve' of matter. Lucretius is not just copying Epicurus; he is twisting, turning, and swerving him in new directions. Lucretius was not deaf to the resonances of the word *ver-* in *ver-tere* in his '*Latinis ver-sibus*' (1.137; verses are things that 'turn') in which he is considering the question of 'truth' [*ver-um*] by associating it with the dynamic changes of 'spring' [*ver*].[9]

Argumentation

The fourth axis is composed of several argumentative theses directly supported by the close textual reading. These are: 1) Lucretius was not an Epicurean atomist, 2) Lucretius developed his own unique philosophical system in which movement and matter were primary, and 3) Lucretius developed a unique kinetic and materialist ethics, epistemology, and aesthetics consistent with his ontology and physics from Books I and II.

I also believe that Lucretius' ethical theory is a promising starting point for thinking about contemporary ethical issues. However, this book will not be able both to argue that such an ethics exists and then apply it to all our contemporary problems. If the reader is interested to see more precisely how the philosophy of movement contributes to thinking about the big contemporary events of our time, I refer them to my other books on these topics.[10] My hope for this book in particular is that others will find this unique movement-oriented ethical framework useful in their own ways to issues they care about.

Each chapter of this book thus uses close reading, original translation, and argumentation together to show the big picture of what is going on in the text.

Conclusion

If we are entering a century of motion, then we are going to need some new ethical and theoretical tools to think through some of the biggest events of our time. Although it might seem strange that such a new ethics would come from such an old and apparently obscure book, I would like to remind the reader that every epoch, since the rediscovery of *De Rerum Natura* in the fifteenth century, has returned to this incredible book. Virtually all the greatest minds of Western culture, including scientists, philosophers, artists, and political thinkers, have read this book and derived new inspiration.

Importantly, however, each age has also differed significantly in its interpretations and translations.[11] Each age has made Lucretius answer *its* questions. There is thus not one Lucretius forever and for all time. Each age has its own Lucretius. This is what I think we are rediscovering today and what I hope this book can contribute to: a Lucretius for our time.

Notes

1. Samantha Page, 'World's Glaciers Melting Faster Than Ever Before Recorded, Study Finds', *Think Progress*, 5 August 2015, https://thinkprogress.org/worlds-glaciers-melting-faster-than-ever-before-recorded-study-finds-3ee73aa09038/ (accessed 10 September 2019).
2. Craig Welch, 'Half of All Species Are on the Move – And We're Feeling It'. *National Geographic*, 27 April 2017, https://news.nationalgeographic.com/2017/04/climate-change-species-migration-disease/ (accessed 10 September 2019).
3. Geoff Brumfiel, 'Sea Levels Rose Faster Last Century than in Previous 2,700 Years, Study Finds', National Public Radio, 23 February 2016, https://www.npr.org/sections/thetwo-way/2016/02/23/467813673/sea-levels-rose-faster-last-century-than-in-previous-2-700-years-study-finds (accessed 10 September 2019).
4. See Thomas Nail, *Lucretius I: An Ontology of Motion* (Edinburgh: Edinburgh University Press, 2018).
5. See Thomas Nail, *Marx: The Birth of Value*, unpublished manuscript, under review with Oxford University Press; Thomas Nail, *Theory of the Earth*, unpublished manuscript, under review with Oxford University Press.
6. See Mel Chen, *Animacies* (Durham, NC: Duke University Press, 2012).
7. See Thomas Nail, *Being and Motion* (Oxford: Oxford University Press, 2018), ch. 3 and Part III for a critique of the vitalist tradition up to Gilles Deleuze. Even Baruch Spinoza's atomistic vitalism is part of the historical fear of death and inorganic materialism.

8. See Nail, *Being and Motion*.
9. Jane M. Snyder, *Puns and Poetry in Lucretius' De rerum natura* (Amsterdam: Gruner, 1980).
10. Thomas Nail, *The Figure of the Migrant* (Stanford: Stanford University Press, 2015); Thomas Nail, *Theory of the Border* (Oxford: Oxford University Press, 2016); Nail, *Being and Motion*; Thomas Nail, *Theory of the Image* (Oxford: Oxford University Press, 2019); Thomas Nail, *Theory of the Object*, unpublished manuscript, under review with Oxford University Press; *Theory of the Earth*, unpublished manuscript.
11. For a study of the reception of Lucretius, see Catherine Wilson, *Epicureanism at the Origins of Modernity* (Oxford: Clarendon Press, 2008).

Book III

1. A Matter of Desire

Lucretius provides us with an ethics of motion relevant to the twenty-first century. Ethics, however, for Lucretius, is also inseparable from the physics of motion, the mind, and the body that compose ethical beings. To understand what ethics is and how an ethical life is lived, we must first understand something about the nature of ethical beings themselves. This is why Lucretius frames Books III and IV around the physical nature of mind and body. Lucretius has already alluded to the ethical importance of physics at the beginning of Books I and II, but in Books III and IV he connects these general physical principles to the working of the body and mind as they create, reproduce, and change their ethical practices.

The aim of this chapter is to begin our description of Lucretius' ethics of motion. We therefore begin where Lucretius begins, at the beginning of Book III, by introducing the main inspiration for his ethical theory: Epicurus (3.1–30). In these lines, the two main areas of the ethics of motion are introduced: the material nature of desire and the primacy of movement.

Briefly though, before we develop Lucretius' ethical theory, we first have to set up the basic philosophical orientation of his work, *contra* Epicurus. In short, the argument of this chapter is that Lucretius was inspired by, but does not adopt, the Epicurean ethics of *ataraxia* and *katastematic* pleasure.[1] By contrast, ethics, for Lucretius, is grounded in the physical movement of desire and expenditure. This is the starting point of his materialist ethics.

Against Religion

The primary enemy of ethics, for Lucretius, is *religio*. The Latin word *religio*, which is also the etymological origin of the English word 'religion', comes from the Latin root *lig*, meaning 'to bind' or 'confine'. Lucretius understands all transcendent values as kinds of bindings that restrict our movements. Epicurus is celebrated in Book I for *traversing* a limitless universe [*peragravit*] (1.74) just as Lucretius says he traversed [*peragro*] (1.926) the 'pathless' ground of the Muses' mountains.

Book III thus begins its ethics of motion by recalling the most important historical contribution to the critique of religion: Epicurus' philosophy.[2] Lucretius describes Epicurus' revolt against religion in detail in Book I (1.61–5), but in Book III he explicitly connects it to the conditions of ethical life [*commoda vitae*] (3.2). This is achieved in the two opening lines of the proem of Book III (3.1–2).

*E tenebris tantis tam clarum extollere lumen
qui primus potuisti inlustrans commoda vitae,*

You were the first who was able to lift up so clear a light
amidst such deep shadows and illuminate the conditions of a pleasurable life,

Epicurus was the one who first discovered the material-kinetic conditions for all that is [*sunt omnia*] (1.61) and thus for ethical action as well. In Book I Lucretius dramatised Epicurus' critique of religion by saying that before Epicurus, humans had crushed themselves under the weight of religion. Before Epicurus, humanity appeared [*oculos*] as a foul and rotting form of life [*Humana ante oculos foede cum vita*] (1.62) which lay fallow, idle, and inactive [*iaceret*] (1.62) because it was crushed into the ground by the gravity and weight of religion [*in terris oppressa gravi sub religione*] (1.63), whose horrible head [*quae caput horribili super*] (1.64–5) stretched down from Heaven [*a caeli regionibus ostendebat*] (1.64) and stood upon mortals [*mortalibus instans*] (1.65). In other words, the dark shadows [*tenebris*] (3.1) that Lucretius is referring to in the opening lines of Book III is the darkness that humans see when they are crushed by the weight of religion with their faces down in the muck. Religion and all metaphysical abstractions that posit the existence of values that transcend all of nature and history do not exist for Lucretius. Religion is dark because it is practically blind to nature.

However, since religion is an abstraction of the mind, humans are not crushed by anything *outside* themselves. There is nothing external to critique or destroy. Therefore Epicurus' great revolution, according to Lucretius, was simply to stand up with his feet crushing down religion [*religio pedibus subiecta*] (1.78) lifting himself up [*tollere*] (1.66) into the light.

In the opening lines of Book III Lucretius combines these ideas from Book I beautifully by saying that Epicurus lifted up so clear a light [*extollere lumen*] (3.1). This is not metaphysical light, the light of absolute truth, reason, or God outside Plato's cave. It is 'the external appearance and *inner conditions of nature*' [*naturae species ratioque*], the material conditions [*ratioque*] for the appearance [*species*] of nature [*naturae*] (1.148; 3.93). Epicurus opened his eyes and began his ethics and philosophy with sensation and nature.

Before Epicurus stood up he first lifted his *eyes* [*oculos*]; then made a stand [*obsistere*] against religion. His eyes provided the evidence for his 'standing up' to religion. The reference to eyes is important and links lines 1.66–7 to 3.1–2, because in Latin poetic idiom, the eyes can be referred to as *lumina*, 'lights'. Thus the 'light' that Epicurus lifts up for us is what he has observed with his own 'lights'. This is the kinetic and pedetic source of Epicurus' ethics.[3]

What Epicurus found under his feet, Lucretius says, was the real material basis of ethics and of religion: the collective conditions for favourable or pleasurable life [*commoda vitae*] (3.2). The Latin word *commoda* is a composite of *com*, 'together', and *moda*, 'way or method'. *Commoda vitae* is, therefore, a collective way of life or set of actions. The conditions for all ethical life are, for Lucretius, thus collective. Ethics is not just something individuals contemplate and follow on their own. All ethical action takes place in a social and sensuous world. Furthermore, Lucretius does not call this Epicurean discovery a maxim or commandment. *Commoda vitae*, or 'collective ways of pleasurable life', are the conditions for the emergence of ethical life as such and are thus not reducible to any single law or principle of action.

False Footsteps

Lucretius follows the Epicurean ethical revolt against religion but only so far. Lucretius says politely that he is trying to follow Epicurus but that his footsteps are not the same (3.3–6).

> *te sequor, o Graiae gentis decus, inque tuis nunc*
> *ficta pedum pono pressis vestigia signis,*
> *non ita certandi cupidus quam propter amorem*
> *quod te imitari aveo;*

> it is you I follow, O glory of the Greek race, and now
> in the tracks you have laid down I feign to place my feet,
> not so much eager to compete with you but because from love
> I desire to imitate you.

Lucretius uses the language of walking along paths and following traces [*vestigia*] throughout *De Rerum Natura*. It is an absolutely central methodological principle of his philosophy. He talks about walking the path of truth (2.80), about the paths of matter as it falls and swerves (2.124, 2.250), and about the footprints of matter on the sensuous body (2.356). Matter has always been swerving in its path.

Contrary to the common interpretation of the rectilinear rain of atoms in the void, Lucretius is explicit in Book II that matter is always 'in the habit of swerving' [*declinare solerent*] (2.221) and if it were not [*nisi*], 'all would fall like raindrops' [*caderent*] (2.222). Matter moves, and its movement is always a swerving, indeterminate, and deviant movement. For Lucretius the 'path of truth' is not straight but rather curves and twists. This why we need the poet as our guide. The truth is not a static place we reach, or a set of fixed principles, or even a straight path from A to B. Lucretius' poetic method follows precisely the matter he is studying in its swerves and patterns. Philosophical knowledge, like matter, is on the move. We thus understand by walking.

This idea is simply not compatible with the Epicurean idea of *ataraxia*. Lucretius' method overlaps but is not identical to Epicurus', because Lucretius is also following the epic poetic tradition in which thought and speech are directly coordinated with the motion and rhythm of walking, breathing, and speaking. In archaic Greece the poet composed, memorised, and recited by walking.[4] In the tradition of the great philosophical poet Empedocles, Lucretius is composing poetry about nature while on the move. The hexameter regulates one's breath and composes one's thoughts. Epicureans did not reject poetry entirely, but the greatest Epicurean pupil, Philodemus, says, in *On Poems*, that poetry is useless and of no philosophical value.[5] This is obviously *not* Lucretius' position. Philosophy and poetry both happen *in motion*.

So when Lucretius says he follows [*sequor*] (3.3) the footprints [*pressis . . . signis*] (3.4) that Epicurus laid down, we should pay careful attention to his use of the word *ficta*, from the Latin word *fingo*, meaning 'feign', 'falsify', or 'form'. Lucretius' use of *ficta* indicates that he both follows

Epicurus, 'fixes his feet in his tracks', but also deviates, 'feigns or falsifies' them at the same time.[6]

There is no doubt that Lucretius followed Epicurus just as Epicurus followed Democritus, but the three are not identical. The word *sequor* can also mean 'to come after'. Just because someone comes *after* someone else under whom they studied does not mean that they are identical. In this case Lucretius puts his own footprints in his master's, but in doing so leaves new footprints over the top of the master's prints – just as Memmius, the patron of *De Rerum Natura*, tried to build his house on the ruins of Epicurus' house in Athens.[7]

This difference between Lucretius and Epicurus is made especially clear in the fact that Lucretius says he is not staging a direct competition or battle [*certandi*] (3.5) with Epicurus as he did with Empedocles (1.719). Rather, Lucretius desires [*cupidus*] (3.5) to imitate [*imitari*] (3.6) his master out of love [*amorem*] (3.5). But the Latin word *imitari* does not necessarily refer to the Platonic metaphysics of the superiority of the original. In Latin, the rhetorical term *copia*, which vestigially survives in phrases such as 'reporter's copy', means 'source material'. Thus, the ambiguity in the Latin word *imitari*, meaning 'to copy' and 'to counterfeit',[8] and the Latin word *copia* indicate that Lucretius was following Epicurus but also producing something new and not necessarily inferior. It is precisely Lucretius' *desire* to imitate that throws into question his mere passivity as an inferior copy. The true Epicurean does not seek truth or follow the master for the *purpose of pleasure* but for the removal of all pleasure (and pain).

There is thus something about Lucretius' poetic method that is left out and untranslatable into Epicurean philosophy: *the movement of desire*. Lucretius follows the Greek epic and philosophical tradition at the same time and thus remains unfaithful to both in different ways. Lucretius, we could say, is a bit too passionate a follower to be a good and pure Epicurean or even Stoic.[9] The rational tradition of philosophy is not supposed to be seeking pleasure but wisdom. Pleasure, like poetry for Epicureans, has no philosophical value on its own. At worst it can mislead us from the true path.

Lucretius is therefore one of the first in the tradition of philosophy to acknowledge and even affirm philosophy and truth as products of desire: what Friedrich Nietzsche will later call 'the will to know'. In this way truth is not something objective and universal for Lucretius, as it was for Epicurus. Lucretius was not 'first and foremost a missionary', as the famous Lucretian scholar Cyril Bailey once wrote.[10] Ethics, for Lucretius, is not about contemplation – it is about *movement* and *desire* (which are the same thing).

Pedetic Ethics

One of the boldest and most beautiful statements confirming Lucretius' self-awareness of his original method is in the next passage, where he explicitly describes his own poetic failure, or *ficta*, to properly put his feet in the footsteps of Epicurus (3.6–13).

> *quid enim contendat hirundo*
> *cycnis, aut quid nam tremulis facere artubus haedi*
> *consimile in cursu possint et fortis equi vis?*
> *tu, pater, es rerum inventor, tu patria nobis*
> *suppeditas praecepta, tuisque ex, inclute, chartis,*
> *floriferis ut apes in saltibus omnia libant,*
> *omnia nos itidem depascimur aurea dicta,*
> *aurea, perpetua semper dignissima vita.*

> For why would a swallow contend with
> swans, or what can young goats with their shaky legs
> produce in a race to match the powerful energy of a horse?
> You are our father, the discoverer of how things are, you supply us
> with a father's precepts, and from your pages, O illustrious one,
> just as bees sample everything in the flower-strewn meadow,
> so we, too, feed upon all of your golden words,
> golden they are, and always worthy of eternal life.

Lucretius is not just self-deprecating here. It is a classical technique of Roman satire [*satura*] to hide one's novelty behind the mask of inferiority.[11] This is important because Lucretius bases his whole ethics of motion on kinetic action and desire – not rational obedience. Matter is pedetic, swerving, and unpredictable for Lucretius, as is his poetic method and the animals to which he compares himself. The three (materialism, poetry, and animality) are intimately connected in this passage. Understanding this connection is crucial to making sense of Lucretius' materialist ethical deviations from Epicurus and his ecstatic relation to philosophy that comes like a jolt of lightning in lines 3.28–30.

Therefore, to understand what is so unique about Lucretius' philosophical, poetic approach to ethics, we need to look closely at the interconnection of images that he uses to describe himself in relation to Epicurus: the swallow, the goat, and the bee.

Materialist Ethics
Lucretius says he is like a swallow compared to Epicurus the swan. This comparison is absolutely critical but is typically ignored in favour of more rationalist readings of *De Rerum Natura* that ignore Homeric and poetic influence and treat the text as a series of philosophical propositions. This rationalist method of interpretation has completely obscured the originality of Lucretius' poetic and philosophical genius.

The swan is an image of beauty, grace, and steady, rectilinear flying.[12] More specifically, it is a mythological image of Zeus, who transformed himself into a swan to seduce Leda.[13] Lucretius thus compares Epicurus with the steady rectilinear fall of atoms and the peaceful rational contemplation of them. In short, Lucretius compares the mythological god Zeus with the philosophical master Epicurus. Lucretius' brilliance here is that he naturalises epic myth at the same time as he destabilises and renders poetic Epicurean philosophy.

In Greek mythology the baby Zeus was hidden from his father, Cronos, in a cave and raised by birds, bees, and a goat, under the care of the Earth (Gaia).[14] It is therefore *absolutely no coincidence* that Lucretius compares himself precisely to these three animals in this passage. Here we have an extremely clever critique of Epicurean rationalism.

Zeus was only a powerful male sky-god because of the sensuous and material conditions of the earth, birds, bees, and goat that raised and protected him. Similarly, Epicurus could only have become the master philosopher he was because the earth and its creatures supported his material body with their desire. In other words, Epicurus can rationally endorse stasis and *ataraxia* only on the more primary condition of a moving, material, and desiring world of which he is part. Epicurus, like Zeus, is immanently constituted by his material natural conditions, but then strives to dominate them and deny their constitutive role. Epicurus and Zeus, in their own ways, both disavow the caring labour and material knowledge of the women and animals that make their action possible. The denial of the desiring labour that conditions ethical action in Epicurean *ataraxia* and Olympian authoritarianism is at the heart of Lucretius' critique of both ethical systems.

The conditions of ethical action, for Lucretius, however, are based on the primacy of the materiality of the earth and the caring/desiring labour of women and animals. Under the satiric veil of self-deprecation, Lucretius thus identifies himself with them against Epicurus and Homer. Ethics, for Lucretius, is neither contemplation nor divine authority. But let's look more closely at the animals to which Lucretius compares himself, as they tell us about the nature of ethical practice.

The Swallow

First, Lucretius says he is a swallow, but how is the swallow a poetic image of ethical practice?

Pedesis. Swallows are known above all for their chaotic and unpredictable flight paths as they hunt insects in mid-air. Swallows spiral, circle, dive, and make sharp turns and twists that few other birds can manage. Since humans cannot see these insects, it looks as though the swallows are moving 'randomly', when in fact their erratic-looking movements are the result of a highly relational and responsive entanglement with their prey. From the perspective of those who do not hear the music, the dancers (*pedetes*) appear insane.

For Lucretius, the swallow is the perfect animal to express the pedetic movement of matter as it continually swerves and twists. The fall and flow of matter is never perfectly straight nor is it completely random. The flow of matter is not random because it is relational and responsive to itself, like the dance between swallows and insects. Since each is responding to the other, neither alone is the cause of the other. Causality is collective and immanent precisely because matter responds to itself through sensation.

Wisdom. Swallows are also known for being prophetic birds. For example, the ancient Greek and Roman practice of augury was a way to divine truths about future events from the behaviour of birds based on what noises they made, how they flew, what kind of bird they were, and their direction (Fig. 1.1). Swallows, in particular, were signs of spring, fertility, and fidelity since they always returned home to the same place year after year in spring to mate.

This is particularly appropriate in the context of Lucretius' amorous poetic invocations of Venus (1.1–30), Favonius (the west spring wind) (1.11), Dionysus the fertility god at Delphi (1.734–41), the smiling spring weather that brings so much pleasure to bodies (2.29–33), and countless others. Lucretius is a poet of springtime, of nature's fertility as well as destructive expenditure. Lucretius was well aware of the Homeric

Figure 1.1 Romulus receiving the augury. Wikimedia Commons.

and Roman practice of bird-prophecy. He even explicitly describes it in lines 5.1083–6. However, Lucretius does not invoke augury because he believes in prophecy, but because he believes bird movements tell us something about nature, the weather, and so on (which they do). Lucretius the swallow is thus the wise and wily bird that announces the pleasures of springtime.

Desire. Swallows are also associated with desire, specifically in Homer.

The homecoming return of the swallow's migration is associated with fertility, wisdom, beauty, and poetry. In the *Odyssey*, Athena (a goddess of wisdom, beauty, and poetry) turns into a swallow when Odysseus returns home to Ithaca (22.239).[15] When Odysseus fights off Penelope's false suitors, Homer says that the sound of the bowstring from his bow and arrow was like the note of a swallow (21.411). The sound of the bow paired with the appearance of Athena at the battle connect Odysseus' homecoming with the renewal of life, springtime, desire, and poetic song at the same time. The importance of the swallow's song is also crucial to mating. Swallows 'sing before coition, and perhaps during it'.[16] Lucretius, the philosophical poet of desire, calls himself a swallow in this mythopoetic context.

Song. The swallow's song is also known for its erratic twittering noise. In contrast to Epicurus, the Zeus-swan of *ataraxia*, Lucretius compares himself with the erratic and pedetic noises of the swallow. A parallel occurs in the case of Zeus. According to Hesiod and Homer, and as repeated by Lucretius (2.633–9), the cries of the baby Zeus were hidden from his father, Cronos, by the loud noises of the Curetes, who banged their shields and swords in front of the cave.

There is an important philosophical consequence to be gleaned here from Lucretius' perspective. The material conditions of *ataraxia* are not immobile. Stasis and *katastematic* pleasures occur only on the condition of a more primary movement and motion that protects, bears, and supports them. *Ataraxia* is not static but rather a kind of metastable state supported by deeply turbulent but patterned movements, like the swallows or Odysseus' pedetic homecoming. Lucretius' noisy swallow song shows us a different ethical orientation in which desire and action take primacy over tranquillity and contemplation.

The Goat

The second ethical animal to which Lucretius compares himself is the goat. Epicurus is like a powerful horse [*fortis equi vis*] (3.8), associated mythologically with Poseidon, the brother of Zeus, who made the first horse in an attempt to create the most beautiful animal for Demeter. The horse is also associated with Zeus, who, after failing to seduce Aphrodite, spilled his seed on the ground and gave birth to horse-men, or centaurs.

Lucretius, by contrast, says he is a goat. The goat shares four common ethical features with the swallow in this context.

Pedesis. Unlike horses, the movements of goats are rarely in a straight line for very long. They swerve all over the place. Lucretius further qualifies himself as a young goat whose legs shake [*tremulis*] (3.7) at their joints [*artubus*] (3.7). If we take Lucretius seriously, how are we to believe that a shaking goat is able to truly follow in the footsteps of the Epicurean master? Lucretius is telling us explicitly that his footsteps are shaking like the swerving flows of matter that define nature itself. A goat cannot follow a horse but moves differently, more pedetically.

Furthermore, in epic myth, the horse is associated with urbanisation, warfare, and chariot races, and with Pegasus, the immortal winged horse of the gods. The goat, on the other hand, is associated with pastoralism and agriculture. The horse is a high-class animal associated with Greek power and the gods. The goat, however, is a low-class animal associated with pre-classical, Cretan, or archaic agricultural life. Since the goat follows the pedetic and indeterminate patterns of rain, sun, and fresh grazing grounds, so do the pastoral-agricultural societies that follow them.

These two animals express two different modes of ethical life and thought. The goat moves through the undivided countryside, the *nomos* or *chora*, without rigid walls or social forms. The Cretans, about whom Homer sings, for example, had no walls around their towns.[17] The horse, on the other hand, moves through highly striated spaces such as the *polis* (walled city) and *imperium*, as transportation and military power. Epicurus' philosophy represents this tradition of power, reason, contemplation, and peaceful law, but only on the condition of the supportive *chora* or agricultural countryside that maintains and materially reproduces the city in the first place. Lucretius' philosophy expresses the tradition of practical action, open society, and the materiality of knowledge through nature.

Desire. The goat is also an epic figure of desire. More specifically, the goat, goat-man, or ancient satyr is a figure of desire, fertility, laughter, and pleasure. Roman representations of satyrs are of men with a goat's ears, tail, legs, and horns. The satyrs are tricksters, mischief-makers, and dancers. Their movements are erratic, and they roam the countryside with Dionysus, their leader, having sex, getting drunk, singing, and laughing.

However, the goat is not only the subaltern figure of wild desire but is also a figure of nurturing desire and care. For example, the she-goat Amalthea was a mother to Zeus in the cave on Crete. Her milk was nectar and ambrosia for him. Her broken-off horn became his cornucopia, and her hide became his indestructible armour (*aegis*). The goat is therefore both the material and desiring condition for the creation of Zeus and divine laws, but also the wild abandonment of those same laws in the bacchanal. Lucretius is the goat because his ethical theory shows us the conditions for the creation and destruction of ethical value as such through kinetic expenditure. Epicurus, like Zeus, ascends to the peaceful sky, while the goats and satyrs remain on the earth to create something new (Fig. 1.2).

Wisdom. The goat-satyr is also a figure of wisdom. However, the satyr acts as if he knows nothing, just as Lucretius defers in the proem of Book III and elsewhere to Epicurus' knowledge. The satyr dissembles [*ficta*] that he knows nothing but in fact holds profound wisdom. This hidden knowledge mirrors Lucretius' own poetic knowledge about the hidden *nature* of things. The satyr's knowledge is a strange knowledge because it dissembles and even, like the satyr, changes shape, just as the swerving and shape-changing flows of matter change.

The satyr's wisdom is also related to the wisdom of Dionysus and his satyr companion Silenus, whom the satyrs follow. Dionysian and satyric wisdom is not propositional wisdom but rather a kind of inspired, poetic knowledge, not of things but of *processes*; of strange and ambiguous truths like the one Silenus espoused when he said that 'not to be is best'.[18] Similarly, for Lucretius there are no beings, only *becomings* – only flows of matter in constant composition and decomposition. An ethics of static beings and static values will only end in tragedy by trying to hold on and accumulate in a universe defined by energetic expenditure. This is not the endpoint of ethics, of course, but an important starting point. Lucretius says that Epicurus discovered something about 'things' [*es rerum inventor*] (3.9) but not that he discovered the *nature* of things, which Lucretius always writes as *corpora*, *rerum primordia*, or *materies*, never conflating them with *rerum*. Atoms are still too discrete and 'thingly' for Lucretius, who is more interested in flows, threads, weavings, and becomings, as we will see. It is significant that Lucretius always uses the *plural forms* of matter, thus resisting any reduction to a metaphysical 'one' of abstract matter.

In Book I, Lucretius explicitly likens his own philosophical and poetic inspiration to being stabbed in the heart by Dionysus' *thyrsus* (1.922–30). After he is stabbed, Lucretius says that his mind 'blooms' and opens up like a flower. Then he wanders, much like the satyrs, through

A Matter of Desire 27

Figure 1.2 Rhea and the infant Jupiter. Wikimedia Commons.

the obscure regions of the Muses' mountains, drinking spring water and eating herbs, just as the prophetic Dionysian bee priestesses did at Delphi.[19] It is an extremely psychedelic and ecstatic scene like few others. This is *not* Epicurean methodology. Nothing, in fact, could be less Epicurean.

To complete Lucretius' parallel of himself as Dionysus to the Epicurean Zeus, Lucretius calls Epicurus his father [*pater*] (3.9), just as Zeus was Dionysus' father. If Epicurus is the rational and contemplative sky-god or Zeus-swan, then Lucretius is the desirous materialist earth-god or horned Dionysus, failing to follow properly in his father's footsteps. Dionysus was born from the thigh [testicles] of Zeus, but Dionysus deviates from his father in important and dramatic ways. Since Dionysus is born from Zeus's body, Dionysus effectively turns Zeus into a second, or prosthetic, mother goddess – certainly nothing that Zeus, like Epicurus, would have intended.

There is one final piece of Zeus's infancy that Lucretius invokes to describe his relationship with Epicurus: the Curetes described in Book II (2.633–9). The Curetes, who made a loud noise outside the cave of the baby Zeus to hide his cries, also presided over the birth of Dionysus and later became his followers. The Curetes practised a form of wild ecstasy in their worship of Cybele, whom Lucretius calls *Mater Materque*, 'the Great Mother' (2.598), and presents to the reader as a naturalistic (not deistic) model for his kinetic materialism.[20]

All these images share a common geographical and historical origin on the pre-classical island of Cretan Crete.[21] The myth of Dionysus was born on Crete; Dionysus was the horned (bull or goat) god-son of the mother goddess worshipped by the Cretans (Fig. 1.3). During their new year's celebrations, they gathered honey from beehives in their caves and fermented it into mead to accompany their ecstatic rites at the birth of spring. Even the name of the cave on Crete where Zeus was born (Dicte Mountain) comes from the Cretan net goddess Dictynna (*dictyon* means 'net').[22] Lucretius therefore takes up the Homeric tradition, but only insofar as the Homeric tradition itself takes up a much longer and older tradition of naturalism, materialism, and ecstatic poetry from Crete. Lucretius leaves behind the exaltation of warfare, killing, and violence in Homer but also leaves behind the divine worship of the Cretan mother goddess as a monistic deity.

Song. The Curetes' wild movements and fluting noises are similar to the swerving of matter in its expression of nature but also to the wild

Figure 1.3 Minoan stone bull's head. Wikimedia Commons.

movements, noise, and flute-playing of the ecstatic satyrs and swallows. More importantly for our discussion here is that the Curetes were also magicians, seers, prophets, and metallurgists. Metallurgy was considered an almost magical art but was also directly connected to the shape-changing nature of matter. Metallurgy was therefore one of the first kinds of philosophical materialism, which rejected the idea that matter had natural Platonic forms.[23] The sparrow, the goat, and the Curetes form three of the four parts of Zeus'/Epicurus' conditions of possibility.

The Bee

Next, Lucretius compares himself to a bee that jumps around the pages of Epicurus' books as if they were a flower-bearing meadow [*floriferis*]. Lucretius drinks and perhaps spills everything [*saltibus omnia libant*] (3.11). This is an extremely heterodox approach to Epicurean philosophy – or any philosophy, for that matter. 'Father Epicurus hands down his propositional commandments' [*tu patria nobis suppeditas praecepta*] (3.10), but then Lucretius treats the 'papyrus paper' [*chartis*] of Epicurus' books like the real leaves or unfolding, unrolling flowers of plants (alluded to in *praepandere* in 1.144 and *evolvamus* in 1.954), as if he were a bee jumping around a field drinking nectar from unfolding plants/papyrus scrolls. He thus emphasises the performative and kinetic nature of philosophy and ontology itself in the materiality of its techniques of inscription and description.[24]

This is strikingly odd for a number of reasons. The first is that virtually every time Lucretius mentions flowers in his poem they occur in the context of springtime and goddesses. Flowers bloom during the birth of Venus [*summittit flores*] (1.8), [*floribus herbas*] (1.33), then again in the celebration of Cybele or *Mater Materque* [*rosarum floribus*] (2.628), and then again in her flower crowns [*coronis floribus*] (5.1396). Even more dramatically, Lucretius himself on his drug-induced Dionysian trip to the mountains of the Muses (1.921–34) picks new flowers and makes the same flower crown for his own head [*capiti . . . coronam*] (1.927–8). The flower crown is, of course, an ancient Greek and pre-classical Neolithic symbol of fertility, desire, and spring festivals.

Immediately after Lucretius gathers flowers from the Pierides mountains, he then says that he will use what he has gathered to make a honey cup (1.938) with medicine inside, 'and touch it, so to speak, with the sweet honey of the Muses' (1.947). He will then give this medicinal honey mixture to others to let their minds bloom open as well.

Although Lucretius explicitly mentions the medicinal drink as *absinthia taetra* (1.936), *absinthi laticem* (1.941), the poetic image itself also invokes other honey-based beverages, such as the mead consumed on Crete and at Delphi in honour of Dionysus.

We can now draw the following parallel to Book III. Just as Lucretius drank the honey-wine of poetic knowledge from the Muses in Book I, so now he eats the leaves of Epicurus' books with an excess of desire that leads him to jump around, chew them up, and make them into an intoxicating medicinal honey, that is, Dionysian mead. Immediately after drinking this inspired gathering of Epicurus' flowers, Lucretius enters an intoxicated state of ecstatic rapture, shaking and convulsing (3.28–9), like the theoleptic states of the bee priestesses at Delphi and butterfly priestesses of Crete, and the swerving flows of matter in his philosophy. Philosophical materialism means that knowledge is both performative and transformative; it means that ethical theory is itself a practice and an action, not contemplation and idealism. Ethics is not a theory about the good, but rather an *action* that really happens in the world. Lucretius shows us the way that even propositions are full of desire and require desire for their transmission, like bees drunk on flower wine.

No doubt the English translators of the Loeb edition of *De Rerum Natura*, Smith and Rouse, never dreamed of the wild interpretation I have just given. But even they are highly suspicious of Lucretius' own use of the Latin word *libant* to describe his method of interpreting Epicurus. They go so far as to say in a footnote that Lucretius' use of this word was 'inappropriate here, because, it might imply that Lucretius studied Epicurus' sayings in a casual and superficial manner'.[25]

On the contrary! I think *libant* is the perfect word because it means both 'drink some' and 'spill some'. One raises a glass of honey-wine to Dionysus to drink some and pour some out as a libation in his honour. Poetic and performative knowledge is not about representation but about a kinetic expenditure of bodily energy. Ecstatic knowledge is an act of physical excess. It is a *libant*, gift, and sacrifice back to nature: a kinetic excess of life that connects it with death. This is an old tradition that goes all the way back to the pre-Greek Cretan tradition of libation for the goddess.[26]

In contrast to the patriarchal dissemination of father Epicurus' rectilinear commandments, Lucretius takes some seed and scatters the rest around like the pedetic and swerving flows of matter, or instead transforms Epicurean seed into something else, some other fermented idea. Mead or opiates made from poppy seeds, known as the 'fruit of transformation', have a long oracular tradition beginning on Crete.[27] Lucretius continues this tradition.

Lucretius' critique of dissemination also allows the binary gender divisions of his primary sources to break down. Nature is not just some kind of all-nurturing mother, but also a destroyer, an erratic origin and waster of seed – like the castration of Ouranos, which gave birth to Aphrodite. Aphrodite was not the product of patrilineal reproductive seed but the swerving and pedetic product of expended and wasted seed, cut loose and indiscriminately spread into the ocean.

Just as the Cretan Dionysus' artificial birth transformed Zeus into a mother, so Lucretius transforms father Epicurus into a nectar-laden flower goddess. The whole gendered opposition between flower and seed, feminine and masculine reproduction, breaks down entirely, because bees are the trans-species, transexual prostheses that allow plants to have sex. Sex and sexuation are not primary ontological categories but rather products of a more primary movement of queer matter, or 'bees' that traverse sex, making sex artificial, and thus exposing the material heterogeneity that is the condition for sexual difference as such.

In other words, sexual difference begins as a non-biological material milieu. Sexual differentiation is thus, first of all, material and not biological. Sexual difference is performance, but the performance is always collective and *material* – not just cultural.[28] Or rather, culture is already itself a material practice. Lucretius the (non-human) bee subverts father Epicurus and mother Cybele at the same time through his movement, bee-dance, or *bee-coming*, which is irreducible to the static masculine or feminine 'beings' being performed. The movement of performance is the material condition for the cultural production of masculinity and femininity alike. Epicurus' seed is wasted/spilled out, and Cybele loses her transcendent divinity in one and the same movement.

The bee also echoes all the same key features of the other animals Lucretius has so far invoked to describe his relationship to Epicurus.

Pedesis. Lucretius says that he 'jumps' [*saltibus*] (3.11) around like a bee. But the flight of the bee is not random or 'superficial' at all. On the contrary, the flight of bees is a highly relational pattern that depends on which flowers are in bloom in what places at any given time. Similarly, in Lucretius' ethics of motion, no blueprint or ethical maxims can be given in advance of the relational singularity of the situation. Bees, like humans, have general habits and first steps they typically take, but if these become set in stone, dogmatic, and unresponsive to the situation, they must adapt and change paths. Like the swallow's flight, the bees' path only appears to be random from the perspective of a Cartesian grid placed on top of the situation.

Desire. Bees are how plants have sex. Botanical desire expresses itself by non-botanical methods: insects and bees. Desire, for Lucretius, is not merely reproductive or even species-specific. Desire is action or movement. The Latin word *inclinatio* means not only 'inclining' but also 'desiring'. The swerve of the bees jumping around is yet another image of the swerving *corpora* desiring one another. In ancient mythology bees were used to celebrate fertility and spring – a theme Lucretius continually invoked as a primary aspect of nature but also as a source of simple pleasure for humans and nature more generally.

Wisdom. Just as there were ancient bird oracles, so there were also bee oracles, attested to throughout epic poetry from Homer to Virgil and going back to Cretan Crete. Bee speech is a material kind of knowledge tied directly to Dionysus and to pre-Greek goddess worship. For example, after the Dionysian sacrifice of the bull, its head was filled with bees, which would swarm from its skull like the living souls of the dead, producing life from death. The sound the bees made was the buzzing knowledge of new life, hence the description of the Pythian maidens as 'Delphic bees', whose unintelligible speech was associated with the sound of bees and with their knowledge.[29] The Curete sages who protected Zeus were not only metallurgists and shepherds but also beekeepers. They used the bees to provide the baby Zeus with honey, just as Lucretius believes that all Epicurus' philosophy comes from desire in nature, not abstract fatherly precepts (Fig. 1.4).

Song. The buzzing of bees sounds chaotic, just like the unpleasant twittering of the swallows, the clanging sounds of the Curetes' metal shields (another Cretan goddess symbol), and the wild fluting of the satyrs. The humming of the bees is heard as the 'voice' of the goddess, and the 'sound' of creation. Virgil describes the sound of bees as 'the cymbals of the Great-Mother'.[30]

Our threefold image of Lucretius' self-portrait is now complete. Together, the swallow, the goat, and the bee form an interconnected and much more kinetic foundation for philosophy and ethical theory than that of Epicurus and the idealist tradition of moral philosophy. In the next lines, Lucretius says precisely that Epicurus' philosophy 'springs from

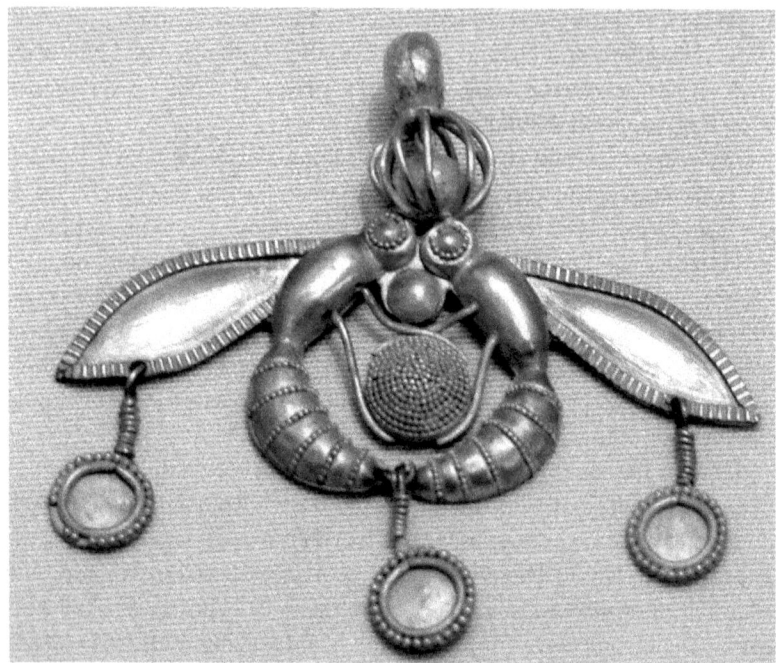

Figure 1.4 The 'Bees of Malia'. Wikimedia Commons.

his divine mind' [*divina mente coorta*] (3.15). This is exactly how Lucretius contrasted his own methodology in his book with earlier Greek philosophers, whose ideas all came from the divine temples of their minds [*divinitus invenientes ex adyto tam quam cordis responsa dedere sanctius*] (1.736–7). Philosophical method fails, according to Lucretius, because it is tainted by the history of idealism and mental contemplation.

Epicurus gets very close, but it is no coincidence that immediately after describing the 'divine ideas from the minds' of Greek philosophers in lines 1.736–7 and 3.15, Lucretius contrasts this with his own materialist philosophy of ecstasy in lines 1.734–41 and 3.28–9, respectively. Just as earlier Greek philosophers built their temples over the top of Telphussa's spring at Delphi and covered over the archaic and Neolithic knowledges of the oral and feminine traditions of oracular speech,[31] so Epicurus (like Zeus) covered over the material and sensuous conditions of his own philosophy. Lucretius, however, brings both traditions together in a (new) materialist and sensuous philosophical practice. He does this by invoking the birds, goats, and bees that are explicitly connected to the historical-mythological figure of the Curetes and thus to their movement, dance, and materialist practices of indigenous knowledge. This is the new materialist tradition that Lucretius brings to the Epicurean one.

The Birth of Spring

A brilliant demonstration of this novel approach is Lucretius' beautiful description of Epicurean *ataraxia* as Mount Olympus in Homeric verse. Based on Homer's description of Olympus in the *Odyssey* (6.42–5), Lucretius completely changes the meaning of Homer and Epicurus. He naturalises Homeric mythology and materialises Epicurean *ataraxia*, thus significantly altering both their images of the 'good' at the same time. This move is absolutely central to understanding the materialist philosophical basis for Lucretius' ethics of motion (3.18–24).

> *apparet divum numen sedesque quietae,*
> *quas neque concutiunt venti nec nubila nimbis*
> *aspergunt neque nix acri concreta pruina*
> *cana cadens violat semperque innubilus aether*
> *integit et large diffuso lumine ridet:*
> *omnia suppeditat porro natura neque ulla*
> *res animi pacem delibat tempore in ullo.*

> The divinity of the gods appears, and their quiet dwelling-places,
> which neither winds buffet nor clouds soak with violent
> rains, nor does snow formed from biting frost, falling
> white, disturb them, but an always cloudless atmosphere
> spreads over them and smiles with light diffused in all directions.
> Nature, moreover, supplies all their needs, nor does anything
> nibble away at their easy breathing at any time.

Strikingly, Lucretius begins by saying that the divine [*divum numen*] appears [*apparet*] to us (3.18). This is in direct contrast to Homer's *mythos* in which Olympus is something that 'they say' exists (6.42) and in contrast to Epicurus' *logos*, in which *ataraxia* is a static place of 'mental tranquility'.[32] For Lucretius, ethics begins with sensation and bodily affect, as we will discuss further in Book IV. Implicitly there is a contrast with the Platonic 'good', which remains fundamentally insensible as well.

Lucretius' poetic image of the good is neither divine nor ideal but a sensuous image of the birth of spring, which is not just a time of desire and pleasure for humans; all of nature comes to life and enjoys itself in spring (1.1–30, 2.29–33). New desires are created in the spring. Goodness is therefore not some transcendent place, idea, or value but continuous with the process of material and natural creation on Earth and of Earth itself. There is a thus a kind of geological ethics in which nature's own flourishing and diversity is a kind of desire and pleasure – something that climate change negatively affects, we might add. Summer and winter are taking over spring and destroying species at alarming rates. The conditions for the creation of new desires are ones in which there is not too much violence or disturbance. But this is precisely what the history of ecocide has done to our planet. It has expended energy in such a way that it has destroyed the ability of other life forms to expend their own energy. The result is increasingly dramatic storms.

By contrast, Lucretius describes Olympus as a resting place [*sedesque quietae*] (3.18) that is not beaten by wind or soaked too violently [*violat*] (3.21) with rain or snow. It is a cloudless sky overflowing [*large*] and pouring out radiant light [*diffuso lumine*] (3.22). He says that the spring sky smiles, curves, and laughs above [*ridet*] (3.22). Lucretius therefore directly and explicitly connects this whole Olympic scene to the birth of Venus, where he uses almost exactly the same phrase [*rident . . . diffuso lumine*] (1.8–9).

Nature, Lucretius says, lays everything at our feet in abundance [*omnia suppeditat porro natura*] (3.23). He also says that nature spreads out before us everything to lie on [*substernere*] (2.22) at almost the exact same line number in the proem of Book II, in his description of nature's excessive supply of desire. These lines from Book II are in turn based explicitly on lines in the *Odyssey* (7.100–2). The excessive and bountiful desire of nature refers both to the infinite movement of matter [*corpora*] and to the excessive desires of 'desirous, bountiful Venus' [*voluptas, alma Venus*] (1.1–2). The smiling curvature of the sky echoes the smiling waves on the shore, which echo the curving and shaking (laughing) nature of matter, which is the source of all material pleasure. This is not the Epicurean 'contemplation of eternal truths' that defines the 'mental tranquility' of *ataraxia*.[33] There is no stasis, or *katastemasis*, here.

When Lucretius says '*res animi pacem delibat tempore in ullo*' (3.24), he is not referring to static contemplation but rather to breathing [*animi*], from the Latin word *animus*, meaning 'breath', 'wind', 'soul', or 'physical life'. Lucretius makes a consistent terminological distinction between mind [*mente*] and soul [*animi*], which is key to understanding his theory of mind, soul, and body in Book III. The only reason to translate *animi* in this passage as 'mind' is because translators assume that Lucretius is merely Romanising Epicurus' mentalist idea of *ataraxia*. However, in this passage, Lucretius is drawing instead on the proem of Book I, in which the peaceful spring wind [*favoni*] (1.11) is invoked [*venti*] (1.6), and on the proem of Book II in which the wind (2.1) and smiling [*ridant*] weather (2.32) are invoked. These are all kinetic pleasures of the body, not *katastematic* ones of the mind. This is not an 'anti-Lucretius in Lucretius', as a number of scholars have suggested. Such an idea still assumes that *De Rerum Natura* was just Epicurean dogma.[34]

If there were any doubts left in the reader's mind about the materialist and kinetic foundations of ethics in Lucretius' philosophy *contra ataraxia*, lines 3.28–30 shatter these completely and force us to think seriously about the genuine philosophical novelty of *De Rerum Natura*.

The Ecstasy of the Sensuous

After drinking the philosophical mead that he has made from the foraged leaves [*chartis*] (3.10) and flowers [*floriferis*] (3.11) of Epicurus' books, the birth of spring appears to Lucretius in a sensuous vision [*apparet*] (3.18) that seizes and shakes him [*percipit atque horror*] (3.29) with divine desire [*divina voluptas*] (3.28–30).

> *his ibi me rebus quaedam divina voluptas*
> *percipit atque horror, quod sic natura tua vi*
> *tam manifesta patens ex omni parte retecta est.*

> Then, from these things a kind of divine desire
> and shivering awe seizes me, because in this way nature
> by your power has been uncovered and laid open in all directions.

This is no failed Epicureanism; it is something else entirely. Lucretius transforms and consumes a fermented Epicureanism and allows this beverage to transform him. Lucretius does not contemplate like a rationalist but says he sees [*video*] (3.17) matter in motion; he sees [*apparet*] (3.18) Epicurean-Helicon; Acheron does not appear [*apparent*] (3.25). The language of vision is continuous with the much longer pre-Greek tradition of ecstatic and epiphanic knowledge grounded in sensation that the Greeks adopted from Cretan Crete[35] and that Empedocles and Homer both invoked.[36]

This mutual transformation of theory and action *through matter* is at the foundation of Lucretius' ethics of motion. Lucretius describes his material transformation as a *divina voluptas*, which is an explicit reference to the *divomque voluptas* of Venus in the opening line of Book I. Just as Venus is the desire immanent to humans and gods [*hominum divomque voluptas*] (1.1), so now Lucretius lays the ground for an immanent philosophy neither human (Epicurean) nor divine (Homeric). 'Divine desire' invokes the same contradiction between ideal transcendence and bodily immanence embodied in Venus' 'sacred body' [*corpore sancto*] (1.38). Lucretius, in this poetic state, thus *becomes* the movement of desire immanent to both. Lucretian philosophy is therefore neither a mechanistic materialism nor an ontological vitalism.

Lucretius is seized and shaken [*horror*] (3.29) by this desire just as the flows of matter [*materies*] are moved by inclination and are shaken by their swerving laughter [*rident*] (1.919), and just as the legs of the goat shake [*tremulis*] (3.7) and the swallow and bee jump [*saltibus*] (3.11) around. It is only through desire and movement that the whole of nature is uncovered and unfolded through sensation. Contemplation cannot achieve this because it tries to cut itself off from nature. It tries to freeze itself in stasis. Sensation, however, is immanent in all of nature. Thought itself is not an abstraction of nature into maxims, eternal truths, and unchanging atoms: it is the sensuous transformation of nature itself. Through sensation and desire, the human animal becomes the matter that it is. We are, like other matters, a creaturely articulation or region of nature's own sensation of itself.[37] This is what we share in common with all of nature at the most basic level, not mental ideas of peace and Epicurean immortality.

Lucretius therefore begins philosophy not with thought but with material sensation and transformation: the ecstasy of nature. As Marx writes in his second thesis on Feuerbach,

> The question whether objective truth can be attributed to human thinking is not a question of theory but is a *practical* question. Man must prove the truth – i.e. the reality and power, the this-sidedness of his thinking in practice. The dispute over the reality or non-reality of thinking that is isolated from practice is a purely *scholastic* question.[38]

Philosophy, for Lucretius, is not Epicurean, 'sober reasoning' (*ataraxia*), 'pain avoidance' (*aponia*), and static (*katastematic*) 'non-sensual pleasure' (10.131), but material practice and desire. As Marx says, 'The coincidence of the changing of circumstances and of human activity or self-changing can be conceived and rationally understood only as *revolutionary practice*.'[39] The ecstasy of the sensuous is Lucretius' revolutionary practice. The point is not to contemplate the world but to change it through movement.

Conclusion

The purpose of this chapter was to lay out the basic orientation of Lucretius' philosophy, which forms the foundation of his ethical theory. More specifically, this chapter showed that Lucretius was inspired by, but did not adopt, an Epicurean ethics of *ataraxia* and *katastematic* pleasure. By contrast, Lucretius mixes Homeric myth and Epicurean philosophy together in order to produce a new hybrid materialist philosophy neither divine nor idealist. The result is an ethics that begins with the primacy of sensation, desire, and motion.

The point I think we should take away from lines 3.1–30 is that, for Lucretius, philosophy and ethical theory in particular are not 'ideas about the good' and certainly not withdrawn contemplation. Philosophy and ethical theory are material practices that transform the world and are transformed by it at the same time. The philosopher is sensually enmeshed or 'ennetted', as Lucretius says (3.384), in the world. The only truth or good is the one that can be performed in this world. The physical movements of bodies are inseparable from the ethics of their habits and compositions. Theory and action, physics and ethics, are entangled: this is the starting point of Lucretius' ethical theory. Several major ethical consequences follow from this starting point – as we will see in the next chapter.

Notes

1. 'There is in the *De Rerum Natura* no dedicated discussion of, for example, the Epicurean distinction between "kinetic" and "katastematic" pleasure or the role and purpose of rhetoric'; James Warren, 'Lucretius and Greek Philosophy', in Stuart Gillespie and Philip Hardie (eds), *The Cambridge Companion to Lucretius* (Cambridge: Cambridge University Press, 2012), 21.

2. Before Karl Marx ever read Friedrich Hegel, he read Epicurus and Lucretius. His first and lasting orientation to philosophy was based on the critique of religion, determinism, and idealism.
3. Educated Romans often contrasted religion (*religio*) with superstition (*superstitio*), praising the benefits of the former and the harmfulness of the latter. Lucretius rejects this distinction, maintaining that religion as the Romans practised it was a harmful error and, in effect, no different than superstition. In the words of Seneca, '*religio* [religion] honours the Gods, *superstitio* [superstition] wrongs them'. See Mary Beard, John North, and Simon Price, *Religions of Rome: Volume 1, A History* (Cambridge: Cambridge University Press, 1998), 216.
4. Milman Parry and Adam Parry, *The Making of Homeric Verse: The Collected Papers of Milman Parry* (New York: Oxford University Press, 1987).
5. 'This is in fact the line that Lucretius' contemporary Philodemus takes in *On Poems*: while accepting that poetry can give pleasure, he firmly denies that it can have any utility qua poetry. If it happens to be beneficial to the reader, that must be entirely the result of its content, and the same effect could presumably be achieved just as well if not better by employing prose-form.' Monica Gale, 'Lucretius and Previous Poetic Traditions', in Stuart Gillespie and Philip Hardie (eds), *The Cambridge Companion to Lucretius* (Cambridge: Cambridge University Press, 2012), 59–75, 73.
6. Lucretius even uses the same Latin verb, *fingere*, in Book I to describe *falsities* (1.104).
7. In a letter that Cicero wrote to Memmius, we learn that Memmius was living in Epicurus' ruined house in Athens. The Epicureans living in Athens wanted Memmius to leave, but Memmius refused to give it up. Lucretius might have thus been directing his comment about feigning or forming over the footsteps of Epicurus towards Memmius, who was literally living in the imprint of Epicurus' house against the orthodox Epicureans. My great thanks to Ryan Johnson for drawing my attention to this fact and for this fascinating historical interpretation regarding the ambiguity of the word *ficta* with respect to Lucretius' advice to Memmius.
8. For a long list of Latin authors using the word *imitari* as 'to copy' and 'to stand in the place of' or 'counterfeit', see Lewis and Short, *Oxford Latin Dictionary*, http://www.perseus.tufts.edu/hopper/morph?l=imitari&la=la#lexicon (accessed 10 September 2019).

9. Lucretius' affirmation of poetic desire is also a critique of Stoic asceticism and Epicurean fundamentalism.
10. 'Lucretius . . . is first and foremost a missionary.' Cyril Bailey, *Lucretius: De Rerum Natura. Edited, with Prolegomena, Critical Apparatus, Translation and Commentary (Three Volumes)* (Oxford: Oxford University Press, 1947), 13.
11. See T. H. M. Gellar-Goad, 'Lucretius' De Rerum Natura and Satire', PhD dissertation, University of North Carolina, 2012.
12. For a list of Latin references to the beauty and song of the swan, see Lewis and Short, *Oxford Latin Dictionary*, 'cycnus', http://www.perseus.tufts.edu/hopper/morph?l=cygnus&la=la#lexicon (accessed 10 September 2019).
13. M. Ebbott, 'Lede (λήδη)', in M. Finkelberg (ed.), *The Homer Encyclopedia* (Hoboken, NJ: Wiley, 2011).
14. Anne Baring and Jules Cashford, *The Myth of the Goddess: Evolution of an Image* (London: Arkana, 2000), 316.
15. For a great article on the significance of swallows in Homer, see E. K. Borthwick, 'Odysseus and the Return of the Swallow', *Greece & Rome*, 35.1 (1988): 14–22.
16. Edward Armstrong, *A Study of Bird Song* (London: Oxford University Press, 1963), 136, 159.
17. 'Cretan towns were not enclosed with defensive walls, and nowhere in their art is war or violence celebrated'; Baring and Cashford, *The Myth of the Goddess*, 132.
18. Plutarch, *Plutarchi Scripta Moralia, Volume 1*, ed. Friedrich Dübner (Paris: Firmin Didot, 1841), 137–8.
19. See Thomas Nail, *Lucretius I: An Ontology of Motion* (Edinburgh: Edinburgh University Press, 2018), ch. 8.
20. See Nail, *Lucretius I*, 233.
21. The term Minoan was invented by Arthur Evans, the archaeologist of Crete, c. 1900 for the culture he unearthed. In classical times what is called 'Minoan' nowadays would have been referred to as 'Cretan'.
22. Baring and Cashford, *The Myth of the Goddess*, 130.
23. 'The Kouretes are also, as all primitive magicians are, seers (μαντεις). When Minos in Crete lost his son Glaukos he sent for the Kouretes to discover where the child was hidden. Closely akin to this magical aspect is the fact that they are metal-workers. Among primitive people metallurgy is an uncanny craft and the smith is half medicine man.' Jane Ellen Harrison, *Themis: A Study of the Social Origins of Greek Religion* (Cambridge: Cambridge University Press, 1912), 26.

24. See Thomas Nail, *Being and Motion* (Oxford: Oxford University Press, 2018).
25. Lucretius, *De Rerum Natura*, trans. William H. D. Rouse and Martin F. Smith (Cambridge, MA: Harvard University Press, 2002), 189.
26. Baring and Cashford, *The Myth of the Goddess*, 112.
27. Baring and Cashford, *The Myth of the Goddess*, 115.
28. See Karen Barad's critique of Judith Butler in *Meeting the Universe Halfway* (Durham, NC: Duke University Press, 2007), 34: 'I argue that Butler's conception of materiality is limited by its exclusive focus on human bodies and social factors, which works against her efforts to understand the relationship between materiality and discursivity in their indissociability.' See also Vicki Kirby, *Judith Butler* (London: Continuum, 2007).
29. 'The tombs at Mycenae were shaped as beehives, as was the *omphalos* at Delphi in classical Greece, where Apollo ruled with his chief oracular priestess, the Pythia, who was called the Delphic Bee. In the Greek Homeric *Hymn to Hermes*, written down in the eighth century BCE, the god Apollo speaks of three female seers as three bees or bee-maidens, who, like himself, practiced divination.' Baring and Cashford, *The Myth of the Goddess*, 119.
30. 'This intense drama of epiphany suggests that, as well as these connotations, the humming of the bee was actually heard as the "voice" of the goddess, the "sound" of creation. Virgil, for instance, describing the noise of howling and clashing made to attract swarming bees, says: "They clash the cymbals of the Great-Mother." Virgil, *Georgics*, IV, 63.' Baring and Cashford, *The Myth of the Goddess*, 119.
31. Nail, *Lucretius I*, 139–40.
32. There is extensive citation of Epicurus by the ancient biographer Diogenes Laertius, whose work is now available in an excellent new translation: *Diogenes Laertius: Lives of the Eminent Philosophers*, trans. Pamela Mensch (Oxford: Oxford University Press, 2018). Book 10 of Diogenes Laertius is exclusively devoted to Epicurus and contains his three extant letters. See 10.83 for this citation.
33. *Diogenes Laertius: Lives of the Eminent Philosophers*, 10.83–4.
34. For more modern evaluations of this hypothesis, see Peter Toohey, *Epic Lessons: An Introduction to Ancient Didactic Poetry* (London: Routledge, 1996), 103–7; Alexander Dalzell, *The Criticism of Didactic Poetry: Essays on Lucretius, Virgil, and Ovid* (Toronto: University of Toronto Press, 1996), 41–4; James J. O'Hara, *Inconsistency in Roman Epic: Studies in Catullus,*

Lucretius, Vergil, Ovid and Lucan (Cambridge: Cambridge University Press, 2007).
35. See Baring and Cashford, *The Myth of the Goddess*, ch. 3.
36. See A. A. Long, 'Thinking and Sense-Perception in Empedocles: Mysticism or Materialism', *The Classical Quarterly*, 6.2 (1966): 256–76.
37. What Maurice Merleau-Ponty called 'flesh', in *The Visible and the Invisible*, ed. Claude Lefort, trans. Alphonso Lingis (Evanston: Northwestern University Press, 1992).
38. Karl Marx, *Early Writings* (London: Penguin, 2005), 422.
39. Marx, *Early Writings*, 422.

2. Kinophobia

Death is woven in with the violets . . . Death and again death.

Virginia Woolf[1]

The source of all unethical action is 'the fear of death' [*mortis formidine*] (3.64, 3.79). This a bold philosophical claim. How can the fear of death lead to unethical action?

The aim of this chapter is to defend Lucretius' claim through a close reading of 3.31–93. More specifically, the argument of this chapter is that the fear of death (necrophobia) is also a fear of matter (hylephobia) and a fear of motion (kinophobia). These three interrelated phobias are at the heart of unethical action and unnecessary suffering. They are also, unfortunately, at the heart of Western civilisation. The ethics of motion is opposed to this fear, which is at the heart of ethical theories based on stasis.

Lucretius is not a life-worshipping vitalist who, like Spinoza, 'thinks of death least of all things; and his wisdom is a meditation not of death but of life' (EIV, P67).[2] *De Rerum Natura* is just as preoccupied with decay, death, and destruction as it is with the birth of spring, desire, and creation. Lucretius begins Books I, II, and III with proems about spring, life, and creation and ends them with reflections on death, entropy, destruction, and expenditure. The whole book of poetry itself is structured around this Empedoclean twofold movement between life and death. Book I begins with a dedication to Venus (not Epicurus), and then Book VI concludes with the deadly plague at Athens. The fact that the French philosopher Gilles Deleuze could accuse Christians of falsifying the final chapter of *De Rerum Natura* because it concluded with death shows just how deep the vitalist and Spinozist prejudice has been in Deleuze's, and others', misreading of Lucretius.[3]

Epicurus might have been the first philosopher to understand the nature of *things* with his *mind* (3.14), but Lucretius was the first to understand the *nature* of things *as nature itself*. This is why Lucretius dedicated *De Rerum Natura* to Venus and *not* Epicurus. This is why there are almost as many references to Empedocles' *On Nature* as there are to Epicurus' *On Nature*.[4] All this is important because the ethics of motion directly follows from the ethics of death and from materialist ontology. Let's see how.

Death Matters

Lucretius' materialist ethics is based on his ontology of motion. Before there were any humans thinking about ethics – or anything else, for that matter – there was matter in motion. The human mind and body that engage in ethical practice emerged from a historical, material, and kinetic process of deep time and space. This does not mean that an ontology of motion tells us what to do. It does, however, tell us that nature tends to increase its rate of kinetic expenditure as it moves. It is a kind of hypothetical ethics. *If* we want to survive, then our best chance is to go with the flow of cosmic expenditure – to do as nature does, *not* to hoard, accumulate, and try and escape death. Nature is matter in motion and we are part of its flow. For this reason, immortality is impossible. These are the necessary, but certainly not sufficient, conditions for an ethics of motion (3.31–7).

> *Et quoniam docui, cunctarum exordia rerum*
> *qualia sint et quam variis distantia formis*
> *sponte sua volitent aeterno percita motu,*
> *quove modo possint res ex his quaeque creari,*
> *hasce secundum res animi natura videtur*
> *atque animae claranda meis iam versibus esse*
> *et metus ille foras praeceps Acheruntis agendus,*

> And since I have shown how the whole material body of nature is woven together into all things, and how, differing in their various shapes,
> they fly around on their own, stirred up by eternal motion,
> and how from them all things are able to be created,
> next after these things it appears that the nature of the mind
> and soul must now be made clear in my verses,
> and the fear of Acheron must be thrown violently out the door.

In Books I and II, Lucretius showed us how the whole material body of reality [*cunctarum*] (3.31) is woven [*exordia*] (3.31) together into relatively discrete things [*rerum*] (3.31). The Latin word *exordia* means 'first' and 'woven web', which fits perfectly with the poetic language of weaving used throughout the poem [*textum, contextum, nexum*]. Lucretius' emphasis on the constitutive power of matter to move and to weave already makes clear that we are not going to receive a theory of pre-existing, ideal, and immobile forms, or 'atoms', but rather a theory of how things [*rerum*] are the formed metastable products of the 'weave' of corporeal and material threads.

Furthermore, the Latin phrase *qualia sint et quam longe distantia formis* (2.334, 3.32) used above indicates that the *qualia* or qualitative constitution of things occurs over a 'long distance of formation'. Lucretius importantly does not say that there are simply different pre-existing forms, but rather that there is a long or large distance or difference between the forms.[5] The invocation of weaving here is directly related to the Homeric, poetic, and feminine tradition of craft knowledge, and not to Epicurean rationalism.

Matter flies around freely swerving [*sponte sua volitent*] and not caused by anything other than its own immanent and unlimited motion [*aeterno percita motu*] (3.33). Every thing [*rerum*] is created by the warp and weft of matter in motion (3.34). These are the material and kinetic conditions for the appearance [*videtur*] (3.35) of human minds and bodies that *do* ethics. Lucretius' verse will make it clear [*claranda*] (3.36) to us like cloudless skies (3.21) how the human mind and body emerged, and how the material-kinetic conditions of this emergence show us how to throw the fear of death out of the door *head* first [*et metus ille foras praeceps Acheruntis agendus*] (3.37).

All of nature is in continuous motion. Death therefore cannot possibly be a static, passive non-existence. There simply is no such state in nature. Death is, as the epic tradition describes it, like a river (Acheron) that flows continuously with the rest of nature – in constant transformation (Fig. 2.1). The Homeric image of death has been intimately associated with water throughout antiquity and up to the present.[6] Death is the expenditure and decomposition that all matter is continuously undergoing. Life comes from death. There is no movement without decay, entropy, and death. Death is not a bug in the system; it is a built-in *feature* of nature. The only thing that does not die is that which does not move, and there is no such thing, according to Lucretius (and contemporary physics). Our bodies and minds are borrowed energies riding on a much larger material wave that will eventually crash on the luminous

Figure 2.1 Charon, the ferryman of Hell. Wikimedia Commons.

shores of nature [*luminis oras*] (1.22). As Virginia Woolf writes, 'There is nothing staid, nothing settled, in this universe. All is rippling, all is dancing; all is quickness and triumph.'[7]

The fear that death is a passive state of non-existence or negativity is a real feeling that we can overcome by throwing our minds and bodies back into motion [*agendus*] (3.37). We have to understand and practise this knowledge of death *in motion*, as motion, and recognise that we ourselves are the process of death. This is 'joy before death'.[8] All of nature expends vastly more energy than it conserves.[9] Human bodies emerged historically as natural processes in this context, like everything else, aimed towards increasing the kinetic dissipation and expenditure of the cosmos. The most fundamental error of civilisation is to think and act as if this is not happening and that we can escape it: that we can escape death.

Liquid Desire

What is the fear of death? Lucretius offers us a materialist description of this fear as something that pours, like a river, over itself [*suffundens*] (3.39) in an excess of turbulence [*turbat*] (3.38) and covers over the clear, moving flow of desire (3.38–40).

> *funditus humanam qui vitam turbat ab imo*
> *omnia suffundens mortis nigrore neque ullam*
> *esse voluptatem liquidam puramque relinquit.*

This fear throws human life into deep and utter confusion,
staining everything with the black darkness of death,
and leaves no pleasure clear and pure.

The fear of death is not a purely mental or cognitive fear. Rather, the fear of death occurs when the movement of our own bodies and minds begins to suffuse over the larger natural and material world that supports us. When we think or feel that our bodies are something radically distinct, separate, or cut off from nature, we worry that death will destroy 'them'. When human life feels or seems to be a 'depth' [*funditus*] cut off from nature, then this dark internal depth can feel as if it is drowning the free flow of liquid desires [*voluptatem liquidam*] (3.40) that typically move the body. When the body and mind inhibit themselves according to rules or laws that feel external to them, then they feel crushed under the weight of *religio* and the *moenera*, the closed circle of political and military power described in Book I and that I discussed in *Lucretius I*.

The movement of matter, body, and mind, including their death, however, is a continuous transformation of liquid desire. *Death* is not dark; the *fear* of death is. When the body and mind think that they can cut themselves off from nature, it is as if they try to create an internal darkness untouched by the 'material light of nature' [*naturae species ratioque*] (1.148). The fear of death is thus a kind of pleasure turned back against itself; stultifying itself, and prohibiting itself from desiring and moving for fear of being destroyed. This is precisely how Nietzsche describes consciousness and morality when he says that 'the existence on earth of an animal soul turned against itself, taking sides against itself, was something so new, profound, unheard of, enigmatic, contradictory'.[10]

The fear of death is dark, according to Lucretius, because it is life turned against itself into a closed fold or cycle, just like the *moenera*. Life that rejects the reality of sensation tries to hide inside its mind through contemplation, which it believes to be immortal and unchanging. However, since the body is always already thrown into motion, death is a constant source of change and decomposition to be feared. The fear of death is therefore not just an *idea*; it is a real historical practice by which humans have tried to enclose life in darkness through temples, palaces, city walls, and their own minds and actions. But desire, like death, for Lucretius, is liquid and flows without cease.

Historically, the connection between death, the river Acheron, water, and liquid desire comes from the pre-classical Cretan tradition in which there was a triple goddess of light above, dark below, and earth in between. The Roman goddess Diana has three names for this reason. Her desire for her son-lover Dionysus (the green man) flows continually between these stages. The fear of death comes from trying to isolate one stage from the others and thus arrest the whole movement.

Lucretius does not contrast life and death as two ontologically separate stages but rather as two types of motion: an open flow moving between all three like the water cycle (above, surface, below) and a closed circle that tries to lock itself into a single stage (life) forever. This is why Lucretius described *moenera* and *religio* in Book I as closed, dark, rotten patterns of motion. They lock humans into militaristic and divine circles of social debt, credit, and slavery. We fear death and look to the gods to help us. We can thus see that the whole history of the technologies of enclosure are attempts to ward off death and motion: a whole kinophobic politics, architecture, and social world of *borders*.[11]

Practical Ethics

The problem is that everyone seems to acknowledge the constant process of movement and change, but no one seems to act as though it is real (3.41–7).

> *nam quod saepe homines morbos magis esse timendos*
> *infamemque ferunt vitam quam Tartara leti*
> *et se scire animi naturam sanguinis esse,*
> *aut etiam venti, si fert ita forte voluntas,*
> *nec prorsum quicquam nostrae rationis egere,*
> *hinc licet advertas animum magis omnia laudis*
> *iactari causa quam quod res ipsa probetur.*

For although people often assert that sickness and a bad reputation
are more to be feared than the infernal regions of death,
and that they know the nature of the mind is made up of blood,
or maybe of wind, if by chance they want it that way,
and further, that they have no need at all of our philosophy,
you can tell from the following that they proclaim all this to gain
praise rather than because the idea itself is thought to be true:

Roman society, and perhaps most of our own contemporary society, acknowledges the basic physical fact that everything is in motion. It admits that the river of death [*Tartara*] (3.42), or what we call entropy, is unavoidable; that the mind is made of flows of moving blood; and that our life is contingent on moving breath [*venti*] (3.44). However, we also think that human desire [*voluntas*] (3.44) somehow exceeds these laws and that human life does not need to put this practice *into motion*. We think that everything is already in motion 'out there'. So we do not act and live as though matter were moving through us.

According to Lucretius, people thus only verbally accept the existence of constant motion so that they do not look stupid in the face of science. People literally 'throw these ideas around' [*omnia . . . iactari*] (3.46–7) in grand, boastful gestures, but fail to *act* as if they were true [*laudis . . . causa*] (3.46–7) through their practices, habits, and lives. The point here, for Lucretius, is that ethics *is practical action* and not just espousing belief in this or that. Ethics is not merely mental or verbal acknowledgement of precepts but has to be grounded in the material and kinetic technologies of movement that define reality. The truth of poetry is that 'you must change your life', as the poet Rainer Maria Rilke writes.[12]

The Mask of Materialism

In this way, idealists wear a mask of materialism. Practically, we must all act in the world as if it were real and as if matter and motion were primary to our existence and our relation with and as nature. On the surface everyone is, in one way or another, a naturalist who accepts the reality of the senses in order to survive – even if they verbally or conceptually deny or abstract them afterwards into gods. Without the primacy of sensation there is nothing to deny, conceptualise, or abstract in the first place (3.55–8).

quo magis in dubiis hominem spectare periclis
convenit adversisque in rebus noscere qui sit;
nam verae voces tum demum pectore ab imo
eliciuntur et eripitur persona manet res.

Wherefore it is more effective to gauge a person in times
of flux, and to learn what they are like in adversity.
For then at last real voices are extracted from the bottom
of the heart, and the mask is ripped off: Reality remains.

When we look [*spectare*] (3.55) at the flow and flux [*in dubiis*] (3.55) of human life, we can see something about the kind of thing [*rebus*] (3.56) that we are. Everyone moves. However, when they are in trouble, we hear their voices calling out from the depths [*imo*] (3.57) of their hearts or minds [*pectore*] (3.57) (the mind is in the heart for Lucretius), for immortality. Below the mask of practical movement lies a popular belief in a world without motion (the soul, heaven, Helicon, etc.), precisely because people fear that death is a passive, static state.

Here we see that the static idea of life and the static idea of death are at the heart of the hatred and fear of motion. In order to avoid a static, passive death, we dream of an absolutely static yet somehow active life. But these are two sides of the same idealist abstraction in the dark depths of an internalised mind cut off from its body and from nature. Both abstractions (active life and static death) are predicated on a hatred of the movement that unites and sustains them.

When movement becomes particularly dangerous or overly turbulent, humans often seek out stasis. The twins of eternal mental life and passive material death emerge at this moment, and the mask of practical materialism reveals the real motivating habits of people to sacrifice, meditate, build temples, seek wealth, office, and so on in the hope of avoiding death. We can thus diagnose such abstractions by looking at the kinetic habits of people who fear death. In these following passages Lucretius aims to tear off the mask of Roman society to reveal its deep-seated motivation in the hatred of movement and matter.

Statism and the Wound of Life

The collective fear of death manifests itself in the form of the state. The state, for Lucretius, is essentially a group of people who have been possessed by greed and power to act against a population (3.59–64).

> *denique avarities et honorum caeca cupido,*
> *quae miseros homines cogunt transcendere fines*
> *iuris et inter dum socios scelerum atque ministros*
> *noctes atque dies niti praestante labore*
> *ad summas emergere opes, haec vulnera vitae*
> *non minimam partem mortis formidine aluntur.*

> So too, greed and blind burning after elected office,
> which coerce wretched people to go beyond the boundaries
> of what is right, and at times as allies in crime and accomplices
> they exert themselves night and day with outstanding effort
> to rise to the level of the greatest wealth – these lacerations of life
> are nourished in no small way by the fear of death.

Desire and motion, for Lucretius, is at the heart of all of nature and ethics. Blind desire [*caeca cupido*] (3.59), however, is blind because its desire is for something abstract, symbolic, and immobile that will not directly confer the immanence of sensual pleasure. Elected office [*honorum*] (3.59) is not just honour in general, but a very specific structure of official and political power related to the Roman *munus* and *moenera*. The blind striving for elected office is, for Lucretius, an attempt to escape death because it is a symbolic position of power and memory in the eyes of the population that will remember the official after death.

Here Lucretius clearly rejects a major theme in Homeric epic: the desire to live forever through heroism or glory [κλέος, *Kleos*]. Such a desire is not consistent with Lucretius' emphasis on matter, movement, and desire. In epic poetry, the hero lives forever through the song of the poet who sings him. For Lucretius, this kind of drive for *kleos* in general and political office in particular is nourished by a fear of death and gives birth to groups of people who collectively engage in violence, warfare, and political domination [*miseros homines cogunt*] (3.60) for the sake of maintaining office and attaining immortality. The result, unfortunately, is simply an increase in overall suffering and death.

The fear of death is not just about individuals; it is also about 'social or associational wickedness' [*socios scelerum atque ministros*] (3.61), which takes a specific social form: the state. The state can be historically defined precisely by the existence of a small group of office-seeking and -holding people who maintain their offices through the management of a population by force.[13] Even if we admit that there could be some good statesmen, the fact that the very existence of such a state and its positions already presupposes a fear of death would make Lucretius at the very least highly suspicious of any holding, seeking, or maintaining of office for the 'good of the people'.

The purpose of holding this office, as Lucretius says, is to accumulate things that only came into existence with the state itself: *opes* (property, wealth, riches, treasure; military or political resources, might, power, and so on). The only reason it is possible for anyone to accumulate any of these *opes* is that the state-form and its officeholders have already created the conditions for this accumulation in the first place: war and theft. Given Lucretius' bold statement that such things are the objects of a blind desire to escape death, it seems unlikely that his critique of such desire would not apply more broadly to the state itself and the existence of the very positions he thinks are unethical. There is therefore, in Lucretius, at least a deep-seated suspicion of all state positions and the people who seek them. At most there is kind of general anti-statism, as we will see in Book V and as we have already seen in Book I, with his critique of warfare and the whole structure of the *moenera* that it assumes.[14]

In fact, Lucretius explicitly connects these two critiques of statism with the concept of the wound [*vulnera*] (1.34, 3.63). The wound of love in Mars is also a battle wound that exposes the shared vulnerability of all life and thus the condition of collective love and union between wounded humans: Venus. The wound of material vulnerability is both the condition of violence and the condition of love. The state, the *munus*, and *moenera* try to close up the wound within the dark immobile confines of city walls and palaces, but Venus opens it up, lays Mars down, and breathes her kiss into his wound. The historical rise of the state was associated strongly with the rise of the idea of immortality, the fear of death, and a hatred of motion.[15]

54 Lucretius II

Primitive Accumulation

In addition to the rise of the state, the fear of death is also historically connected with hatred of the working or labouring classes. This hatred follows directly from the desire for statism and political power. If it is possible to escape death through military and state honour, then the reverse must also be true: being poor and of low social status must be closer to death. The rise to symbolic power and the fear of death thus nourish the murder and enslavement of the working classes, or what Marx calls 'primitive accumulation' (3.65–73).

turpis enim ferme contemptus et acris egestas
semota ab dulci vita stabilique videtur
et quasi iam leti portas cunctarier ante;
unde homines dum se falso terrore coacti
effugisse volunt longe longeque remosse,
sanguine civili rem conflant divitiasque
conduplicant avidi, caedem caede accumulantes,
crudeles gaudent in tristi funere fratris
et consanguineum mensas odere timentque.

For low social standing and bitter poverty nearly always
seem to be far removed from a calm and pleasant life,
and to be a kind of loitering, so to speak, before the gates of death.
This is why people, attacked by false fears,
desiring to escape far away and to withdraw themselves far away,
amass wealth through civil bloodshed and in their greed double
their riches, piling up slaughter on slaughter.
Unmercifully they rejoice in the sad death of a brother
and they disdain and fear eating with their relatives.

The fear of death, for Lucretius, is the source of statism and classism. The labouring classes are associated with death because they are treated as passive slaves, craftspeople, or women. Since this group of people is captured and does the bidding of the wealthy and powerful, then they must be more passive and thus more material. Since they must do physical labour with their bodies, they must be both more mobile and more passive compared to those who order them around. The logic here is straight out of the first chapters of Aristotle's *Politics* and Plato's *Republic*. Plato and Aristotle were philosophers of the state.

Lucretius, on the other hand, rightly identifies the logic of domination inherent in all such statist philosophies. Matter has been relegated to the bottom of the great chain of being. Physical mobility (nomads, barbarians), labour (slaves, craftspeople, women), animals, and nature are all 'closer to matter' because, like matter, they are more passive stuff that *gets moved* around by powerful political men. The labouring and slave classes have to move to survive, while the wealthy and powerful can remain relatively immobile while they make everyone else move – like Aristotle's 'unmoved mover'.

The whole Greek division between the walled *polis* and the open *oikos* is predicated on an even more primary necrophobia, hylephobia, and kinophobia. This is why Aristotle says that barbarians (non-Greeks) are 'natural slaves' and not fully human, and that women and animals are more bodily: they are all more like inert passive matter than active mind or form. However, this whole phobic trinity is based on a fundamental misunderstanding about the nature of matter and motion, according to Lucretius.

Matter in motion is what immanently supports all natural and social life in the first place. Greece and Rome were built and maintained by slaves and women, and yet it is precisely this materiality of society itself that must be denied, brutalised, and overcome through domination and statism. Immortality allows one to escape death, but it comes through state office, and state office comes through the domination of using wealth and power to steal from the poor, enslave foreigners (barbarians), kill one's neighbours through warfare, and manage women's wombs to reproduce more soldiers, and so on. Nature is passive stuff that must be pacified and made into wealth so that statesmen can join immortal history.

Historically speaking, Lucretius is describing precisely the history of the Kurgan, Mycenaean, and eventually Greek domination of old European and Cretan Neolithic peoples and their cultures. Older Neolithic and newer Bronze Age cultures mixed, but it was an asymmetrical mixture. Lucretius thus draws us back to the pre-classical poetic and philosophical tradition.

Karl Marx, who wrote his first book on Lucretius and Epicurus, calls the expansion of society through the use of direct violence and theft 'primitive accumulation'. By this he means that the prior condition of accumulation has historically always relied on colonialism, slavery, theft, and war. This is true not only of the capitalist mode of production but of every major civilisation back to antiquity.[16] This is true even in civil war, as Lucretius says. Groups of people will kill and expropriate their own people to amass wealth and accumulate political power. Primitive accumulation is directly related to the founding and reproductive mechanisms of state military power. This is where new natural materials and enslaved human beings come from, who are seen as being so close to matter, movement, and death. The creation of labouring and slave classes through war, theft, and colonialism is not the exception of statism; it is the rule. This is why a stronger case can be made for an ethical anti-statism in Lucretius. If there is no state that has not fallen prey to classism and militarism of some variety, then there is no state that Lucretius can ethically endorse. This is true for ancient states and all modern states based on primitive accumulation.

Of Stasis, Statues, and States

To envy those who march down the streets in official glory [*claro qui incedit honore*] (3.76) is to envy a symbolic fiction of immortality. Lucretius says this fear of death and envy of official honour is so strong that it causes some people to risk their lives or to die to have a statue [*statuarum*] (3.78) made of them.

The personal state statue is a perfect image for people who fear death and hate matter and motion. The statue is made of matter, but it is matter frozen in perfect form and immortalised as an individual. The Latin word *statuarum* comes from *statuō*, meaning 'to stand', from the ancient Greek words ἵστημι (*hístēmi*) and στάσις (*stásis*), from which Epicurus' term *katastematic* pleasure is also derived. Lucretius thus connects the desire for immortality to the desire for stasis and statism. The state produces status and statues in an attempt to render the individual static and thus immortal. Not all statues do this, of course, but state statues in particular immortalise a mortal individual. Although not explicit, this also might be a satiric dig at the statues of Epicurus that Memmius worshipped. The subtle message Lucretius is trying to convey to Memmius here is that life and philosophy move on and change beyond Epicurus, and that Lucretius himself is taking him in a new direction.

An ethical consequence of Lucretius' rejection of stasis is that ethics cannot be an ethics of static moral commandments or duties but must be something more like a living set of habits that is responsive to the people who practise and change them. In other words, the ethics of motion is more like the structure of poetic mythology than the rationalist doctrine of Epicurus.

Hatred of the Body

The belief in the immortality of the soul and its attendant fear of death go hand in hand. If we believe that the soul is immortal, then it follows that the material body and its entropic movements are the active cause of all our sufferings. The hatred of the body is implicitly and explicitly at the heart of the Western metaphysical tradition. Asceticism and morality, as Nietzsche writes, is a disease in which life turns against itself and says, 'You shall renounce yourself and sacrifice yourself.'[17] For Lucretius, the hatred of the body is at the core of asceticism (3.79–82).

> *et saepe usque adeo, mortis formidine, vitae*
> *percipit humanos odium lucisque videndae,*
> *ut sibi consciscant maerenti pectore letum*
> *obliti fontem curarum hunc esse timorem:*

> And often through fear of death such a great hatred of life
> and of seeing the light grabs hold of human beings,
> that they inflict death on themselves with a sad heart,
> forgetting that this fear is the source of their cares.

Through the fear of death comes a great hatred of life. Even more generally, Lucretius says, the hatred of life is a hatred of 'seeing the light' [*odium lucisque videndae*] (3.80). The fear of death and the hope for an immortal, static soul is at the heart of the hatred of sensation, of seeing, and of light itself as the material medium of sensation for both organic and inorganic matter. Behind the filthy [*caenoque*] (3.77) sensuous matter of the body, people believe that there is a clean, immortal, static soul waiting to be released. In a ridiculous inversion, these people, Lucretius says, even blame their own fear of death on the body. They think it is the body that makes them sad and not their own belief in a transcendent immortality that is the cause.

Here is a fundamental connection between materialist physics and ethics. If ethics begins with a materialist philosophy, it will avoid the abstract immaterial traps of immortality, the good, and morality that lead to suffering, hatred of the body, hatred of matter, and hatred of motion. If people believe there are static moral duties, virtues, or values, other than what their bodies can do, then they will end up hating their own immoral bodies.

As we have seen, this is not just an individual problem of asceticism and self-hatred, but is intimately connected with the hatred of the labouring classes, women, animals, and nature itself. If nature cannot be moral, then it is fundamentally inferior and passive with respect to human thought. Perversion is the historical name given for the free flow of desire to create new values and practices. As its name suggests, the Latin word *perverse* means 'invert, twist, or curve'. For Lucretius, however, perversion is not the exception to the rule of moral behaviour but the norm and condition for the production and reproduction of ethical habits as such. Ethical practice is the result of the habitual swerving or perversion of matter.

Pietas: Collective Ethics

The fear of death and the desire for the immortality of the soul are at the core of a complete inversion of collective ethical life [*pietate evertere*] (3.83–6).

> *hunc vexare pudorem, hunc vincula amicitiai*
> *rumpere et in summa pietate evertere suadet:*
> *nam iam saepe homines patriam carosque parentis*
> *prodiderunt vitare Acherusia templa petentes.*

> It convinces one to abuse honor, another to burst
> the ties of friendship, and in short to abandon responsible conduct.
> For these days people often betray their country
> and dear parents, trying to escape the regions of Acheron.

The desire for an immortal individual soul pits the individual against all other individuals who stand in the way of individual honour, wealth, power, and domination. This is not only a problem with the fear of death but with a very specific form of immortal life that occurs individually and not collectively. This individualism of the immortal soul is a complete historical inversion of the real, material, social conditions of an individual life. Strictly speaking, for Lucretius, there is no isolated individual – this is an abstraction just like the immortal soul (see Book V). The human being is a social and natural being. The idea of an individual immortal soul is thus a double inversion: it is an inversion of the *social* and the *material* conditions of real sensuous life.

The direct consequence of this individualism of the soul, for Lucretius, is that it causes people to break decency [*pudorem*], burst the ties of friendship [*amicitiai*], and invert the whole social relationship [*pietate evertere*] of which ethical practice is made (3.83–4). The individualism of the soul as well as of values, virtues, or duties grounded in the individual is fundamentally antisocial.

This is a central point of a Lucretian ethics of movement: ethics is fundamentally collective. The ethics of individuals is a horribly inverted abstraction based on the idea that minds are isolated from bodies and that human bodies are somehow cut off from their natural and social metabolic relations. In short, ethical theories centred on the individual and not the *collective* creation of ethical practice is part of the same rotten legacy of Western metaphysics that Lucretius already saw the beginnings of by the first century BCE.

Lucretius thus proposes a materialist ethics grounded in collective practice. Since ethics is collective, there is no possibility of individual 'correctness' or purity separate from social or collective *pietas*. Ethics is a set of constantly shifting habits or patterns of motion that have to be socially negotiated among friends (*pietas* and *amicitiai*). Ethical collaborations are not the discovery of universal principles of pleasure maximisation and their calculus. Debates over ethics are important not because they always get things right or have a better chance of getting things right by certain strategies or ethical theories, but because they dramatise a collective and *ongoing* antagonism. Confrontation and struggle produce changed patterns of action. People change their ethical habits for too many reasons to calculate, so we just have to keep working on them.

For Lucretius, the name of this social process of ethical decision-making is *pietas*. *Pietas* is not a single value, duty, virtue, or way of behaving. It is a social movement of ethical production and reproduction. It is the way we move together and create new ways of moving together. *Pietas*, for Lucretius, does not and cannot possibly mean 'piety' or 'duty to the gods'. There are no transcendent gods, and believing in them leads to the most wicked, unethical, and anti-social consequences (1.83). Lucretius explicitly rejects this definition of *pietas* and sacrifice in Book V (5.1198). Yet again, here is another difference between Lucretius and Epicurus: Epicurus still prayed and sacrificed to the gods.[18]

Pietas, for Lucretius, also does not mean any specific set of duties to family or society. This is because such duties have to be collectively negotiated by the immanent desires of the population that shares the same *pietas*. In short, instead of looking for transcendent values, Lucretius finds collective desires and movements that produce immanent values. *Pietas* is thus the creation of immanent patterns of ethical behaviour or 'immanent values'. For Lucretius it is crucial that we realise that we are the creators of our own values and that those values or habits can change if we want. Value is the performance of collective desire. *Pietas* is the kinetic process of creating the common good.[19] *Pietas* is thus always in motion.

Transcendental Materialism

Lucretius concludes this section of Book III on necrophobia and kinophobia by repeating several lines from Book I on his philosophical method. These lines describe what I call his 'transcendental materialism' (1.146–8),[20] that is, 'the study of the material conditions of what is'. This is in contrast to transcendental idealism or 'the rational or ideal conditions of possible experience', and metaphysical materialism, 'the absolute description of what is'.

Lucretius, following the poetic tradition of Homer and Empedocles, repeats the most important points he wants to make throughout *De Rerum Natura*. In Empedocles and in Lucretius, this repetition is also philosophically important because it mirrors nature's own process of kinetic iteration. Nature destroys old material conditions and produces new ones continually. Lucretius' philosophical method follows suit. The study of material conditions is not an ahistorical study of *a priori* or static conditions but the study of shifting historical and material structures in motion. Therefore, Lucretius does not give us an ontology of being qua being or a metaphysics of nature, but rather a situated material and historical description of nature immanent to nature itself.

Transcendental materialism is the study of the patterns of motion that continually produce and reproduce what is. Accordingly, these conditions can be produced otherwise than they are. This is a crucial material condition of ethical freedom forbidden by all transcendent ethical systems (3.91–3).

> *hunc igitur terrorem animi tenebrasque necessest*
> *non radii solis neque lucida tela diei*
> *discutiant, sed naturae species ratioque.*

> Therefore this fear and darkness of the mind must be shattered
> apart not by the rays of the sun and the clear shafts
> of the day but by the external appearance and inner law of nature.

Here Lucretius completely rejects the typical transcendent view of ethics that posits the existence of values, virtues, or duties beyond the earth, like Platonic rays of sun shining down from beyond. There is no true, beautiful, or good beyond nature to shatter the dark interiority of the abstract and individualist fear of death. There are only the material conditions of nature as it sensuously appears [*naturae species ratioque*] (3.93). The material conditions and ethical practices that emerge historically are completely immanent to nature. Humans do not discover laws of nature shining down from above; they invent, create, and desire systems of collective movement that they call ethics.

The study of these patterns and their creation is part of a materialist and kinetic ethics. It is the study of how we desire to move and how we can desire to move differently. This study is part of the same transcendental materialism that Lucretius described in Book I. If we want to understand nature or ethical practice, we do not need to conceptualise a static value shining down from above; we need to look at the material conditions that allow us to reproduce values and generate new ones. There is no other meaning to an immanent ethics than this.

Conclusion

There are three main takeaway points from this chapter. The first is that the fear of death and the belief in a transcendence beyond nature and motion are the source of unethical action. Unethical action, for Lucretius, is all action that turns against itself and tries to negate its own movement. Trying to create stasis will never achieve stasis and thus will always end in 'empty' cares and unnecessary suffering.

The second point follows from the first: if we believe that the unchanging soul is immortal and that death can be avoided, then all actions necessary to ensure this immortality or good are justified. According to Lucretius, this results in three interrelated problems of civilisation: 1) statism, militarism, and domination; 2) greed, wealth asymmetries, and wars of accumulation by dispossession (civil and colonial); and 3) anti-social individualism, religion, and the hatred of the body.

Third, and more positively, ethics for Lucretius is collective, practical, material, and kinetic. An immanent ethics of motion can never tell anyone what to do forever and for all time. The quest for static, unchanging codes, duties, and virtues of behaviour is fundamentally metaphysical and socially authoritarian. The existence of such values is also contrary to everything we know about nature: that everything moves. Ethical values are products of collective action and desire, not divine principles. Nothing is forever: not souls, minds, bodies, values, nor duties.

This is what Lucretius will show *concretely* in the next lines of his poem.

Notes

1. Virginia Woolf, *The Waves* (New York: Harcourt, 1931), 141.
2. Benedictus Spinoza, *A Spinoza Reader: The Ethics and Other Works*, ed. and trans. E. M. Curley (Princeton: Princeton University Press, 1994).
3. 'I fantasize about writing a memorandum to the Academy of the Moral Sciences to show that Lucretius' book cannot end with the description of the plague, and that it is an invention, a falsification of the Christians who wanted to show that a maleficent thinker must end in terror and anguish.' Gilles Deleuze and Claire Parnet, *Dialogues*, trans. Hugh Tomlinson and Barbara Habberjam (New York: Columbia University Press, 1977), 15. 'In a way, this means that Deleuze thinks that Lucretius is not Spinozist enough. While Deleuze sees Spinoza's "incredible book five" of his *Ethics* as an extraordinary thinking at infinite speeds that ends in the joyful affirmation of the world, *De rerum natura* strangely concludes a book of immanence and pleasure with a gruesome picture of death and destruction.' Ryan Johnson, *The Deleuze–Lucretius Encounter* (Edinburgh: Edinburgh University Press, 2017).
4. See D. J. Furley, 'Variations on Themes from Empedocles in Lucretius' Proem', *Bulletin of the Institute of Classical Studies*, 17 (1970): 55–64. Furley argues at great length for a correspondence between Venus and Empedocles' love. Furley also persuasively argues that the lines also contain reference to the four elements, Empedocles' 'roots'.
5. For a full discussion, see Thomas Nail, *Lucretius I: An Ontology of Motion* (Edinburgh: Edinburgh University Press, 2018), 208.
6. Gaston Bachelard, *Water and Dreams: An Essay on the Imagination of Matter*, trans. Edith R. Farrell (Dallas: Dallas Institute of Humanities and Culture, 2006), ch. 3.
7. Woolf, *The Waves*, 35.
8. Georges Bataille, 'The Practice of Joy before Death', in *Visions of Excess*:

Selected Writings, 1927–1939, trans. Allan Stoekl, Carl R. Lovitt, and D. M. Leslie (Minneapolis: University of Minnesota Press, 2008), 235–9.
9. Thomas Nail, *Theory of the Earth*, unpublished manuscript, under review with Oxford University Press.
10. Friedrich Nietzsche, *On the Genealogy of Morals*, trans. Walter A. Kaufmann (New York: Vintage, 1969), 85.
11. See Thomas Nail, *Theory of the Border* (Oxford: Oxford University Press, 2016); and Thomas Nail, *The Figure of the Migrant* (Stanford: Stanford University Press, 2015).
12. Rainer Maria Rilke, *Selected Poems*, trans. C. F. MacIntyre (Berkeley: University of California Press, 1978), 93.
13. For this historical definition of the state, see James C. Scott, *Against the Grain: A Deep History of the Earliest States* (New Haven, CT: Yale University Press, 2018).
14. See Nail, *Lucretius I*, ch. 2.
15. See Thomas Nail, *Being and Motion* (Oxford: Oxford University Press, 2018), Part II: 'Being and Eternity'. See also Riane Eisler, *The Chalice and the Blade: Our History, Our Future –Updated with a New Epilogue* (New York: HarperOne, 2014), and Anne Baring and Jules Cashford, *The Myth of the Goddess: Evolution of an Image* (London: Arkana, 2000).
16. 'It seems, therefore, that the Greeks and the Romans had a process of production, hence an economy.' Karl Marx, *Capital, Volume 1*, trans. Ben Fowkes (New York: Penguin, 1976), 175.
17. Friedrich Nietzsche, *The Gay Science: With a Prelude in Rhymes and an Appendix of Songs*, trans. Walter Kaufmann (New York: Vintage, 1974), 94.
18. W. H. Shearin, *The Language of Atoms: Performativity and Politics in Lucretius' de Rerum Natura* (Oxford: Oxford University Press, 2014), 31–2. Plutarch says that Epicurus sacrificed alongside common ritual; saying that he sacrifices to all the gods, 'I was sacrificing to all the gods who fail to pay attention to me.'
19. See Thomas Nail, *Marx: The Birth of Value*, unpublished manuscript, under review with Oxford University Press.
20. See Nail, *Lucretius I*, 67.

3. Critique of Kinetic Reason

Ethics is the study of moving well. The desire for immobility is therefore antithetical to ethical practice and is the source of the hatred of death, matter, mobility, and the body. It is absolutely central, according to Lucretius, to understand and live according to a materialist theory of the soul that is fundamentally kinetic and mortal. What we need for ethics, then, is a materialist theory of knowledge that can describe the basic conditions for ethical practice and remove us from the epistemological fear of death. Epistemology, or the theory of the mind, soul, and body's knowledge, for Lucretius, is completely continuous with ethics and provides a key weapon against the fear of death.

The aim of this chapter is to introduce the reader to Lucretius' kinetic and ethical theory of mind through a close reading of lines 3.94–237. The unique thesis of this chapter is that Lucretius was the first to develop a *kinetic* and *affective* theory of mind and emotion. This is in contrast to the Epicurean interpretation in which Lucretius is understood to be following a static theory of mind (*ataraxia*) and a static theory of emotion (*katastematic*).

The kinetic theory of mind developed in this chapter is therefore at the heart of a kinetic ethics that does away with any residues of immobility or immortality, and thus with the fear of death and the hatred of matter still at the heart of contemporary biopolitics (based on the valorisation of life over death). This chapter is also the first, to my knowledge, to argue that Lucretius was the ancient father of what is now called 'affect theory'.[1]

The Material Conditions of Reason

When the German philosopher Immanuel Kant wrote his *Critique of Pure Reason* in 1781, his purpose was to give an immanent description of the operations of the human mind. By 'critique,' he therefore meant a description of the conditions for all possible experience. His question was, 'What does the mind have to be like such that it can experience nature as spatial and temporal, one and many, and so on?'

Lucretius was not a transcendental idealist like Kant, but his method was similarly 'transcendental' insofar as it offered a description of the *material conditions for sensation* or what he calls '*naturae species ratioque*' (1.148). Lucretius' theory of mind and the soul, just like his theory of nature, is not a metaphysical or ahistorical description of the laws of nature or mind forever and for all time. Rather, given the existence of sensuous nature and the emergence of sensuous human minds in nature to ask such a question, what must sensation be like such that it has produced the kinds of moving bodies and minds that we are using? This is what we might call Lucretius' 'critique of kinetic reason'. Unlike Kant, therefore, this theory is not about the logical and idealist structure of reason but about the sensuous, material, and kinetic conditions of our minds and bodies *in* nature and *as* nature.

The first condition of materialist reason, according to Lucretius, is movement (3.94–7).

Primum animum dico, mentem quem saepe vocamus,
in quo consilium vitae regimenque locatum est,
esse hominis partem nihilo minus ac manus et pes
atque oculei partes animantis totius extant.

First, I say that the mind, which we often call the intellect,
in which the rational and guiding principle of life is located,
is part of a person no less than a hand and a foot
and eyes are parts of the whole living creature.

The first and most important point Lucretius makes in this passage is about the *material-kinetic* connection between the mind [*animum*] (3.94), the soul [*anima*], and life [*animantis*] (3.97). All three of these words come from the same Latin root word, *animus*, meaning 'breath', 'life', and 'thought'. The Greek word *psyché*, used by Epicurus, expresses the same three ideas as well and has proto-Indo-European roots going back thousands of years, attesting to a long-held belief in the material and kinetic nature of the soul and its unity with the mind and body. For example, in the pre-classical Cretan and Homeric tradition in particular, *psyché* is described as a fluttering butterfly. In part this is because the butterfly is defined by the rhythmic movement of beating wings and because it is a symbol of life that comes from death (the husk of the chrysalis). The Cretan butterfly goddess, for example, holds a double-bladed butterfly axe symbolising the double-winged cycle of life and death (Figs 3.1 and 3.2).[2] This contrasts quite sharply with the classical Greek and Christian ideas of the soul as immaterial, immortal, and unchanging.

The flow and cycle of air, or breath, is what brings together mind, body, soul, life, and wind in a single, constantly moving and rhythmic process of creation and destruction, inhalation and exhalation. Without the movement of air, atmosphere, weather, and wind breathing and circulating in and out, much of what we see would not exist. The primacy of the metabolic and respiratory movement of nature and the human body is therefore the first material condition for the emergence of human reason or mind. To have a mind or spirit is to continue the breath of nature by other means.

Lucretius makes this connection explicitly when he describes conscious reason [*consilium*] (3.95) as being like a 'rudder' [*regimenque*] (3.95) that simply guides movements by adjusting its own movement. Reason is not an absolute or ideal structure that unilaterally controls everything

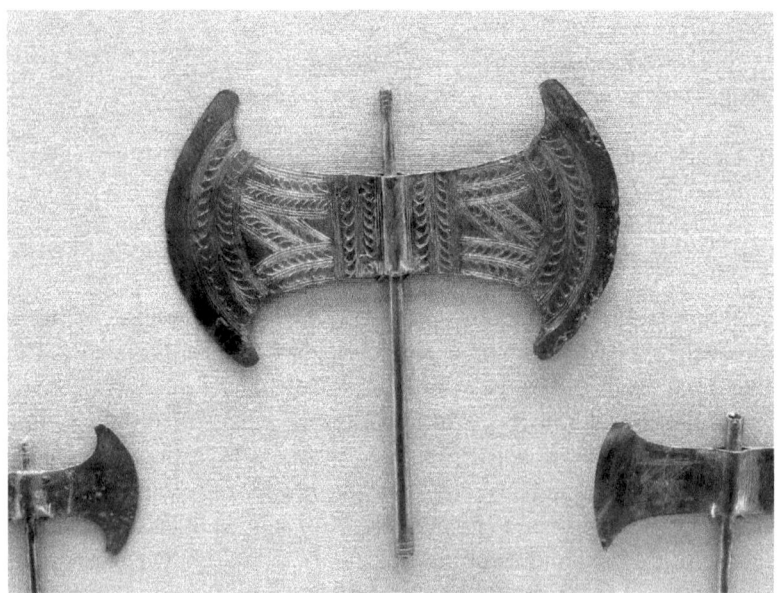

Figure 3.1 Gold Minoan labrys (double axe). Wikimedia Commons.

Critique of Kinetic Reason 67

Figure 3.2 Sarcophagus of Agia Triada (1600–1450 BCE), detail: priestess sacrificing a liquid at an altar adorned with double axes. She is followed by another woman and a lyre-player. Wikimedia Commons.

else in the body; it is a part of the human, just like a hand or foot. The whole living being [*partes animantis totius extant*] (3.97) is in constant rhythmic motion, and conscious deliberate reason is just one aspect alongside all the others, with its own activity and passivity to affect and be affected. It is also, and we will say more about this later, *not* a mental representation of the body and world. A rudder does not represent anything; it acts and is acted upon. Mind similarly performs some kind of movement that plays a role along with other agencies in the world.

Critique of Harmonic Reason

These three aspects of the Latin *animus* (mind, soul, and life) *do not form a harmony*, Lucretius says. The harmonic theory of the soul and its Platonic legacy is nothing but idealist necrophobia (3.98–105).

> *sensum animi certa non esse in parte locatum,*
> *verum habitum quendam vitalem corporis esse,*
> *harmoniam Grai quam dicunt, quod faciat nos*
> *vivere cum sensu, nulla cum in parte siet mens;*
> *ut bona saepe valetudo cum dicitur esse*
> *corporis, et non est tamen haec pars ulla valentis,*
> *sic animi sensum non certa parte reponunt;*
> *magno opere in quo mi diversi errare videntur.*

> However, certain philosophers have thought
> that the mind's power of sensation is not located in a particular part,
> but is a certain state of the body that produces life,
> which the Greeks call a 'harmony,' something which gives us
> life and sensation, although there is no intellect in any part –
> as when often the body is said to possess good health,
> and yet this health is no part of the healthy person.
> They thus do not locate the mind's consciousness in a particular part;
> in this they seem to me to wander seriously astray.

We know that Epicurus absolutely despised Plato and his theory of the soul as well as the harmonic theory of the soul that Plato contrasted with his own.[3] The harmonic theory of the soul was put forward by Simmias, a character in Plato's *Phaedo* (86b–c), and was likely inspired by Pythagoras' theory of musical and mathematical harmony. Since Lucretius' theory of the soul also has three aspects, it is important to clarify precisely how and why his theory is different from the harmonic theory which also puts forward a relational theory of body and soul.

The body, according to Simmias, is like the lyre, and the soul is like the harmony produced when a specific ratio of notes are plucked. In this way the soul is dependent on the inert material body, but once the harmony emerges, it gives life and sensation [*vivere cum sensu*] (3.101) to the inert body. As such, the mathematical harmony has no *physical* part called the intellect [*mens*] (3.101).

It is absolutely crucial for Lucretius to reject this harmonic theory for two reasons. The first is because this theory assumes the *a priori*, transcendent, and metaphysical existence of immaterial mathematical 'ratios'. When the body-lyre plays, the ratio is physically activated and the body is given life from an immaterial mathematical form. Second, Lucretius rejects this theory because it assumes that the mathematical harmonic ratio is itself immortal even if its activation by a particular body is not immortal. This only brings us back to the fear of death and the hatred of the body in favour of immortal musical ratios.

Lucretius' rejection of the harmonic theory is also an implicit rejection of the Platonic theory of the soul, which is defined by immortality and immobility. In the *Phaedo*, Socrates rejects the harmonic theory of the soul because it is still too dependent on the body, which means the soul would pass away when the lyre stopped playing and the body died. Socrates instead takes the idea of the Pythagorean mathematical ratio and completely abstracts it from its material context or body. Plato's immortal soul is like a ratio that needs no music to play it. The harmonic relation is thus inverted: the body merely participates fleetingly in the eternal form of the soul (100d). Thus, the soul is indestructible and immortality is preserved (106e–107a). Socrates thus says that this immortality will make us good because the souls will be judged in the end in the underworld (107d–108c).

However, following this logic, the wisdom of Silenus is appropriate: 'It is better not to be.' If Socrates is right, then the body and nature can only bring corruption and wickedness to the soul. The soul cannot be made any better by something inferior such as the body, which merely participates in the soul. The filthy body is always confusing and corrupting the soul with sensuousness and disrupting its pure contemplation. Socrates says he does not fear death as he drinks his hemlock only because he has properly hated and renounced his life in the world through his rigorous idealism.

However, this only *proves* Lucretius' argument in the previous chapter that belief in immortality nourishes the fear of death, which in turn teaches us to hate our bodies and the bodies of others. Socrates has lived a wicked life nourished by a fear and hatred of movement, matter, and nature. He fantasised about expelling poets and artists such as Lucretius from the *polis* and placing himself, the philosopher king, in the highest political office – just as Lucretius says the hater of life would do.

The hatred of matter and the immortality of the soul have a long legacy, taking us all the way up to Immanuel Kant, who made a perfectly emblematic remark about the etymology of the Greek word *psyche*. Kant says it 'means butterfly. Thus in this naming of the soul there lies an analogy with a butterfly, which is hidden preformed in the caterpillar, which is nothing more than its husk . . . Matter cannot live for itself.'[4] Kant thus goes out of his way to completely invert the natural and material process of change so as to posit instead the Platonic and idealist soul as something 'preformed' in the husk of the caterpillar. Naturalistically speaking, this is completely wrong – as is the theory of the soul modelled on this false analogy. Kant even follows this harmonic legacy with his own theory of the 'harmony of the faculties', in which the different faculties are united in the transcendental ego.[5]

The Discordant Harmony of the Soul

Lucretius gives us several concrete examples that refute any kind of centralised, idealist, immobile, or formalist harmony of the soul. For example, if the body is sick we can often still think about things that bring us joy (3.106–7). Inversely, if the mind is unhappy the body can often still feel pleasure (3.108–9). This is the same physical principle at work when our foot is in pain but our head feels fine (3.110–11). Even when we are unconscious, the body still moves around and feels the motions of joy and anxiety (3.112–16). Therefore there is no proper or *a priori* harmony in the soul and no single 'I' that unites them. Mind and body can do distinct things without harmony.

Philosophers, Lucretius says, took the idea of harmony from musicians, who dragged it down [*traxere*] (3.133) from the Muses of 'high' [*alto*] (3.132) Helicon. Or perhaps they carried it over [*transtulerunt*] (3.134) from somewhere else. Either way, the origins of this abstraction are kinetic in nature and should be returned to whoever mobilised them in the first place, Lucretius says (3.134–5).

For Lucretius, the mind, soul, and body are not harmonically related according to any such immaterial mathematical forms. The whole human being, like nature itself, is filled with a multiplicity of swerving motions. Each has the power to affect and be affected by the others. No part of the human being has autonomy over the others. There is no unilateral command centre or single agent to which all action and motion can be attributed – such as Aristotle's 'unmoved mover', Kant's 'ego', or René Descartes' 'I think'.[6] The human being struggles with and against itself in a kind of disharmony of the soul.[7]

Lucretius was therefore one of the first thinkers in the Western tradition to posit a radical discordant theory of the soul. This is an original move that also distinguishes him from Epicurus and the ascetic tradition of 'mental tranquillity'. Tranquillity is not the same as harmony, of course, but for Lucretius both are out of the question because of the mobile and distributed nature of agency. Lucretius gives numerous other examples of this disharmony and the multiplicity of desires moving through the body in the following sections.

Critique of Pure Emotion

The discordant harmony of the soul is the foundation upon which Lucretius makes yet another strikingly prescient and original move in the history of philosophy. Lucretius develops a brilliant new affective theory of emotion. Affects are all the ways that the whole human being is materially and kinetically affected or moved. For Lucretius, emotions are not mental representations of bodily affects, nor are our mental states the sole source of emotions. Instead of a harmony between mind, body, and soul there is a feedback system of mutual transformation (3.136–42).

> *Nunc animum atque animam dico coniuncta teneri*
> *inter se atque unam naturam conficere ex se,*
> *sed caput esse quasi et dominari in corpore toto*
> *consilium, quod nos animum mentemque vocamus.*
> *idque situm media regione in pectoris haeret.*
> *hic exultat enim pavor ac metus, haec loca circum*
> *laetitiae mulcent: hic ergo mens animusquest.*

> Now I maintain that the mind and soul are held joined together
> with each other and make one nature from each other,
> but that the rational principle which we call mind and intellect
> is the head, as it were and lords it over the whole body.

It is situated and stays in the middle region of the breast.
For here leaps panic and fear, around this location
feelings of pleasure radiate; here then is the intellect and mind.

For Lucretius the mind and soul hold each other [*teneri*] (3.136) in a mutual embrace or conjunction [*coniuncta*] (3.136). What Lucretius calls 'the mind' we refer to today as 'awareness' and what he calls 'the soul' is what we call 'the nervous system'.[8] The word *coniuncta* means 'with' or a coordination of two junctions or *iuncta*, meaning 'join', 'connection', or 'yoke'. The meaning of the Latin word *iuncta* by this definition, and as Cicero[9] used it, is almost identical to the word *nexus*, 'a tying or binding together', as Lucretius used it throughout to describe the process by which the flows of matter fold over and join themselves to themselves and produce a haptic bond. *Iuncta* is even more explicit in that this junction or fold is produced by joining something to itself in a yoke, as a moving animal is bound to something else through the circular yoke around its neck. The yoke is the loop or fold that, by curving back around itself, touching itself, captures or harnesses a flow of motion. In general, therefore, the *iuncta* is not conceptually dissimilar from the *nexus*; both terms describe the process by which flows are joined to themselves in a bond or yoke. *Coniuncta* are therefore the connection of two or more *iuncta*, *nexum*, or folds.

This is an important first definition of 'mind' and 'soul' because it means that they are not discrete things but rather kinetic processes. The conjunction of mind and soul is therefore a kinetic coordination between junctions. Mind and soul are not connected to each other like two pieces in a puzzle, but 'hang together' like threads in a spider's web or in a woven cloth. Mind and soul hang together because they move and change together. This is the meaning of *coniuncta* and of *nexum*, which Lucretius also uses in this section (3.217) to describe the soul.

Lucretius says that the mind is 'the head, so to speak' [*sed caput esse quasi*] (3.138) because it can play a directorial role in guiding, like a rudder [*regimenque*] (3.95), the body's movements. The mind, though, is located not in the physiological head but rather in the chest for Lucretius. The reason for this is crucial for Lucretius' theory of mind. The mind is not merely conscious mental awareness, as we typically use the term today, but rather a more general emotional-mental awareness that we feel in a certain location in our body: our chest. The mind, as we will see shortly, is not the only steering organ in the human, but is simply one 'head', 'origin', 'source', or 'spring' (5.270, 6.636, 6.729) among others. The source of the mind's awareness is its emotional awareness, where 'pleasure flows out from' [*laetitiae mulcent*] (3.142) and where 'fear leaps out from' [*exultat enim pavor*] (3.141).

Emotion, for Lucretius, is explicitly a movement that travels through and across the mind, soul, and body. Lucretius does not use the Latin word *emotum* here, but his description is fully consistent with the Latin use of the word *emotum*, from *ex*, meaning 'out', and *moveo*, meaning 'to move'. Emotion, for Lucretius, is therefore quite literally a movement of sensation that travels in the human body, and not merely a mental representation. In fact, the mind, for Lucretius, is no different from emotion at all.

Here, in contrast to the long tradition of idealist theories of emotion as either the 'origin' or 'conscious awareness of physical changes', Lucretius gives us a theory of emotion as a real kinetic process of flowing, leaping, and so on that is unified with the mind. Emotion is the movement that defines the mind's own movement. Lucretius knows that the brain is in the skull, but he sees no reason to confine 'awareness' to the strictly mental awareness that we often associate with brain activity. Our body, most frequently the chest, is also an important site of awareness, where we feel 'butterflies in the stomach', or our heart pounding in our chest from fear, joy, and other affects.[10]

Lucretius does not strictly divide consciousness from the unconscious or mental from emotional awareness. All are completely continuous with the mind's kinetic activity. There is no radical break between the affective changes throughout the whole body and our conscious awareness of these movements. There *is* a difference between regions of the body, of course, but it is a strictly topological and kinetic difference [*loca circum*] (3.141), not a substantial or cognitive difference.

The next lines of the poem give several examples of the differentiated interconnection between mind, soul, and body (3.143–74). 'The mind', Lucretius says, 'has a sense of itself and has its own enjoyments even when the soul and body are not moved together as one' (3.145–6). Just because our eye hurts does not mean the whole body hurts. Just because we are thinking or feeling something joyful does not mean that the limbs will feel a new sensation because of it (3.147–51).

However, sometimes when the mind is upset, it can move the whole body, as when we are afraid (3.152–8). Similarly, the movements of the body also can move the mind because mind and body 'feel together' [*consentire*] (3.169) and are equally affected [*pariter fungi*] (3.168) by the same corporeal movements [*corporea natura*] (3.167). The mind can affect the body, and the body can affect the mind, and the soul can affect both mind and body, or each can affect itself without significantly moving the other. This is the same threefold relationship that Lucretius described in Book II between the mind [*mens*], heart [*corde*], and limbs [*membra*] (2.269–80), which I discussed in *Lucretius I*.[11] We have here an iteration of the same threefold conjunction in which mind, body, and soul are three topologically folded regions or circuits of the same continuous material circulation (Fig. 3.3).

Lucretius believes that all matter inclines (desires). All matter has *voluptas* and *voluntas*. If it did not, there would be no swerve and therefore no things. It therefore follows that the human body, which is made up of things, has many wills or inclinations. Lucretius' theory of the mind, soul, and body is thus not a command model but a kind of agonistic model in which various parts of the human affect and are affected by one another. The human is a multiplicity of material desires and flows connected to one another regionally through circulation, and not as a single unified substance or single will. Lucretius was thus one of the first philosophers to invent a materialist epistemology that also de-centred the subject. This is clearly not an abolition of the subject by any means but rather an ennetting, entangling, or weaving of the subject into the material and multiple processes of its kinetic opera-

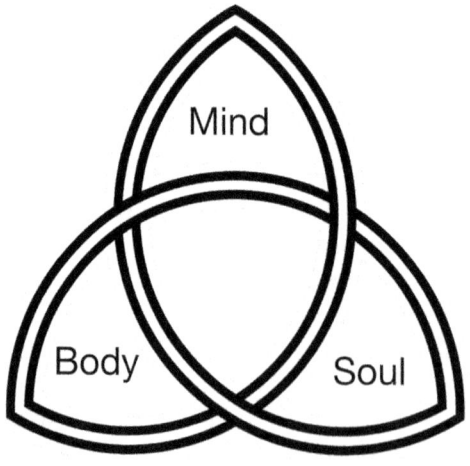

Figure 3.3 Mind, body, and soul.

tions. Instead of a natural harmony, we therefore have *a non-equilibrium disharmony of the soul*.

Furthermore, the fact that the mind is emotional, material, and fundamentally kinetic means that there is no *ataraxia* or static mind for Lucretius. The mind is moving all the time, even when we sleep. Emotion is a real movement that is continuous with the movement of the mind – not something to be contrasted with and suppressed by reason.

Affect Theory

Lucretius' theory of mind thus prompts us to completely reconsider what we today call 'affect theory' in philosophy and psychology. This modernist tradition has completely ignored Lucretius because it has wrongly associated him with the rationalist and ascetic tradition of Epicurus, where the mind subordinates desire and emotion to achieve *ataraxia*. However, upon closer reading, I think we find that Lucretius is actually the historical source for much of what is now called affect theory.

Affect theory is defined by the idea that emotions occur first as affects in the body and only later as 'feelings' *about* these affects in our conscious awareness. When scholars go in search of the historical precursors of this idea they typically arrive at Baruch Spinoza. There is good reason for this. All modern theories of emotions that begin with the affects of the body as primary can be traced back to Spinoza, who directly inspired William James's theory of emotions,[12] which in turn inspired the emotional psychology of Silvan Tomkins (1911–91) and the neuroscience of Antonio Damasio (b. 1944) and, through them, most contemporary psychological theories of emotion. Spinoza also directly inspired the French philosopher Gilles Deleuze's (1925–95) theory of affect, which in turn inspired Brian Massumi's (b. 1956) theory and, through him, most of today's philosophical theories of affect.[13] What has not been seen, however, is that Spinoza's theory of affect is based directly on the materialist physics and theory of emotion in Lucretius.

For Spinoza, all bodies, including the human body, are made of nothing but matter in motion. When atoms of matter bump into one another, they produce affects or sensations. Spinoza took this idea straight from Greek atomism. However, where he breaks with the atomists and materialists is precisely in his theory of mind. For Spinoza, the mind is immaterial and completely unaffected by the movements of matter. An emotion begins first in the affects of the body but is then thought in the mind as an 'idea' or 'feeling' about the body's affective state. Spinoza says very clearly, 'The first thing which constitutes the actual being of a human Mind is nothing but the idea of a singular thing which actually exists' (EII, P11).[14] This means that emotions, for Spinoza, do not originate in the mind, *contra* the idealist tradition. The same is true for Lucretius. The affective movements of the body are primary. This is the basic idea that Spinoza borrows from Lucretius' theory of emotion and the main feature that has defined the history of affect theory. Lucretius and Spinoza *both agree* that the material-kinetic physics of the body is the primary motor of affect and emotion.

Here, however, is where the similarity ends and where Spinoza, and the history of affect theory that has followed him, has held on to an idealist theory of emotion. For Lucretius, the movements and affects of the body can produce direct material changes in the mind because the mind and body are both *material* and *emotional*. There is simply no division between mind and body in the first place such that one functions as a 'representation' or 'idea' of the other. There is no such thing as mental or ideal representations in Lucretius' theory of sensation, as we will see in more detail in Book IV. Rather, there is a kinetic and topological difference between parts or regions of the body that continually transmit and receive movement from one another. The mind is no less materially affective than any other region of the body.

This stands in contrast to almost all major strands of modern affect theory. When William James says that 'emotion is nothing but the feeling of a bodily state', he defines 'feeling' as the 'thought of a bodily state' and thus as different from a bodily state.[15] James thus divides bodily states from mental states that represent bodily states.[16] Antonio Damasio adds to James's theory the very non-Spinozist idea that the causality between idea and affect can go the other way as well and enter into a kind of feedback 'loop'. However, he still holds on to a representationalist theory of mind when he says that an idea 'may be the representation of the body "as if" rather than the body "as is"'.[17] Massumi has been the most aggressive defender of the Spinozist and Deleuzian distinction between emotion as mental representation and affect as intensive bodily movement. 'It is crucial', he says, 'to theorize the difference between affect and emotion' so that 'psychological categories' do not 'undo the considerable deconstructive work that has been effectively carried out by poststructuralism'.[18]

For Lucretius, in contrast with all these modern affect theorists, mind and emotion are, like the rest of the body and soul, *completely affective and material*. Emotion is an affective state and a mental state at the same time. Affect simply manifests differently in different regions of the body. Sometimes micro-affects, such as the movement of bacteria in our microbiome, occur in our stomach by themselves and we are not aware of them. At other times these movements directly affect our limbs and our minds. This is not a representation but a direct material transformation and thus goes both ways. For the mind to be aware, it must be materially affected or altered. The mind, body, and nervous system, or what Lucretius calls the soul, are all affected to different degrees. This is the difference between the kinetic theory of emotion and the merely affective theory, which still holds on to a distinction between mental representation and affect. Lucretius was thus the first and most radical affect theorist, for whom there are nothing but affects all the way down without any representation or residue of idealism.

Weaving the Soul

Lucretius describes the soul as a process of 'weaving' [*nexam*] (3.217) 'spread throughout the entire body' and 'moving along with the movement of the mind' [*cetera pars animae per totum dissita corpus paret et ad numen mentis momenque movetur*] (3.143–4), like the body's nervous system. The soul is made out of matter so thin [*minutis*] (3.187), smooth [*rutundis*] (3.186), and fast [*celeri*] (3.182) that it must be like 'lightning' (2.373–80), Lucretius says. The matter of the soul must be moved exceedingly easily by the slightest beginnings [*seminibus*] (3.187) of motion.

Lucretius does not share the same electrical theory of neurodynamics that we do today, but his account here does not directly contradict it either. The nervous system is spread through the body, and electrical impulses travel very quickly and are very lightweight indeed. Yet electrical impulses are still completely material, just as Lucretius described the soul. Lucretius even describes the movement of this material in terms strikingly consistent, although obviously not identical, with how contemporary neuroscience talks about them today. He likens the movement of this matter to the way 'water is moved and ripples at the slightest impulse' [*namque movetur aqua et tantillo momine flutat*]. The soul spins or oscillates in waves [*volubilibus*] and must be thinner than sticky honey and lighter than poppyseeds that are so easily blown out of their pods by the wind (3.190–200).

Lucretius thus describes the soul as a kind of fluid, electrical, kinetic process. More importantly, however, he also describes it as a kind of spinning or oscillation moving rapidly back and forth like a weaver. The soul is not just some static part of the body but an active and creative process or fabric spread [*dissita*] (3.143) throughout the body.

Additionally, it is absolutely no coincidence that Lucretius uses the poetic images of water, honey, and poppyseeds to describe the features of the soul. Prepared mixtures of these three substances as mead and opiates are the ecstasy-producing fluids historically ingested by poets, philosophers, and Cretan priestesses. Bee and poppy goddesses abounded on the island of Crete and in archaic Greek oral culture precisely because of their relationship to poetic and sensuous knowledge (Fig. 3.4).

Lucretius thus compares the soul to intoxicating fluids to show both its sensuous nature and the ecstatic connection to philosophical truth found in and through the soul. In other words, philosophical thought is not a representation of the world but a performance of the soul in and as the world. Nature is ingested and transformed into the soul as the soul is materially transformed and rewoven at the same time.

Critique of Atomic Reason

The fact that Lucretius describes the soul as a process of weaving is here, as elsewhere, completely incompatible with the idea that the soul is made of discrete atoms or particles. Particles simply cannot be woven. They do not thread together like veins, flesh, and nerves. Only flows of moving matter can be the source [*seminibus*] of the woven soul (3.216–17).

ergo animam totam perparvis esse necessest
seminibus nexam per venas viscera nervos,

> Therefore the whole soul must be made up of very thin
> beginnings and woven through veins, flesh, and sinews.

This description of the soul is in stark contrast with the Orphic and Platonic theories of the soul as the space or gap *between* the woven net of the body.[19] For Lucretius, the *soul itself is what is woven* and is completely material. The soul is like a rippling electrical fluid that moves around throughout the whole body via the veins, flesh, and nerves.

Lucretius' description of the soul as something *woven* is no coincidence. Poetry from Crete to Homer is frequently described as an act

Critique of Kinetic Reason 79

Figure 3.4 The poppy goddess. From Arthur Evans and Joan Evans, *The Palace of Minos: A Comparative Account of the Successive Stages of the Early Cretan Civilization as Illustrated by the Discoveries at Knossos*, by Sir Arthur Evans (London: Macmillan, 1921), I, 341.

Figure 3.5 Silver drachma, Knossos, 300–270 BCE. Obverse: head of Hera, wearing ornamented stephanos, triple-pendant earring, and necklace; reverse: labyrinth, flanked by A–P, KNΩΣI(ΩN), 'of Knossians', below. Wikimedia Commons.

of weaving.[20] In his description of the construction of Achilles' shield (another prominent symbol of the Cretans) in the *Iliad*, for example, Homer says that Hephaestus weaves [*daidala poiei*] and folds [*triplaka . . . ptukhes*] the liquid flows of metal together (18.478–89). Homer thus draws an explicit connection between Daedalus [*Daidala*], the master architect of Crete, and Hephaestus, the later Greek god of craftsmen. In the *Iliad* Achilles' shield, according to Homer, then becomes a dance floor like the one that Daedalus designed in Knossos for Ariadne, the Cretan goddess of weaving. The dance floor at Knossos was shaped like a folded-up labyrinth, which was an old image taken from images of Neolithic meander patterns, serpents, and water waves (Fig. 3.5). The word 'labyrinth' is not Greek in origin but refers to the double-headed butterfly axe of the goddess who oversaw the ecstatic mysteries of the temple at Knossos. Young men and women performed fertility rituals by entering the folded labyrinth, spiralling towards one another and then away in the epiphany of creation.

In the *Iliad*, Homer next depicts young women with 'woven garlands' on their heads dancing with young men with 'woven tunics' around their waists. Homer describes all of this beautifully by mixing together his song about the shield with the active performance of the shield itself as a *material kinopoetics* (*Iliad* 18.590–609). In short, in this incredible section of text, Homer completely overthrows the whole division between representation and presentation, subject and object through performative weaving.[21]

Lucretius similarly invokes this Cretan and Homeric tradition by comparing the movements of the soul to the sweet smell of Bacchus' flowers (3.221). This is, first of all, a description of the soul as something very light. This is technically correct with respect to what we know about the electrical impulses in our nervous system, which Lucretius is essentially describing. However, there is also an important philosophical point to be made about this electrical flow through our bodies.

The soul is the material basis for pleasure and pain in our bodies and thus relevant to a materialist ethics. If we are looking to distinguish good from bad ethical motions, we cannot defer to any absolute value, behaviour, or set of rules. We must look to the material patterns of the soul that are strictly and historically unique to their bodies and to the milieu in which those bodies exist. In short, ethics is, like poetry, a question of weaving well. This does not mean the strict avoidance of pain but rather the Dionysian creation of new patterns of motion that we collectively desire. We do not always desire pleasure or the elimination of pain, nor can we ever know the Epicurean 'whole life' of our body's future in order to calculate the total value of pleasures and pains properly. This calculus approach is entirely misguided. The soul, for Lucretius, is much more Dionysian insofar as it is seeking to give birth to something new – hence the flowers, fertility, bees, the marriage of Dionysus to Ariadne the Cretan weaver, and the epiphany of intoxication (mead and poppies).

Pleasure is not the 'alpha and omega' of ethics, as Epicurus said. For Lucretius, ethics is instead about creating new values and weaving new patterns *together* [*pietas*]. These new ways of acting do not come from ethical treatises or the 'divine minds' (1.738) of great masters, but from collective performances: previous practices and habits iterated differently. This is why Lucretius is always focusing on desire and inclination, which all moving matter has, and which is not strictly identical with the maximisation of pleasure or *ataraxia*. The epiphany of poetic intoxication is simultaneously a great joy but also a great shaking or turbulence that breaks us out of our old behaviours and thoughts.

The point is this: Lucretius draws on these same themes in *De Rerum Natura* to describe the kinetic nature of poetic epiphany, matter, and the material nature of the soul as something that is woven and folded up through the whole body. The soul is not just a woven *thing*; it is a performative weaving *process*. Poetry is not just a philosophical proposition about the woven soul; it is itself a weaving of the soul. Theory is always theoretical practice. The myth of 'Lucretius the Epicurean fundamentalist' has completely covered over this important poetic and performative dimension of the text.

Poetry weaves words and sounds through metre as the soul is woven throughout [*dissita*] (3.143) the body. Movements of rhythmic oscillation define them both. Both do not represent the truth but perform and express it in a certain way. In fact, Lucretius' use of the word *dissita* to describe the way the soul is woven through the body invokes his earlier use of this term, *disserere* (1.54), in Book I as a double way of describing both the poetic method of 'discussion' and the material performative 'act of sowing', from 'dis-' plus *serō*, 'I join, bind together', or from 'dis-' plus *serō*, 'I sow, plant'. This term links the performative act of poetry and speaking to the beginning flows of matter [*semita*], to the weaving of the soul itself, and to the performance of this soul to express itself in poetry. In short, philosophy, for Lucretius, is not a series of propositions about the world but nature's own performance of itself. The material flows of nature, the soul, and poetic speech are all woven together from the same movements. There is no ontological division between the world as it is for us and the world as it is in itself. Our bodies and souls are the same stuff of the weaving world.

The consequences of this woven theory of the soul are enormous. We are only recently discovering that our nervous system is fundamentally *plastic*. Based on our current understanding, damaged nerves can repair themselves, add new nerve cells, and even change what we still call our neural and synaptic 'nets'. I am not saying that Lucretius understood the finer points of contemporary neuroplasticity, but simply that his description of the soul as a creative and kinetic process of weaving does not basically contradict it, and in fact prefigures what we know today about neurodynamics. This is much more than we can say for almost every other philosopher in the Western tradition who has upheld an immaterial and eternal theory of the soul. Even medical science continued to think about the nervous system as a static tree for thousands of years, thanks to Plato. With the idea of a discordant and kinetic theory of a moving and woven soul, the basic insights of neuroplasticity are already in Lucretius.

Conclusion

In this chapter, we have moved Lucretius' ethical theory forward in three ways. The previous chapters established the materialist starting point of Lucretius' method (Chapter 1) and showed what unethical consequences come from a non-kinetic ethics (Chapter 2). This chapter has built on the previous ones to argue more precisely that since the human mind, body, and soul are all in motion (and cannot stop moving), ethical theory must begin from the kinds of nature that we are: moving nature.

More specifically, this chapter argued 1) that Lucretius was one of the first to develop a discordant theory of the soul in which there is no central ego or 'I' to unify all the affects of the person; 2) that Lucretius was thus also the first to develop a purely affective theory of emotion that rejects the division between mental representation and material affect; and, finally, 3) that Lucretius also put forward one of the first theories of the 'weaving soul' consistent with, but obviously not identical to, contemporary understandings of neuroplasticity.

In the next chapter, Lucretius takes us one step further by arguing that the ethical affirmation of death follows directly from the material mortality of the soul just described. Ethics is not just about life and pleasure; it is also about movement and death.

Notes

1. For an interesting comparison between Lucretius' theory of the soul and Gilles Deleuze's Kantian-based theory of the 'discordant harmony' of the soul, see Ryan Johnson, *The Deleuze–Lucretius Encounter* (Edinburgh: Edinburgh University Press, 2016), 193.
2. Anne Baring and Jules Cashford, *The Myth of the Goddess: Evolution of an Image* (London: Arkana, 2000), 73.
3. James Warren, 'Psychic Disharmony: Philoponus and Epicurus on Plato's *Phaedo*', *Oxford Studies in Ancient Philosophy*, 30 (2006): 235–59.
4. Immanuel Kant, 'VII – Metaphysik K2, early 1790s (selections) (Ak. 28: 753–75)', in *Lectures on Metaphysics*, ed. and trans. Karl Ameriks and Steve Naragon (Cambridge: Cambridge University Press, 2013), 393–414, https://doi.org/10.1017/CBO9781107049505.010 (accessed 11 September 2019).
5. Except in rare cases in which the sublime shatters the harmony between concept and sensation.
6. See Thomas Nail, *Lucretius I: An Ontology of Motion* (Edinburgh: Edinburgh University Press, 2018), 197–8.
7. 'A multiplicity of forces, connected by a common mode of nutrition, we call "life".' Friedrich Nietzsche, *The Will to Power*, trans. Walter Kaufmann (New York: Random House, 1968), 341.
8. For a detailed note on this, see Lucretius, *On the Nature of Things*, trans. Walter G. Englert (Newburyport, MA: Focus Publishing, 2003), 208.

9. For a long list of Cicero's usages of the term as such, see Charlton Lewis and Charles Short, *Harpers' Latin Dictionary: A New Latin Dictionary Founded on the Translation of Freund's Latin-German Lexicon*, ed. E. A. Andrews (New York: Harper and Bros, 1879).
10. Lauri Nummenmaa, Enrico Glerean, Riitta Hari, and Jari K. Hietanen, 'Bodily Maps of Emotions', *PNAS*, 111.2 (2014): 646–51, https://doi.org/10.1073/pnas.1321664111 (accessed 11 September 2019).
11. Nail, *Lucretius I*, 199–203.
12. Kate Stanley, 'Affect and Emotion: James, Dewey, Tomkins, Damasio, Massumi, Spinoza', in *The Palgrave Handbook of Affect Studies and Textual Criticism* (New York: Palgrave, 2017), 97–112, 98.
13. Melissa Gregg and Gregory J. Seigworth, *The Affect Theory Reader* (Durham, NC: Duke University Press, 2011).
14. Benedictus Spinoza, *A Spinoza Reader: The Ethics and Other Works*, ed. and trans. E. M. Curley (Princeton: Princeton University Press, 1994).
15. William James, *The Principles of Psychology: Vol. 1* (New York: Dover Publications, 2012), 459.
16. William James, 'What is an Emotion?', *Mind*, 9.34 (1884): 16; James, *Principles: Vol. 1*, 503.
17. Antonio Damasio, *The Feeling of What Happens: Body and Emotion in the Making of Consciousness* (New York: Harcourt, 1999), 191.
18. Brian Massumi, *Parables for the Virtual: Movement, Affect, Sensation* (Durham, NC: Duke University Press, 2007), 28, 27.
19. The soul is something captured and bound by a woven net of geometrical triangles. 'Eventually the interlocking triangles around the marrow can no longer hold on, and come apart under stress, and when this happens they let the bonds of the soul go. The soul then is released in a natural way, and finds it pleasant to take its flight.' Plato, *Timaeus*, 81d. For the connection with Orpheus, see Radcliffe G. Edmonds III, 'A Lively Afterlife and Beyond: The Soul in Plato, Homer, and the Orphica', *Études platoniciennes*, 11 (2014), http://journals.openedition.org/etudesplatoniciennes/517 (accessed 11 September 2019).
20. Giovanni Fanfani, Mary Harlow, and Marie-Louise Nosch (eds), *Spinning Fates and the Song of the Loom: The Use of Textiles, Clothing and Cloth Production as Metaphor, Symbol and Narrative Device in Greek and Latin Literature* (Oxford: Oxbow Press, 2016).
21. I thank Chris Gamble for bringing my attention to this incredible passage in Homer.

4. Dark Materialism

> Through loss man can regain the free movement of the universe. He can dance and swirl in the full rapture of those great swarms of stars. But he must, in the violent expenditure of self, perceive that he breathes in the power of death.
>
> George Bataille[1]

Lucretius' kinetic ethics begins from two basic ideas: that all of nature is matter in motion and that the belief in transcendent or immortal principles is the primary source of unethical action. If ethics is about moving (living *and* dying) well together, this means we need to understand what the human body and mind are and how they live and feel – as we saw in the last chapter. However, it is equally important to see how our bodies and souls change, die, and decompose. In short, *death*, for Lucretius, is also at the core of the ethics of movement.

The purpose of this chapter is to argue that death is not something that merely comes at the end of a life as its opposite, and thus something to be feared as a lack, but rather is something integral to living motion. The human being is not a static container filled with an immortal soul. Rather, the whole human being is woven, unwoven, and rewoven together. This is a movement of entropy and expenditure. This is the key idea missing from the previous chapter, which focused on life. Living and dying are two names for the same kinetic process of weaving. Lucretius articulated this thesis in what he calls 'the fourth nature' of the soul: the continuous weaving of matter. This is not a fourth separate thing [*rerum*], but a continuous movement or *change of the whole* and is continuous with the rest of nature.

In this chapter, I would like to argue that neither pleasure, pain, nor life are at the heart of Lucretius' ethics of motion, but are rather only co-primary with weaving and death. There is no *katastematic* escape from motion and no *ataraxic* pacification of death through contemplation. Death, like motion, is not a bug in ethical systems to be avoided, but rather is an important feature of it. As Marx says, 'In history as in nature, decay is the laboratory of life.'[2]

Folded Matters

According to Lucretius, the soul is not something simply woven once and for all but is a continuous process or movement of weaving. Its motion is what links it to death. Only that which does not move is immortal. Therefore Lucretius' material and kinetic theory of the human being is quite explicitly one that links it to entropy, decay, and death. This point is absolutely foundational to the ethics of motion. The human being is not a static thing in any sense but a process that is continually changing, moving, and, most importantly, dying. The moving body is, as Bataille says, a destructive expenditure of self, a rhythmic respiration of death.

The 'nature of the soul and mind is not purely simplex' [*Nec tamen haec simplex nobis natura putanda est*] (3.231) but 'many first-threads move through it' [*inter eum primordia multa moveri*] (3.236). 'The nature of the mind/soul is therefore threefold' [*iam triplex animi est igitur natura reperta*] (3.237). The mind is composed of air, heat, and breath [*vapor*] (3.231–7). However, each of these is in turn composed of a 'multiplicity' [*multa*] of 'moving first-threads' [*primordia . . . moveri*] (3.236).

The Material Soul

This is an extremely radical theory of the human for several reasons. First of all, the mind and soul are completely material and thus literally made of the stuff of nature. Furthermore, this same matter is what composes the minds/souls of animals, plants, and all living creatures, for Lucretius. The mind/soul in its basic materiality is not discontinuous with inorganic or organic nature. Humans are certainly different from other creatures in certain ways, but so are hedgehogs. Difference and singularity do not necessarily entail anthropocentrism. The materialist theory of the soul/mind, however, completely undermines a key feature that has bolstered anthropocentrism for centuries in the West: the immaterial soul. That is, the human is not different in kind from the rest of nature but different in degree or pattern of motion, like everything else.

The Folded Soul

Second, Lucretius defines the human mind/soul/life [*anim-*] as something folded [*plex*] and woven [*ordia*] of a multiplicity of material flows. The mind/soul (Lucretius goes back and forth in his terms) is not a simplex or unfolded flow of matter. He therefore uses the weaving term *ordia*, related to the Latin words *ordo*, meaning 'ordering', *ordior*, 'to lay the warp of a web', and *exordium*, 'the warp set up on the loom before the web is started'. The prolific use of weaving words that I discussed at length in *Lucretius I*, and touched on in the previous chapter, is crucial to understanding the human being and its ethical practice in Books III and IV of *De Rerum Natura*. Therefore, I have chosen to translate *primordia* here as 'first-threads' to emphasise the definition of the soul as a kinetic process and to make clear that the language of 'atoms' and 'particles' has no place in Lucretius' philosophy. Instead, the running description of the mind and soul in Book III is as threads and flows of matter that are folded and woven together and apart.

The Elemental Soul

Third, Lucretius' theory of the mind/soul weaves together Epicurus' and Empedocles' theories. Air, heat, vapour, and matter express both the triplex theory of Epicurus' soul and the elemental theory of Empedocles (air, fire, water, and earth). However, Lucretius breaks with Epicurus by defining the 'unnamed' fourth aspect of the soul as a multiplicity of folding and moving matters (3.236) and thus complicating the idea of a simple three- or four-part composite. This also distinguishes him from Empedocles for the same reason: the fourth elemental term becomes a processural manifold and not merely another element. Furthermore, and most important, Lucretius subordinates all three or four aspects of the mind/soul to a continuous movement of weaving and folding, such that the soul is neither one nor many but a kinetic multiplicity of threads.

The Ethical Indeterminacy of Matter

The 'fourth term' of the soul is the most important. Air, heat, and vapour on their own are not capable of the 'sensuous movements' [*sensiferos motus*] (3.240) that are 'twisted or folded together in the mind' [*mente volutat*] (3.240). This fourth nature is the most 'mobile' [*mobilius*] (3.243), 'thin' [*parvis*] (3.244), and 'lightweight' [*levibus*] (3.244) element [*elementis*] (3.244), which 'sets everything into motion' [*omnia mobilitantur*] (3.248).

The fourth element is not an unmoved mover but precisely the opposite: the moving mover. The same movement brings life but also death.

However, Lucretius is extremely careful in choosing his words when he describes this fourth nature. He says 'it completely does not partake of a name' [*east omnino nominis expers*] (3.242). This is a complicated sentence to unpack, but everything hinges on it. If the fourth nature has no name, how can a poet sing about it? But how can something so mobile and in flux have a single fixed name that captures it? To solve this problem Lucretius draws on the same strategy that Homer used in the *Odyssey* to describe his mobile hero: Odysseus.

When Odysseus is trapped in the cave of the cyclops Polyphemus, Odysseus says his 'name is nobody' [*oútis/métis*] (*Odyssey* 9.366–7). The word *oútis* means 'no one' but its synonym *métis*, as well as suggesting 'nobody' (i.e. *mē tis*), means 'some clever or crafty process'. Odysseus, the hero, is therefore indeterminately someone/everyone, no one, and a cunning form of craft-like intelligence, associated with weaving. This is a brilliant solution to a central problem of philosophical poetry: how do you poetically or sensuously describe that which cannot be named or fixed into a static substance?

Lucretius follows Homer's same performative solution. Instead of capturing the indeterminacy of motion with a single immobile concept or making it something mysterious, Lucretius *performs* the indeterminacy of this moving matter in poetic speech. In order to pull this off, Lucretius brilliantly weaves together three key Latin terms with the same ambiguities as the Homeric ones: 1) *nominis*, meaning both 'name' and 'knowledge'; 2) *omnino*, meaning both 'everything' and 'entirely'; and 3) *expers*, meaning 'having no part in'. So when Lucretius says that the fourth nature '*east omnino nominis expers*' there are actually three translations that peformatively demonstrate the indeterminate nature of this most primary, pedetic, and mobile of all matters in the soul. The fourth nature is therefore:

1) That which is completely without name.
2) That which is wholly without part or division.
3) The practical or working knowledge of nature that nature has of itself without external division.

Why is this such an important point? This is the ontological basis of the ethics of motion. The human body is a celestial body continuous with the rest of the cosmos and subject to the same indeterminate material conditions of entropic decay.

First of all, the primordial flows or threads of matter do not have a single fixed name or abstract concept. This is because they are not substances. A substance can have a single name, 'matter', but a process requires a performative description of multiple names such as first-threads [*primordia*], matters [*materies*], bodies [*corpora*], roots [*radices*], sprouts [*semina*], flows [*flux*], folds [*plex*], fabrics [*nexum*, *textum*], and so on. The name 'atom', or Greek *atomos*, is no good. It treats nature as if it were made of a single substance. Since nature and matter are processes, however, not substances, they are neither divided parts nor whole totalities. The concepts of 'whole' and 'part' go together as two sides of the same substance ontology. Without parts there is no '*whole* of the parts', and without a whole there is no '*parts* of the whole'. This is why this fourth mobile nature is completely without a single name.

Second, this is why the fourth nature does not have a part in the whole. It has no ontological divisions and thus is not a whole of parts. Rather it is a whole of a continuous process without cuts or divisions.

Third, the knowledge *of* nature is something continuous with nature itself and thus undivided from it. Nature knows and must know, or else natural beings such as humans would not be capable of knowledge in the first place. The *knowledge of* the fourth nature is not something ontologically different from the fourth nature itself, or known by someone wholly different from that nature. All regional knowledges of nature are expressions of that whole process itself. Therefore, abstract concepts of matter and the good are deeply problematic. The knowledge of nature must be performed *by nature* itself without neutral observers or pure contemplations and transcendent principles. This is why ontology is epistemological and epistemology is ethical. If knowing is a doing, then it is tied to the ethics of moving well.

Therefore ethics is *not* about pain and pleasure, which, for Lucretius, occur at the level of conscious sensation, but the fourth nature is the material and affective condition for the emergence of these sensations in the first place. This is where inquiry into ethical action begins: not with conscious sensations but with the *material unconscious* of woven affects, that is, this fourth indeterminate and performative nature which is everywhere and nowhere the act of knowledge itself.

Touching on Nature

This is precisely why Lucretius worries about the danger of abstraction [*abstrahit*] (3.260) that lurks in the poverty of his native speech [*patrii sermonis egestas*] (3.260). This is not because the Greek language is necessarily superior but because we often forget the materiality of language, with its real haptic and tactile immediacy. We hear a word and mistake the word for a representation of something else.

However, it is the materiality of the word as a sound as it touches our ears and resonates in our bodies that is the direct, non-representational activity of the word itself. It is not enough to contemplate abstract ideas of eternal atoms as Democritus and Epicurus did. Lucretius wants us to be physically transformed and literally touched by his spoken words. In contrast to abstractions, then, Lucretius will literally 'move' us [*attingere*] (3.261) with his earnest desire [*reddere aventem*] (3.259) to touch, affect, or pluck us [*tangam*] (3.261) with his performance.

Ontology and Ethics

Lucretius *touches* on the relation between his materialist ontology developed in Books I and II and his epistemology and ethics developed in Book III. The basic and important point here is that ethical theory and practice are completely continuous with nature's own movements. There are no transcendent values, no *a priori* goods, no gods, and so on. There is not even any substance to the universe. There is only process: matter in motion (3.262–5).

> *inter enim cursant primordia principiorum*
> *motibus inter se, nihil ut secernier unum*
> *possit nec spatio fieri divisa potestas,*
> *sed quasi multae vis unius corporis extant.*

> For the first-threads shoot back and forth with motions
> among themselves, so that none can be separated off
> by itself, nor can its power be separated off by space,
> but they are the multiplicity of powers, of 'one,' so to speak, corporeal
>   being.

Ethics cannot be only a theory of individual action because there is, strictly speaking, nothing individual in nature. Nature is not a substance with individual parts. Rather, nature is first and foremost the ongoing, indeterminate movement of matter. Lucretius thus appropriately follows his previous lines about the 'fourth nature' without part, with a crystal-clear summary of his kinetic ontology in which nature is fundamentally indivisible [*secernier*] (3.263). This is the opposite of Greek atomism, in which the world is cut up into discrete spatio-temporal bits. Instead, Lucretius very clearly says that the movements of these threads/flows cannot be spatially divided [*nec spatio fieri divisa*] (3.264). The movement of matter is neither one nor many but rather a multiplicity of movements in 'one', 'so to speak' (3.265), material or corporeal being.

But why is it only a oneness 'so to speak'? This is because nature, for Lucretius, is not one substance or single thing [*rerum*], as he argued in Books I and II.[3] There is only 'one natural process', but since process is, by definition, neither whole nor part, it can neither be one nor many. Nature is not a thing or even a big collection of things. Thus it cannot be 'one' in the strictly numerical sense. If there is absolutely no spatial division of matter in motion, then there cannot be, by definition, any fundamental discrete atoms. All material differentiations are not fundamentally spatial but kinetic. The inclination of matter does not occur in a given space-time. Space-time, and thus all forms of discreteness and thingness, are emergent properties of kinetic matter.

The ethical conclusion here is crucial: the ethical actions of humans and other creatures are not ontologically separate from the celestial bodies flying through the universe towards self-destruction. Human life is continuous with the expenditure of energy in the rest of nature. This, and not individuals, is the starting point of ethics. Individuality is not foundational, but is an emergent process in ethical relationship with the wider world.

It is therefore this 'fourth nature' that materially connects all of nature with the emergence of individual ethical agents. At the heart of all ethical practice is the movement of matter that gives birth to sensations [*primum per viscera motus*] (3.272) to be practically distributed. This 'fourth nature' is not the base of a mental superstructure but rather the 'whole soul itself' [*animae totius ipsa*] (3.275). Air, heat, and vapour are just aspects or dimensions *of* this fourth nature, without which none would have sensuous movement. The fourth aspect is literally the material movement and interweaving of the three. It is a kind of 'base materialism' in which base and superstructure are woven from the same material threads (Fig. 4.1).[4]

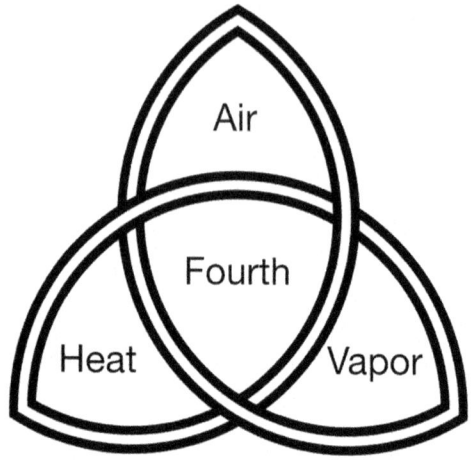

Figure 4.1 Air, heat, vapour, fourth.

The Thermodynamics of Emotion

If the fourth nature is the whole soul, then emotion is simply the movement of the soul, not merely a conscious feeling we have *about* our body. The mind's conscious feelings and the body's affective movements are kinetically continuous with one another. The mind and body are regions of the soul's mobile fourth nature, which makes them capable of sensation.

Again, Lucretius was ahead of his time in his understanding of the material, kinetic, and thermodynamic understanding of emotion. Anger, he says, is a movement of heat 'boiling up' (3.289) through the body. Fear is literally a coldness 'which stirs up trembling in the limbs' (3.291). Heat and anger increase motion, while cold and fear slow it down. This sounds like folk psychology and was treated as such for a long time in favour of more mentalistic explanations. However, the privileging of the mind as the source and origin of the emotions not only marginalised the agency of the body but also neglected the whole range of environmental or atmospheric affects. Changes in the non-human material world, such as temperature, are part of our emotions.

One of the important consequences of a materialist theory of the soul is that it is able to understand the affective thermodynamics of emotion in a way that contemporary psychology has only recently begun to take seriously. For example, numerous studies now confirm that anger actually does increase body temperature. But even more important, we know that increased temperatures increase anger.[5] When we are angry, blood circulates more quickly and moves towards the skin's surface to cool us down. But this also moves oxygen away from the region of the brain that controls impulses. By contrast, fear and anxiety actually move blood centripetally away from the limbs and towards the body's core to protect our vital organs. This often leaves us with cold hands and feet. Warm and pleasant temperatures such as those in spring, or from a hot beverage, or a hug, are related to feelings of happiness, peacefulness, and love.[6] For example, a 2008 experiment conducted at the University of Colorado at Boulder and published in the journal *Science* found that 'participants who briefly held a cup of hot (versus iced) coffee judged a target person as having a "warmer" personality (generous, caring)'.[7]

Heat and anger move blood centrifugally towards the limbs and allow us to move more easily but more impulsively, while cold and fear move blood centripetally away from the limbs, constricting mobility but protecting the organs. Science is only now catching up to this basic kinetic insight about the material and thermodynamic nature of emotion, which, as its Latin root, *movēre*, explicitly indicates, is literally about motion.

This very old but profound idea still has enormous consequences for us today. It means that where there is movement, there is something like sensation and affect. This means that animals, plants, and even inorganic nature directly and materially participate in the circulation of emotion in a general way. Emotion cannot be something just in our heads or even just in our bodies. Emotion is collective and environmental as well since there is a material-kinetic continuum between nature and our bodies. For Lucretius, this is because the 'fourth nature' of the soul is directly woven from the same stuff of nature.

Thermodynamic Ethics

The material kinetics of emotion are also related to our ethical behaviour, not because it tells us what is right or wrong, but because it is a much better description of the thermodynamic effects of emotions on the body. Anger is not wrong, but it does kinetically stress the body's adrenaline system, capillaries, and increase blood pressure in exchange for a rapid burst of impulsive mobility. This is the basic idea behind thermodynamic ethics.

All action is energetic expenditure. The more movement, the greater the energetic expenditure. For example, electric refrigeration preserves our food but only at the cost of taking energy from the natural environment (hydroelectric dams, nuclear power, etc.) and the damage of disposing of the refrigerator when it is worn out. This is a crucial idea for a kinetic ethics because it completely demystifies our actions as being about the 'good', the 'useful', or the 'pleasurable', and allows us to see more clearly the full energetic economy of our actions and make decisions based on the whole range of effects, not just abstract moral imperatives of a regional, isolated, human, or even social 'good'.

It may feel good to expend energy through refrigeration but it also inhibits other material processes on Earth from expending energy, and thus limits our future capacity to expend energy. There are no good principles, only different economies of thermodynamic affect that we can prefer over others. If we want to shape the world and expend our energy in certain ways, the best way to do this is by looking at the whole network of expenditure and its effects. One of the consequences of Lucretius' materialist theory of the soul is that the net of the ethical 'we' is much broader than we often think.

All our actions, thoughts, and emotions take place in a direct material-kinetic continuum with our environment and others. This is not a conceptual argument about how nature influences *our* ideas or *our* feelings. Our feelings and thoughts *are* the natural affective flow itself. We are physically affected and transformed by nature, we internally transform ourselves, and in turn we change nature. These three actions are simply three dimensions of the same process of transformation.

Anger is a risk. Can a temporary burst of less controlled movement change a situation, or is it just damage to the body and others that will limit collective expenditure? Fear is a risk. Can a temporary constriction of blood to the torso protect the body more than an angry counterattack? In either case, it should be clear from Lucretius' emphasis on the thermodynamic character of emotion and the soul that there is certainly no *ataraxia* or *katastematic* pleasure, since the whole soul is in constant motion and circulation, always expending energy, and thus always dying. Tranquillity, for Lucretius, is a metastable kinetic state, like the springtime or a hot cup of tea, not a purely mental state based on the contemplation of the gods, as it is in Epicurus.

Lucretius, however, also makes clear that this is not a behaviourist or mechanistic theory of emotion. There is no absolute causal calculus for ethical action and emotion (3.316–18).

> *quorum ego nunc nequeo caecas exponere causas*
> *nec reperire figurarum tot nomina quot sunt*
> *principiis, unde haec oritur variantia rerum.*

> I am unable now to explain the invisible processes by which emotion occurs
> or to find enough names for all the figures traced by
> the first beginnings, from which the multiplicity of things emerge.

In other words, Lucretius does not claim to provide any absolute causal story of how the vast swerving of matter produces such a multiplicity of emotions and affects. This is another crucial physical and ontological principle at the core of kinetic ethics: pedesis. The movement of matter does not follow predetermined or mechanistic lines because it swerves. The swerve is not caused by something else outside; it is the immanent, unpredictable movement of matter itself. It is the relational agency of matter.

Cicero and Plutarch, and most of the Western scientific tradition, rejected this idea. Matter in the West must always and above all obey something else, for example God, reason, immutable laws of nature, vital forces, and so on. The pedetic agency of matter is an absolutely bold and incredible thesis that even the most militant materialists have not been able to accept.

There are also important ethical consequences that follow from the pedetic and relational movement of matter, one of which is that there can be no ethical calculus. As Spinoza says, following Lucretius, 'They do not know what the body can do, or what can be deduced from the consideration of its nature alone' (EIII, S3).[8] This is because there is an infinite multiplicity of matters in motion. Even the greatest minds of contemporary physics have not been able to create a working mathematical formula for turbulent air arising from a lighted cigarette or to predict the weather with much certainty beyond a day. Even the most high-powered computer simulations of the standard model of particle physics have failed.[9] 'No one knows how to formulate a discrete version of the laws of physics', as Cambridge physicist David Tong says.[10] After 2,000 years we are no closer to mastering the indeterminate and pedetic swerve of matter. Ethics has not fared any better.

This does not mean we should give up experimenting in physics or in ethics, but simply that we would be better experimenters if we accepted that we are dealing with a real pedetic movement in matter that fundamentally cannot be rendered discrete, deterministic, or even probabilistic. Ethical action is relational and changes depending on how one cuts up the agencies involved. Probabilistic thinking in physics and in ethics does not stand outside the situation it is studying. It actively shapes the situation by including and excluding along its cutting limits. Therefore, the question of ethics is not one of right and wrong or the best way to cut. Ethics is the practice of cutting things up together and trying to make something we want to live and die with – not making something we think we *ought* to want.

Ethics is not the application of principles, for Lucretius, but more like the rudder of a ship, which can move only in relation to the rest of the ship and its natural context. None of the motions or emotions of the body are so deep-rooted that we cannot steer the body elsewhere and walk as creators of our own immanent values (3.320–3). As in Homer, even gods can die.[11] In fact, it is the universal process of dying that is at the heart of Lucretius' ethics of motion. Only that which dies well can live well. Only that which moves can move differently.

The Dying Soul

For Lucretius, the soul is not a substance but a kinetic or woven *process*. However, if the soul is material and all matter moves, and 'whatever is changed . . . is immediately the death of that which it was before', then the weaving of the soul is itself a continuous *process of dying* (1.670–1, 1.792–3, 2.753–4, 3.519–20). There is no reason to fear death because we and all of nature are already dying. There simply is no other possible starting point for ethical action than death and no greater obstacle to ethical life than the fear of death and the belief in unchanging values, laws, or gods that stultify and mystify our movements.

Since the soul and body come into being with their matters 'woven' [*inplexis*] (3.331) together and 'roots' [*radicibus*] (3.325) growing together, they are also 'unwoven' or 'untied' [*dissoluantur*] (3.330) together as well. Since the soul and body are in constant motion, it follows that the soul is always weaving. However, it also follows that if all movement is also death, then the soul's movement is also an unweaving as well: death. Weaving, then, just like the movement of the 'first-threads' [*primordia*], is both creative and destructive *at the same time*. There is no binary opposition here, not even an alternation. Living *is* dying, and dying *is* living. The two are united in the same kinetic process.

Atoms, however, do not die and cannot be woven. Lucretius thus continues to mobilise his vast vocabulary of weaving-based images to develop his own unique concept of the soul and its death. The soul is woven together [*nexam, inplexis*] (3.217, 3.331) into a textured fabric [*textum*] (3.208–10), which in turn is woven by his words in the poetic *textum*, which is in turn woven [*exordia*] of the first-threads [*primordia*] or flows of matter [*materies*].

It is then fitting that death, for Lucretius, is the process of unweaving or untying [*dissoluantur*] (3.330). Lucretius borrows the image of Epicurus' *sporos* [*semina*] insofar as matter is like living sprouts or shoots growing out of the ground, but he also borrows the image of Empedocles' *rizomata prōton* or 'primordial roots' [*radicibus*], insofar as it also grows down into the dead earth and feeds from decay. Lucretius thus joins together life and death, shoots and roots, in the same kinetic flow of matter above and below.

The soul and body are completely mixed together like liquid metals [*inter eas conflatur*] (3.335) or like smells [*odorem*] (3.327), according to Lucretius – and not like atoms or particles.

Decaying Life

Life and death are not ontologically separate substances or types, but rather two aspects of a single, ongoing weaving and unweaving, much like Lucretius' own oracular performance (3.417–20).

> *Nunc age, nativos animantibus et mortalis*
> *esse animos animasque levis ut noscere possis,*
> *conquisita diu dulcique reperta labore*
> *digna tua pergam disponere carmina vita.*

> Now come, so that you might learn that the minds and light souls
> of living creatures are born and subject to death,
> I will proceed to set out my poem, sought for so long
> and discovered with such sweet labor, so as to be worthy of your way of life.

Lucretius calls us to move and to walk with him [*age*] (3.417) to learn [*noscere*] (3.418) about how the ongoing process of life and death occurs in the triplex structure of the *anima*: the body, mind, and soul. Lucretius thus again invokes the etymological triplex of *animantibus* (3.417), *animos* (3.418), and *animasque* (3.418), indicating the ontological and poetic unity of the triplex in motion [*age*] (3.417). Lucretius the bee has gathered such sweet honey from the flowers of the Muses and from the leaves of Epicurus' books and now presents them as oracular incantations and ecstatic verse [*carmina*] (3.420), so that we may move well through life [*digna tua pergam*] (3.420). In these few short lines, Lucretius thus links together the movement of the body, mind, and soul in their life and death, the movement of his performance, and the movement of our own understanding of this performance.

Even more important, Lucretius *explicitly* connects the movements of this triplex *anima* to the rest of the natural world in lines 3.425–30. The basic idea that the soul is unwoven [*dissoluantur*] back into nature was already implicit in 3.330. Now, however, it is clear that the *anima* is not something strictly individual nor completely contained inside a single person but something directly affected by flows of moving matter outside the body in the environment [*imaginibus*] (3.430). In fact, Lucretius says, even the finest and lightest flows of nature, such as fog and smoke, directly move our bodies, minds, and souls, 'seeing that it is set in motion by images of smoke and fog' (3.430).

This is a topic that we will explore in Book IV in more depth, but here it is crucial to note the first explicit introduction of this concept and its immediate consequence for the discussion of death. For Lucretius, the body is not simply 'extended' or 'embodied' like a tool of the mind.[12] Rather, the mind is 'intended' nature, or nature folded in on itself. Flows of matter compose the *anima* and continually support and transform the whole creature. If our soul is material, then our soul came from nature and other souls. In other words, our soul is not strictly ours alone but shared with the environment that continually and physically touches it. 'Knowledge is not seeing, it is entering into contact, directly, with things; and besides, they come to us', as Michel Serres writes.[13] Matter is not passively waiting out there in the 'great outdoors'; it is already inside the soul (it is the soul) *and* our knowledge of the soul itself.

When we die, the soul pours out [*diffluere*] (3.435) of our body like dissipated heat, or liquid [*umorem*] (3.435) pouring out of a vessel, from hot to cold. The soul and the body start to become unwoven or untied [*dissolvi*] (3.438) and become the building materials for other creatures. Lucretius is physically correct. The body circulates about 20 watts of energy plus other chemical energies that quite literally dissipate and pour out of our bodies into the surrounding environment upon death. The chemical energy in our cells will eventually be food for other creatures.

But the *anima* is always in a constant state of decay and decomposition. The body is always unweaving and pouring out energy. As we get older, our bodies, minds, and souls together become increasingly tied together in decay. When we get very old, the mind and body become weaker (3.447–54). When the body is ill, the mind and soul are often affected, and vice versa (3.455–73). 'For pain and disease are each architects [*fabricator*] of death' (3.472). For Lucretius, the *anima* (body, mind, soul) is constantly weaving and unweaving itself. It is not a substance but a process of simultaneous composition and decomposition.

The *anima* is moved not only by the environment and by its own decay but also by food, drugs, and medicines (3.476–510). These material flows change our bodies, minds, and souls all together (3.513–16).

> *addere enim partis aut ordine traiecere aecumst*
> *aut aliquid prosum de summa detrahere hilum,*
> *commutare animum qui cumque adoritur et infit*
> *aut aliam quamvis naturam flectere quaerit.*

> For one must add parts or transpose the order
> or take away some tiny bit from the total,
> if someone is trying to alter the mind and gets started,
> or seeks to bend whatever other nature you wish.

The fact that the whole *anima* can be changed by *pharmakon* proves that there is not an immortal soul. because what is immortal cannot change. Rather, because the whole *anima* is a continually moving and changing process, food and drugs simply redirect, curve, or bend [*flectere*] (3.516) the trajectories [*traiecere*] (3.513) of the weaving of the *anima* [*ordine*] (3.513).

Lucretius draws on the image of the inclining and weaving flows of matter to curve, bend, and fold. Just as matter bends and weaves in nature, so it bends and weaves in the soul. 'But what is immortal does not allow its parts to be rearranged, nor anything to be added nor a tiny bit to flow away' (3.517–18). The deluded idea of an unmoved, unchanging, immaterial soul still has an active legacy in the sciences and other disciplines that treat knowledge as objective and their own knowledge performances as neutral or not entangled in their objects of study. The idea of independent observation does not explicitly posit an immortal soul, but it does so implicitly by ignoring the bodies of observers, the environment, their emotions, and the active role of other matters in producing 'an observation'. A relational field theory in physics, for example, is not enough if the act of measuring this field is itself *non-relational*.[14]

The Movement of Death

The soul dies and is in constant decay because movement is death. Lucretius describes death as a kind of walking or movement that leaves tracks across the body [*pedibus*] (3.529). Death is a kinetic process, not a state of being or a substance. Thinking about death as a substance or state is akin to thinking about the soul as state or substance. We imagine, Lucretius says, that the soul is simply a highly contracted eternal point in the body without any sensation (3.534). But this is a complete abstraction.

The existence of atoms is impossible for the same reason. There is simply no infinitely contracted eternal point outside of sensation. Nothing is immortal and unchanging because everything is in motion. All things, substances, and states die. Only process lives forever as death and decay: entropy. Interestingly this desire to imagine the soul as the contracted centrifugal point of the body results in its opposite. The eternal contraction of life into a single point would have to abolish all sensation (so it could avoid being affected or moved) and thus avoid animate life itself. In short, immortal life becomes pure inactive death. The desire of immortal eternity produces its opposite: a dead, unchanging, passive, non-sensuous matter. Immortal life is thus strictly a contradiction by definition. If it lives it moves, but if it moves it dies.

When we look directly at an eternal form in its divine purity, we die. This is why no one sees the face of God. When we look directly at the sun, we do not see the pure form of the circle or sphere; rather, we see the decay and destruction of the eyes. When we look for the purely non-sensuous immortal soul inside us we find instead, Lucretius says, a point of extreme sensation and production in the form of the *anima*'s ultra-fast and violent movements. In other words we find at the heart of life death, decay, and waste. At the heart of weaving is unweaving. The radical production of life is predicated on the continual death and destruction of that same body.

The Woven Vessel
The mind, soul, and body are completely woven [*conexu*] together into a single vessel [*vas*] that hangs together (3.555–7).

> *esse homine, illius quasi quod vas esse videtur,*
> *sive aliud quid vis potius coniunctius ei*
> *fingere, quandoquidem conexu corpus adhaeret.*

> The body appears as the mind's vessel, or something conjoined closely together, since the body hangs together and is interwoven with it.

There are two absolutely crucial points here. First, the body is *not* the vessel *of* the mind/soul. The body, soul, and mind are themselves a process of weaving in all creatures. Mind, body, and soul *are* a triplex vessel. Second, the whole person is a woven vessel or *calathus* made from dead matter.

The *calathus* [κάλαθος] was a cone-shaped basket woven from dried reeds originally used by the Cretans, then by the Greeks, and then by the Romans. The *calathus* was the original cornucopia, or horn of plenty, used to hold wool for weaving, fruit, vegetables, small animals, and other harvest products. As such, it was a symbol of fertility and abundance. However, like most of the poetic figures in *De Rerum Natura*, it is also an image of death. The *calathus* was woven from something dead (dried reeds and twigs) and was used to hold the dying products of the autumn harvest – the time when the goddess and/or her son-lover die (Fig. 4.2).

Homer mentions a silver *calathus* in two different and significant contexts. In the first, Helen descends a flight of stairs 'like Artemis of the golden arrows', and is given a chair to sit on and a *calathus* full of weaving materials to begin weaving (*Odyssey* 4.125). This dramatic scene, much like the older Babylonian 'Descent of Innana', re-enacts the seasonal death of the goddess during harvest. She moves from heaven to earth to the underworld. Artemis is also a triple goddess in Roman mythology, called Luna in Heaven, Diana on Earth, and Proserpina in Hades. Like the Babylonian Innana and Akkadian Ishtar, Diana moves between all three realms like the moon cycle, bringing life, death, and rebirth. Artemis/Diana is both the goddess of birth and death (in the hunt).

Helen thus performs the descent of the goddess who weaves together life and death. The *calathus* also figured in art and literature as connected with the goddess Demeter or Ceres (the goddess of the harvest),

Figure 4.2 A slave presenting her mistress with the *calathus*. Wikimedia Commons.

whose daughter, Persephone, dies and is reborn every year following the seasonal harvests. Penelope, Odysseus' wife, is also regularly portrayed with a *calathus*, as an image of her weaving her father's death shroud during the day and then unweaving it at night, in order to avoid being courted by her suitors while Odysseus is away (Fig. 4.3).[15] The important point here is that Lucretius mobilises this figure to describe the body, mind, and soul as something intimately related to the process of movement, transformation, and death. Like the *calathus*, creatures are woven, unwoven, and rewoven from the first-threads of matter.

Homer mentions the *calathus* again when Polyphemus the cyclops uses

Figure 4.3 Johann Heinrich William Tischbein, *Odysseus and Penelope* (1802), featuring the *calathus*/cornucopia. Wikimedia Commons.

it to strain the whey from his cheese curds in his cave (*Odyssey* 9.247). Here the *calathus* is invoked again as a double image of creation and destruction. The cheese is made but only on the condition that the whey flows out, just as the soul, mind, and body function like a sieve that takes in some images and is affected while others bounce off or flow out of the body. In the end, everything *moves through* the *calathus*.

In sharp contrast to Plato's idea of the body as a watertight vessel that holds an immaterial soul, Lucretius gives us the Homeric image of a dripping sieve defined by movement, filtration, condensation, and entropy: the leaky soul is defined by the constant process of life and death, creation and destruction. Even the *calathus* of the soul/body itself is not static, since Lucretius says that the soul and body are in a constant movement of weaving and unweaving. This is also why Lucretius directly contrasts the *calathus* or woven vessel with the body as a 'cage' [*cavea*] (3.685).

This is a radically anti-vitalist position. Lucretius is not a vitalist, and recent vitalist reinterpretations of *De Rerum Natura*, of which Gilles Deleuze's is the most influential, are deeply ideological and incompatible

104 Lucretius II

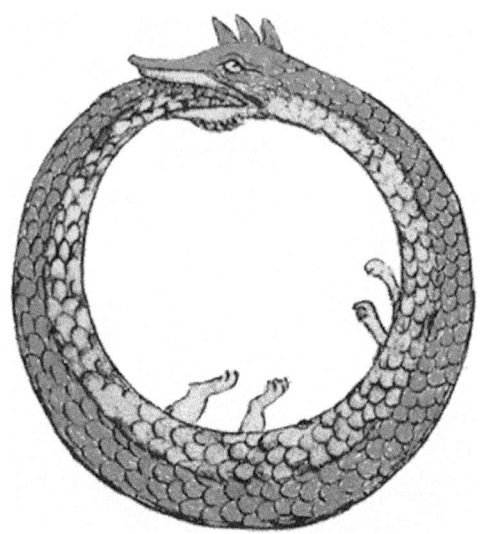

Figure 4.4 Ouroboros. Wikimedia Commons.

with Lucretius' explicit theory of death. Living sensation is completely coextensive with the movement of death and decay.[16] Lucretius says the soul flows or weaves through the labyrinthine folds [*flexus*] (3.587) of the body and unweaves them as well (3.438, 3.455, 3.470, 3.578).

Souls, for Lucretius, do not shed their bodies as snakes shed their skin, as the Mesopotamians and Egyptians believed (3.610). If you cut a snake in half or cut the limbs off a human, the body will flail around spilling gore until it dies, Lucretius says. This is an explicit rejection of an ancient symbol of eternity: the ouroboros, or snake eating its tail (Fig. 4.4). Lucretius says that when the snake is cut in half it will try to bite its own tail but it will fail (3.658). Life and death *do not* form an eternal circle but rather a spiral. This is why Neolithic cultures worshipped the snake and the snake goddess as *spiral* shapes, not as circles (Fig. 4.5). The snake is an image of the soul, not because it lives forever but precisely because its twisting, transforming body is spiral, just like the transformative iterations of life and death.

The Scatology of Spirit

Lucretius even compares the diffusion of the soul in the body to the digestion of food (3.702–12).

Dark Materialism 105

Figure 4.5 Minoan 'snake goddess'. Wikimedia Commons.

dispertitur enim per caulas corporis omnis.
ut cibus, in membra atque artus cum diditur omnis,
disperit atque aliam naturam sufficit ex se,
sic anima atque animus quamvis est integra recens in
corpus eunt, tamen in manando dissoluuntur,
dum quasi per caulas omnis diduntur in artus
particulae quibus haec animi natura creatur,
quae nunc in nostro dominatur corpore nata
ex illa quae tunc periit partita per artus.
quapropter neque natali privata videtur
esse die natura animae nec funeris expers.

> For just as food, when it has been distributed among all the pores of the body,
> and when it is being divided up among the members and all the limbs,
> is unwoven and from itself supplies another substance in its place,
> so the soul and mind, even if they enter whole into the newborn body, still are unwoven in the process of spreading out,
> while, so to speak, through all the pores there are distributed into the limbs particles out of which this nature of the mind is created,
> which now is master in our body, born from that
> which then perished, portioned into parts throughout the limbs.
> Therefore the nature of the soul is seen neither
> to lack a birthday, nor to be deprived of the experience of death.

Our bodies, minds, and souls are literally composed of environmental materials. The mind is not some *a priori* state or substance given to us at birth as whole, but is something made entirely from natural materials from outside us. This is an absolutely radical idea of the soul that connects it to the environment and to a much larger region of nature than most theories of the soul.

An even more radical position follows from these two arguments: first that our bodies, minds, and souls are made from natures outside us (3.708); and second that we are constantly weaving and unweaving these threads as we age or are diseased (3.472). We excrete old, decayed matters as we age, just as threads of the soul can be removed and added through drugs and medicines (3.476–510, 3.513–16). This means that we excrete our souls and that our souls were already the shit of others. Lucretius is thus the first in the Western tradition to write *The Scatology of Spirit*.

Just as food is brought into our body and unwoven, then rewoven into our bodies, so our material soul is actually physically replaced by new matters added and old matters subtracted through excrescence and expenditure. If our souls are material, it follows from Lucretius' comparison here that the waste from other organic and inorganic processes is brought into our body as food, where it is completely woven into our bodies. As we age or are injured, we actually excrete some of our *anima*.

Therefore, for Lucretius, the soul is not just mortal; the soul is shit. Our minds, souls, and bodies are the waste of other bodies, which we in turn waste by living and dying. The soul lacks nothing, not even death (3.712). The only true material plenitude must include the process of death and decay as its material condition. This is a radical condition for thinking about ethics. The ethics of motion, for Lucretius, cannot be about lack. There is no pre-existent wholeness or good form from which we have been separated, and there is no value that is itself not already the excrement or waste product of our dying sun and decaying cosmos. Life is not the struggle to preserve life or even simply to create new values, but to create through collective expenditure. We live to expend and discharge life. This is not a vitalistic ethics based on the mere affirmation of life, creativity, or generativity, but rather an ethics of weaving and moving well together – which always involves a fundamental expenditure or waste. Vitalistic ethics is still attached to a logic of preserving life and thus remains committed, as Deleuze's hatred of Book VI shows, to a fear of death, and thus a fear of the dark material others of history.[17]

Migrant Nature

An ethics of death has nothing to do with pessimism or optimism, but is about migration, movement, and turbulence (3.756–9).[18]

> *quod mutatur enim, dissolvitur, interit ergo;*
> *traiciuntur enim partes atque ordine migrant;*
> *quare dissolui quoque debent posse per artus,*
> *denique ut intereant una cum corpore cunctae.*

For what is changed is unwoven, and therefore passes away.
Indeed, parts are transposed and migrate from their order.
Therefore they must also be able to be unloosened throughout the limbs,
so that in the end they might all perish as one with the body.

Nature is migrant [*migrant*] (3.756). Nature is not a good or bad substance, nor does it tend towards good or evil. Nature is a 'migrant ordering' [*ordine migrant*] (3.757). But since 'what changes passes away', nature's movement is also a movement of death. To be is to move, to migrate, to walk. This is why Lucretius is always talking about his reader walking with him or wandering far from the path. Nature is a movement, and to know it we must walk and move with it. There is no stable ground or static life from which to talk 'about' nature, only paths that we can walk with or away from.

Historically, however, migration is also a state of precarity and an exposure to death. It is both the material condition for creating new forms of life, but also and simultaneously a risk of dying in transit, or dying through transit. Here is the paradox: migrant nature endures [*aeterna*], unlike the soul, because nature repels all blows, because it is nothing other than these blows themselves. In other words, nature is not a thing, state, or substance, and so there are no blows that can break it. It is the continuous [*solido*] (3.807) kinetic process of swerving material blows themselves. Nature is thus not divided from itself such that it could then break itself.

Finally, Lucretius explicitly rejects vitalism. If you think that there are 'vital powers' that hold the soul together and keep it alive, he says, you are *wrong* [*quod vitalibus ab rebus munita tenetur*] (3.820). There is no living thing that is not subject to the blows of nature.

Conclusion

Humans die because nature dies. Ethical practice, for Lucretius, is thus a question of moving and dying well together: weaving and unweaving. Matter is not vital but rather decaying, dissolving, and emerging. Every spring birth is simultaneous with the decay and rot of its composted winter ingredients. Every sensation of pleasure and pain is a transformation, addition, or subtraction of our bodies, minds, and souls.

The thesis of this chapter is that ethical practice begins with the collective vulnerability of death and decay. This includes not only humans but nature more broadly. If all of nature dies, then all of nature is also part of a shared ethical vulnerability or exposure to the entropic conditions of death and waste which are the material conditions of ethical action. Others die so that we may live and we must die so that others in turn may live. To live well is thus to increase the collective expenditure of life; which is also to die well together. Just as the flows of matter curve and bend towards one another in care, affection, and support, so ethical practice is defined by the curvature and mutual support of a woven social fabric of threads.

The consequences of this ethical starting point are radical: death is not something to be feared but the condition of vulnerability and expenditure at the heart of *inclined* ethical practice itself. This requires further explanation in the next chapter.

Notes

1. Georges Bataille, 'Corps celestes', in *Oeuvres complètes, Volume 1* (Paris: Gallimard, 1970), 520.
2. Karl Marx cited in Georges Bataille, *Visions of Excess: Selected Writings, 1927–1939*, trans. Allan Stoekl, Carl R. Lovitt, and D. M. Leslie (Minneapolis: University of Minnesota Press, 2008), 32.
3. See Thomas Nail, *Lucretius I: An Ontology of Motion* (Edinburgh: Edinburgh University Press, 2018).
4. Bataille, *Visions of Excess*, 45–52.
5. See Viki McCabe, *Coming to Our Senses: Perceiving Complexity to Avoid Catastrophes* (New York: Oxford University Press, 2014), and Ajai Raj, 'Feeling Hot Can Fuel Rage: Hotter Weather Sparks Aggression and Revolution', *Scientific American*, 1 January 2014, https://www.scientificamerican.com/article/feeling-hot-can-fuel-rage/ (accessed 11 September 2019).
6. McCabe, *Coming to Our Senses*.
7. Lawrence Williams and John A Bargh, 'Experiencing Physical Warmth Promotes Interpersonal Warmth', *Science*, 322.5901 (2008): 606–7, https://www.ncbi.nlm.nih.gov/pmc/articles/PMC2737341/ (accessed 11 September 2019).
8. Benedictus Spinoza, *A Spinoza Reader: The Ethics and Other Works*, ed. and trans. E. M. Curley (Princeton: Princeton University Press, 1994).
9. David Tong, 'Physics and the Integers', http://www.damtp.cam.ac.uk/user/tong/talks/integer.pdf (accessed 11 September 2019).
10. Tong, 'Physics and the Integers', 7.
11. Even the gods themselves are temporal beings in Homer. See Lorenzo Garcia, *Homeric Durability: Telling Time in the Iliad* (Washington, DC: Center for Hellenic Studies, 2013).
12. Francisco Varela, Evan Thompson, and Eleanor Rosch, *The Embodied*

Mind: Cognitive Science and Human Experience (Cambridge, MA: MIT Press, 2018).
13. Michel Serres, *The Birth of Physics* (New York: Rowman and Littlefield, 2018).
14. See Thomas Nail, *Theory of the Object*, unpublished manuscript, under review with Oxford University Press, ch. 16.
15. Penelope is constantly represented in ancient works of art with the *calathus*. See Hugo Blümner, *Technologie und Terminologie der Gewerbe und Künste: Bei Griechen und Römern, Vierter Band, Erste Abtheilung* (Leipzig: Teubner, 1886), 118.
16. The recent return to Lucretius has been unfortunately vitalist. Vitalist new materialists such as Jane Bennett have followed Gilles Deleuze's Spinozist-vitalist interpretation of Lucretius. However, Stephen Greenblatt has done the most to popularise the vitalist interpretation of Lucretius. 'With its no-nonsense understanding that body and soul "perish completely and forever," Lucretian atomism offers little by way of consolation for mortality, and yet – in Greenblatt's account – that little is just enough to hedge against loss. For all its diversity, the Lucretian renaissance he describes shares one triumphal quality: "a glorious affirmation of vitality" that "somehow extends to death as well as life, to dissolution as well as creation."' Steven Goldsmith, 'Almost Gone: Rembrandt and the Ends of Materialism', *New Literary History*, 45.3 (2014): 411–43, 417. 'It is important that Deleuze, keen to see Lucretius "denounc[e] everything that is sadness" and "mak[e] of thought and sensibility an affirmation," needs to disavow the poem's inconsolable end. It must have been forged by Lucretius's enemies, he suggests, because it is so terribly sad. "I fantasize about writing a memorandum to the Academy of the Moral Sciences to show that Lucretius' book cannot end with the description of the plague, and that it is an invention, a falsification of the Christians who wanted to show that a maleficent thinker must end in terror and anguish." Much of the affirmative vitalism of the new materialist turn, I think, is guided by Deleuze's determined philosophical happiness, which deserves to be assessed in its own right.' Amanda Goldstein, *Sweet Science: Romantic Materialism and the New Logics of Life* (Chicago: University of Chicago Press, 2018), 217.
17. See Peta Hinton, Tara Mehrabi, and Josef Barla, 'New Materialisms, New Colonialisms', for a decolonial critique of vitalist new materialism, https://newmaterialism.eu/content/5-working-groups/2-working-

group-2/position-papers/subgroup-position-paper-_-new-materialisms_new-colonialisms.pdf (accessed 17 September 2019).
18. Christina Sharpe, *In the Wake: On Blackness and Being* (Durham, NC: Duke University Press, 2016).

5. The Ethics of Motion

The ethics of motion is an ethics of living *and dying* well together. The ethics of life, vitality, generativity, animacy, and creativity is, by definition, limited to only a tiny fraction of nature and is thus fundamentally biocentric. Life, for Lucretius, however, is made of inorganic dead flows of matter and lives only through entropic decay. But his material and kinetic ethics is not merely an inversion of the bioethics and biopolitics of most other ethical and normative theories. Lucretius is quite clear throughout Book III that the mere inversion of bioethics and biopolitics entails necroethics and thanatopolitics. In order to preserve the lives of some, others are systematically dominated, destroyed, colonised, enslaved, and their land and wealth accumulated by those wanting to live longer, more, or better. The quest for life is identical with the production and management of regimes of death.[1]

Lucretius' inversion of the ethics and politics of life, however, does not result in merely valorising death over life but rather in rejecting the whole binary opposition itself. Life and death are historical, ethical, and political divisions in the entropic movement of matter. Matter flows, but in moving it creates new life and passes away or dies *at the same time*. There is no ontological necessity to conceptually abstract one part of this process from the other as if they were discrete, static states, or substances or be valued or devalued. Nature does not valorise life over death or death over life. There is only motion.

The argument of this chapter is that Lucretius' ethics of motion offers a critique of three core unethical practices that prevent our attempts to move well together. Lucretius provides us with three guiding suggestions for how to avoid these barriers to ethical action. In other words, Lucretius does not provide us with a normative theory of 'the good' but rather a description of the material conditions by which matter (including living and non-living matters) can collectively decide to move well together.

Kinetic ethics is thus a kind of anti-ethics insofar as the desire for unchanging ethical values is itself what is fundamentally unethical. The bioethical and biopolitical drive to preserve life and fix certain values produces its opposite: the necropolitics of domination and killing. Lucretius' solution is to show that life and death are part of the same movement that must be managed together by all those affected. There is no right or static answer to the question of the good – there are only practices that allow people to collectively direct the processes of living and dying well together (as they understand it), and those that stand in the way of this.

This chapter develops the idea of a kinetic ethics through a close reading of the final lines of Book III (830–1094). Here Lucretius provides, among other things, a kinetic theory of memory, a positive theory of desire (against lack), a critique of private property, and three material conditions for moving well together.

Death has no Value

Death is not a thing, nor does it have any value. Death is anti-value. Ethical values are not transcendent entities, states, or substances. Ethical values are strictly immanent to ethical practices. Ethics is thus not some human practice separate from the rest of nature but an emergent property of nature itself. Ethical practices are nothing other than habits or patterns of moving well together. Ethics is kinetic practice (3.830–1).

> *Nil igitur mors est ad nos neque pertinet hilum,*
> *quandoquidem natura animi mortalis habetur.*

> Therefore death is nothing to us and in nothing does it reach out to us, inasmuch as the nature of the mind has been produced mortally.

Movement, as we have argued in the previous chapters, is the basis of ethical practice. Movement always entails death, dissipation, and decay. We are therefore not alone in dying or in our collective patterns of motion. We are therefore not alone in ethical practice.

In other words, if ethics, for Lucretius, is finally liberated from bioethics and biopolitics, then all of nature can be seen for what it is: regimes of moving together and thus of moving ethically together. Ethics, in this very broad definition, is not anthropocentric – even if humans have invented some of their own methods for deciding how to move together.

If nature is sensuously related and self-affective, as we will see in Book IV, then it can move together with itself. If ethics is fundamentally kinetic, then there are many different ways of moving well together – many of which do not involve humans but are negotiated by other creatures and matters.

Everything dies. The matter of the soul, mind, and body, and the whole of nature breaks down. 'Death is nothing to us' is one of the most famous sayings of Epicurus, but it is rather inert. Lucretius adds to it by suggesting that death does not stretch out [*pertinet*] (3.830) to us directly and make us a unique victim. Our bodies and souls are nothing other than a region of nature moving and dying. From this material basis no immaterial transcendent values can emerge: only ethical practices and ways to live and die together.

After our souls and bodies are unwoven, they no longer have sensation as the woven vessel that we were (3.843–5). After this, the movements of the body and soul are rewoven into other matters and other patterns of motion. Therefore the goal of a kinetic ethics is to move well while we are alive and share that motion with others in death. In life, as in death, this is not totally under our control. During a huge, turbulent storm [*tumultu*] (3.834) or the conflagrations of war [*confligendum*] (3.833), for example, we realise that we have no control over how the future will fall [*cadendum*] (3.836). Movement is affected by chance [*accidere*] (3.841), and thus ethics must be responsive.

The Kinetic Theory of Memory

The belief in immortality is the desire to transcend the swerve of matter. But, for Lucretius, our soul does not survive death. Even if all the matters of our bodies and souls were recombined after our death, the new vessel would not be the same because we would not have the same memories (3.847–60). This is because, for Lucretius, memory is not something immaterial or static, like files in a filing cabinet that can be taken out and put back again.

By contrast, for a strict mechanistic materialist, it is hypothetically possible to produce the same person twice in the universe, because there is a total amount of energy in the universe and all matter is fundamentally identical and exchangeable. Lucretius, though, completely rejects this idea. Nature is an open process of endless delimitation and transformation. Because matter swerves [*inclinare*] indeterminately [*incerto*], the same exact movement of matter cannot happen twice in exactly the same way. Matter is genuinely creative and destructive such that the law of identity of discrete particles does not hold.

Lucretius instead uses the Latin word *repetentia* to describe memory as a kinetic process of *iteration* and differential return. Memory is a cycle or folded process. As such, it is not fixed and cannot be merely reassembled. Only discrete identical atoms can be reassembled, but processes cannot, because they are pedetic and indeterminate.

Nature can weave itself into the same order or spatio-temporal position [*ordine posta*] (3.857) again, but it cannot *move* or *renew* this order in the *same* way that it did before [*repetentia*] (3.851), precisely because it swerves at undetermined times and places. In other words, memory is kinetic. So if 'all the motions have wandered off all over from the senses' (3.860), then there can be only *similar* orders of these motions but no identical or substantial *memory*.

Ethical Abstraction

When we imagine our body suffering after death, we are essentially abstracting ourselves from the present and projecting it on to an inexistent future after our death (3.870–84). This same operation occurs when we abstract ethical habits from the present and project them into the future as if they will judge us after our death or as if they are eternal, unchanging values.

When we ask what the good *is* or what everyone *ought* to do, we are essentially acting as if we ourselves are not practising or influencing the outcome of the question by virtue of who, where, and what we are. We imagine that we can stop our movements in order to contemplate the static form of the good. But the good is not in a single mind; instead it is an emergent property of collective practice. Lucretius' ethics does not tell us what to do, but simply that we can figure out what we want to do together.

If you fear death and hate the body, this will result in both individual and collective suffering. The fear of death is at the core of power, greed, and the search for stasis – as we have seen. It is also, we should note, at the historical core of war, racism, slavery, patriarchy, capitalism, and other tributaries of power, greed, and violence. These unethical consequences are not 'bad' in any absolute ontological sense, but rather are anti-ethical barriers to collectively deciding how to move well together, since they foreclose the possibility of *pietas*. If everyone is not included in the ethical process then there is no *pietas* and no moving well together.

We imagine that when we die we will not be able to have all the pleasures that we had when we were alive. But, Lucretius says, this is an abstraction. We are again projecting our souls and bodies and the detached objects of our desires [*rerum super*] (3.901) into the non-existent future and then imagining 'lacking' them. Lucretius opposes this theory of desire as lack, as we saw in the invocation of Venus: desire is nothing other than motion, and all matter moves.

Kinetically, of course, things can be closer to or farther from one another, but nothing is ever strictly 'missing' or 'lacking' from the situation. The practice of imagining that one's desire for an object is ontologically separate from and unrelated to an object is what Lucretius calls *desiderium* (3.918, 3.922) or 'sad longing for something that one does not have'. *Desiderium* is the effect of the same abstraction that imagines that desire is lacking in the present and fulfilled in the non-existent future.

Ethics for a Leaky Basket

Matter flows through our bodies. It enters through sensation, respiration, and digestion; it circulates and is distributed through the whole body; and it is then excreted. This, for Lucretius, is the basic material-kinetic condition for pleasure. Pleasure is the circulation of affects as matter flows in, around, and out of our bodies. This material process of matter's composition, circulation, and decomposition of the body was explicit in lines 3.708, 3.472, 3.476–510, and 3.513–16, and was discussed at length in the previous chapter on the woven soul.

In the final lines of Book III Lucretius returns twice to the image of the 'woven vessel' [*vas*] or *calathus* from 3.555–7. Here he develops the implications of this image for his kinetic ethics (3.934–9).

quid mortem congemis ac fles?
nam si grata fuit tibi vita ante acta priorque
et non omnia pertusum congesta quasi in vas
commoda perfluxere atque ingrata interiere;
cur non ut plenus vitae conviva recedis
aequo animoque capis securam, stulte, quietem?

Why do you groan and bewail death?
For if your past and former life was pleasing to you

and all its enjoyments have not flowed straight though or gathered in
a *calathus* where everything moved through and ended unpleasantly
why do you not depart like a banqueter who is sated with life,
and embrace untroubled quiet with a calm mind, you fool?

The soul and body are interwoven into a single vessel: the *calathus* (3.555–7). However, the flows of matter and the pleasures they bring cannot be held on to forever. Everything flows through the woven vessel but is also continually refilled at the same time, like the superabundant cornucopia.

Ethically, then, Lucretius says, if 1) matter has not moved straight through us without causing any pleasant sensation or if 2) what matters have moved through our bodies have not caused only suffering, then nature has given us part of its abundant excess to enjoy like an enormous meal. Why not enjoy this excess and die having lacked nothing, 'not even death' (3.712)?

The poetic image here is manifold. First, the soul and body are compared to the woven *calathus* continually filled with all the excesses of the harvest season – connected to Demeter, Dionysus, Fors Fortuna, and numerous other harvest and fertility deities invoked throughout *De Rerum Natura*. Second, these lines explicitly refer back to 3.702–12, in which the soul is literally composed of food, medicines, and other matter we take in, enjoy, and excrete. Ethics is a matter of eating, digesting, and excreting well with others. Thus, the image of the harvest *calathus* is perfect. It is filled and refilled in cycles, just like the body/soul, and is emptied out again. Ethics begins with the material image of a human body composed of and entangled with the natural world. The body is not the cage of the soul.

It is therefore absolutely crucial not to translate or interpret Lucretius here as saying 'as long as you filled your basket and did not let everything run through, then you should be thankful'. This explicitly goes against his whole theory of the material and kinetic nature of the soul and his entire ontology, in which matter is constantly moving (composing and decomposing). Lucretius is extremely clear about this – matter is always flowing through the body. The ethical question, then, is how it *circulates*, what circulates, and whose bodies are affected.[2] Ethics is a question of collective circulation, not damming up, hoarding, or stealing from others.

Ethics is neither a question of filling a basket and capturing its

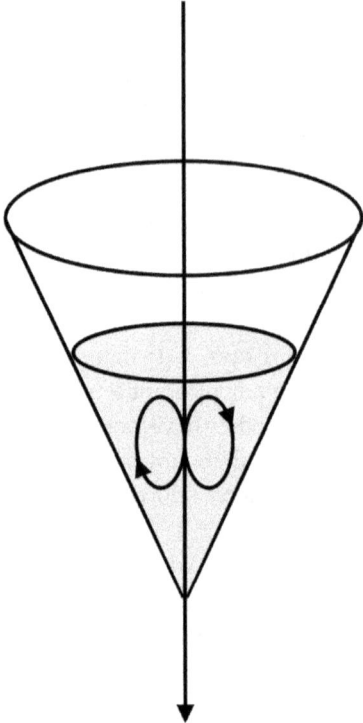

Figure 5.1 The metastable flow and circulation of liquid through the *calathus*.

contents forever, as Plato dreams, or of letting everything run through just as quickly as it is poured in without circulating. Rather, the ethics of circulation is a question of collectively circulating a metastable or homeorhetic pool of flows in the basket, which is continually being drained and refreshed at the same time. Ethics is not about fixed values or 'the good' or even the mere rejection of all values and practices of valuation. Lucretius' kinetic ethics is an ethics of fluid-dynamic equilibrium: a modulated relation of incoming and outgoing fluids (Fig. 5.1).[3] As Bataille dramatically says, in his short ecstatic essay, 'Joy before Death': 'Everything that exists destroying itself, consuming itself and dying, each instant producing itself only in the annihilation of the preceding one, and itself existing only as mortally wounded.'[4]

If what you have enjoyed has poured through (as everything does) and you hate life (which is nothing but this flow going through you), then why keep searching for something that will not flow through your basket? It does not exist. Everything flows (3.940–3).

sin ea quae fructus cumque es periere profusa
vitaque in offensost, cur amplius addere quaeris,
rursum quod pereat male et ingratum occidat omne,
non potius vitae finem facis atque laboris?

But if those things which you enjoyed have been poured out and perished,
and you hate life, why do you seek to add more,
which again will perish badly and pass away unpleasantly?
Why not rather put an end to life and trouble?

To those who hate the body, matter, and nature, Lucretius says, why not just kill yourself? As we saw in previous chapters, the social domination of women, slaves, poor people, the disabled, and the colonised – those seen as 'close to death' (3.65–73) – is connected to the hatred of matter, nature, motion, and death. Why not, Lucretius suggests, instead of killing other people (necroethics) to sustain the aims of your own life (bioethics), just kill yourself instead and save everyone else and yourself unnecessary suffering.[5]

The history of idealism is the history of the hatred of its material others (women, the body, racialised colonies, the poor, animals, and nature). Idealism is a form of asceticism in which the mind turns against the body through philosophy, religion, politics, art, and science. Idealism has thus weaponised culture against its own material conditions.

If one hates the fact that matter flows through our bodies and decays entropically, then one hates what one is. This is not just a hatred of the body and of others but of our entire entropic cosmos. Idealist ethics is self-mortification. The quest for *a priori* principles is a hatred of nature: a kinophobia. There are no *katastematic* pleasures because pleasure is fundamentally kinetic like the rest of nature.

For Lucretius, idealism is a non-starter for ethical practice. We must instead begin with the material physics of the body as the fold and circulation of flows; then we can figure out together [*pietas*] how to move well under these conditions. However, if we think we can actually stop and hoard the flow of matter forever in individual immortal souls, this completely undermines ethical practice.

Lucretius' kinetic ethics is not a mere rejection of individuals in favour of some mystical, Spinozist affirmation of nature in general. If we want to move well together, this cannot be achieved by Epicurean contemplation or Spinozist beatitude. We have to look quite concretely at the circulation of lived experiences and non-living bodies and what they share with one another (3.964–5).

> *cedit enim rerum novitate extrusa vetustas*
> *semper, et ex aliis aliud reparare necessest.*
>
> For old things, pushed out by new things, always
> yield, and one thing must always be built up out of others.

We are literally made of waste (from the cosmos, the sun, minerals, plants, animals, and one another). We are all vulnerable to one another and are entangled with one another's material well-being and movements. We move because something else moves through us. To decay, to waste, and to die is to move back through others and share what you are with them. The mutual vulnerability of *life* is not enough for a broader ecological ethics, because it is still too defined by the biocentrism and bioethics of *life*.

Rather, for Lucretius, we are not merely 'vulnerable life' confronted with the impossible decision of how to treat the human or even non-human other. We are already materially entangled with death insofar as someone or something died for our life and insofar as we are continually producing and sharing waste (carbon dioxide, heat, faeces, vomit, urine, sweat, our own dead bodies, etc.) with others for them to waste and share as well. Ethical practice is not a question of ideal principles or moral values; it is real material practices of sharing our waste and death with others.

By focusing on *ideas* of goodness, ethics has literally *wasted* its time. Lucretius reminds us that ethics is not just something we think. Ethics is something we do with our bodies, always together in a kind of materially entangled *pietas*. Lucretius thus asks us to treat ethics as a material practice of *both* the vulnerability of life[6] and the shared waste of death. The two are completely continuous in a new ethics of circulation.

Property is Theft!

The history of biopolitics is a history of theft and necropolitics. The Western tradition's obsession with and prioritisation of life (especially immortal life and transcendence in all its forms) has come at the enormous cost of human suffering for most of the population, disproportionally those material others of history (women, animals, migrants, the poor, slaves, the disabled, and the racialised and colonial others). In short, at the core of biopolitics and bioethics is the institution of life as property (3.970–1).

> *sic alid ex alio numquam desistet oriri*
> *vitaque mancipio nulli datur, omnibus usu.*
>
> Thus one thing will never stop arising from another,
> and life is no one's permanent property but the usufruct of all.

Property, for Lucretius, is an attempt to stop the constant flow of matter. Matter lives through death and dies through life, but biopolitics tries to arrest the process by trying to preserve one form of life at the expense of the other through property, which is a form of circulatory life that gathers flows of matter inside itself at the expense of the periphery around it (animals, migrants, barbarians, workers, slaves, etc.). It then consumes these matters and excretes them outside itself to maintain the illusion that this social form is distinct from what it consumes and what it wastes. But the soul, like the city, for Lucretius, is not an immortal substance or state but a circulation and cycling of flows. Property tries to delimit and protect a region of life for some by stealing energy from plants, animals, women, and the colonised.

Property, ownership, and the equality of exchange, all entailed by the Latin word *mancipio* (3.971), actually has the opposite of its intended effect. Rather than conserving energy, the protection of property actually *requires* an incredible amount of energy to preserve it, at the expense of the very sources of energy by which it was obtained, that is, ecocide, genocide, etc. For example, the Romans' accumulation of slaves was possible only because of a constant state of war, pillage, and kidnapping around the region. The preservation of a relatively immobile urban life of luxury required an enormous number of men with weapons to go out and kill, colonise, and appropriate new materials to bring back to the capital.

The thermodynamic lesson is clear: the relative stasis of the centre is possible only through an even greater expenditure of energy at the periphery that destroys the ability of ecosystems and others to share in the expenditure. Social and organic life is thus gyroscopic in the sense that its stability is gained not through immobility but through a highly coordinated series of mutual destabilisations. In the case of climate change these destabilisations now threaten the entire biosphere.

Social property and biopolitics is therefore already the secondary effect or product of a more primary practice and belief that life in general can be fixed and rendered static as property as such. Life can be bought and sold because it can be rendered relatively static and immobile. Therefore, the division between life and death (bio- and necroethics) is not an ontological division but a kinetic practice – something that must be performed habitually and reproduced through constant circulation. Movement is ontologically and ethically primary, and bio/necro metastable states are secondary, like eddies in a river sustained by a constant flow of energy from outside.

By contrast, Lucretius says that life is *not* property but *usufruct* [*usu*] (3.971). The Latin word *usus* means 'use, practise, habitually employ, enjoy, consume, undergo'. Life is not something we permanently own or that is ours in any strict sense. Life, for Lucretius, is above all something that we share practically with nature and with one another. Life is a particular region of a process that includes decay and decomposition. Our lives are like little entropic whirlpools, constantly filling with new flows and constantly excreting them in a precarious metastable balance. Life is the habitual and cyclical practice of consumption and excretion. The ethical question is how 'we' (in the broadest sense) can expend this energy together in collective enjoyment.

As a process, life is not a substance or state that can be owned or sold, and certainly not one that can be preserved in property. The process of living and dying is one we share with nature and is not limited to organic life. Our bodies are made of minerals, bacteria, viruses, and all kinds of moving matters that we consume as much as they consume us. When a human or other metabolic process is fully wasted, the matters are shared again.

For Lucretius, our personal use of our bodily matter does not make it *ours*. The flows and folds of the matters that compose our body-mind-soul are not *ours* simply because we happen to be using them right now. Socially speaking, other humans and non-human communities use and depend on our living practices. Our lives are collectively lived and thus collectively *used* and thus not our sole property. This makes us vulnerable before others but also foregrounds the ethical importance of trying to figure out how to move well *with others*, both human and non-human. If we think life is ours only insofar as we use it as individuals, we are still essentially treating our bodies as our useful property. This reintroduces the division between life and death and reproduces the twin anti-ethical practices of bio- and necroethics that have caused so much unnecessary suffering.

Kinetic ethics is therefore a process ethics of commoning and common use. That is, ethics is not merely the common usufruct of shared substances, states, or resources, but the performative sharing of processes that moves through user and used at the same time. Even more, the whole division between user and used breaks down in process ethics. Instead of a substance-based ethics of types and fixed species, subjects and objects, a process-based ethics is based on the constitutive relations of the whole pattern of circulation. The question of moving well together is therefore a *choreographic* question in which the divisions between user and used are blurred. We use bacteria to digest our food, and they use us to enjoy the food and mobilise energy. Nature uses itself to use itself, and so on. There is no 'prime user'. The commons are not merely resources managed by humans but the whole political process of use and mutual circulation among agents human and non-human.

As Marx says, 'Private property has made us so stupid and one-sided that an object is only *ours* when we have it, when it exists for us as capital or when we directly possess, eat, drink, wear, inhabit it, etc., in short, when we *use* it.'[7] Although Marx is speaking here about a specific form of modern *private* property, his point is consistent with Lucretius' critique of property. We tend to treat individual use as identical with property when naturally and socially our bodies are only part of a much larger metabolic circulation of material flows.[8]

The main anti-ethical barrier to figuring out how to move well together is the fear of death and its three primary consequences: 1) political domination, 2) primitive accumulation, and 3) the idealist hatred of the body, movement, and matter. All of these consequences treat the movement of matter as if it could be made into living property and thus weaponised against death and others.

What is the Ethics of Motion?

In the final lines of Book III, Lucretius provides some of his most vivid and explicit descriptions of the ethics of motion. Here, Lucretius describes three major features of his kinetic ethics alongside three anti-ethical dangers we face. Each ethical feature is tied directly to his ontology of motion, and each ethical danger is tied directly to an ontology of stasis.

We therefore conclude our close study of Book III with a careful reading of each of the three mythological examples as they define Lucretius' ethics of motion.

Pedetic Ethics: Tantalus and Fors Fortuna

The first aspect of the ethics of motion is that it is pedetic and relational. For Lucretius, there simply cannot be any deontological principle, utilitarian calculus, or fixed set of virtues for ethics. Ethics must be practical, experimental, and *response-able* to the process and relations that constitute a given circulation (3.980–3).

> *nec miser inpendens magnum timet aëre saxum*
> *Tantalus, ut famast, cassa formidine torpens;*
> *sed magis in vita divom metus urget inanis*
> *mortalis casumque timent quem cuique ferat fors.*

> There is no wretched Tantalus who, as the story goes, is numbed
> by empty terror and fears the boulder hanging in the air;
> rather it is in this life that empty fear of the gods crushes
> mortals, who fear the indeterminate fall that carries us all along.

For Lucretius, as usual, mythology tells us nothing about transcendent deities and powers but rather something about nature. Thus, the story of Tantalus reveals an important aspect of ethical practice. So let us look at each of the three ethical theses contained in this passage: the material and pedetic conditions of ethics, the ethical practice that is responsive to those conditions, and the anti-ethical practice that tries to block them.

Ontology. The first important thesis to note in this passage is that Lucretius' retelling of the myth of Tantalus is actually a description of the first central feature of his materialist ontology of motion: the pedetic swerve. Matter flows, but it does not flow linearly, mechanistically, or causally. Matter is capable of genuine indeterminate motion: pedesis. Matter was always 'in the habit of swerving' [*declinare solerent*] (2.221) and if it were not [*nisi*], 'all would fall like raindrops' [*caderent*] (2.222). Pedesis is not randomness, because if all of matter is swerving together, its movements are relationally connected to one another. One motion follows another, but if the motions themselves are indeterminate or not completely constrained by previous repulsions with others, then they are neither random nor determined, but are pedetic. Motion, as Lucretius says, does not occur in space-time, but space-time is itself a product of indeterminate [*incerto*] matter in motion.

Lucretius dramatises this ontological pedesis in the myth of Tantalus by emphasising the indeterminate [*fors*] (3.983) fall or flow [*casumque*] (3.983) of hanging [*inpendens*] (3.980) inorganic matter [*saxum*] (3.980) whose movement carries everything along [*cuique ferat*] (3.983). Ethical practice, like all of nature, begins not in the well-intentioned minds of moral philosophers but in the material movement and circulation of indeterminate and pedetic flows. Everything flows and dies according to the indeterminate (not random) movements of matter

Ethics. The ethics of motion begins with the ontological primacy of the indeterminate movement of matter. In his description of the indeterminate nature of the fall of Tantalus' rock, Lucretius invokes the Roman goddess Fors, or Fors Fortuna (3.983). Fors comes from the Latin verb *fero*, meaning 'to bring or to happen by chance'. The Roman goddess Fors Fortuna was originally modelled on Tyche, the Greek goddess of chance, who was in turn modelled on older Cretan fertility goddesses.[9] The Roman Fors Fortuna is thus directly associated with indeterminate and pedetic movement. Chance is a goddess who moves, and in moving brings chance. Chance comes through motion, and in motion there is always something deeply indeterminate.

Appropriately, Fors Fortuna, as an ancient fertility goddess, was depicted holding grain and was celebrated on Midsummer's Day, or the summer solstice. Pilgrims would hold a procession on both sides of the Roman river Tiber while decorated boats sailed down the river. Everyone drank wine (in turn associated with fertility, Dionysus, and epiphany) and played games of chance. Dice games in particular were played both as ritual and divination practice.[10] At the temple of Fortuna Primigena in Praeneste there was an oracular practice of divination in which a small boy picked out one of various futures that were written on oak rods. In contrast to serious games of skill and military strategy, dice games introduce an almost profound level of indeterminacy that exposes the players to the impossibility of predicting in advance by any law or knowledge the simple fall of a six-sided die. Only recently has chaos theory forced us to come to grips with the unsolvable, non-linear equations that have tried to predict even the simplest dice throw. A million tiny variables go into a given throw that are beyond the scope of Newtonian and quantum physics to predict in any rigorous way. Celebrants would float down the river to Fortuna's temple outside the city, perform secret rituals, and come back drunk and wearing fertility garlands.

Fors Fortuna was also associated with *virtus* or 'ethical strength'. This is an interesting connection because the ethical practice of responding dynamically to indeterminate motion cannot be fixed in a set of moral commandments or even fixed 'virtues', as we typically describe them. A pedetic ethics is therefore not only about human individuals but about a relational and collective process in which each is *response-able* to the others. There is no ethics of principles for Fortuna but only of flows. This is precisely why Fortuna is associated with rivers, water, and ships. She is depicted with rudders [*gubernaculum*] and wheels [*Rota Fortunae*] for steering because water and weather are pedetic and unpredictable. Ethics is about navigating the unpredictable together – not mastering nature or controlling it. There are no answers in advance but only conditions to respond to with others. We are all carried along in the flows of matter together and will die together. The river is also a river of death [Acheron] that we are ferried along, from the Latin word *fero*.

Fors Fortuna also carries with her the woven *calathus* basket or horn of plenty that brings together images of fertility, harvest, the woven soul-body, the flow that streams through the basket, and the contingency of these fertile water flows (Fig. 5.2). Fors Fortuna brings together all the pedetic but seasonal movements in agriculture, navigation, meteorology, and the material soul in a single image and ethics of relational and collective indeterminacy. Nature, weather, environment, food, and water bear us along and run *through* our baskets. We do not control them but are regional metastable pools of them.

Anti-ethics. Tantalus, however, is the anti-ethical figure who tries to dominate and stop this pedesis. Tantalus, as Homer sings, was the son of Pluto, meaning 'riches and other mineral wealth'. Zeus invited Tantalus to eat in Olympus with the gods, but while he was there Tantalus tried to steal the ambrosia and nectar that would make him immortal. To atone for this error, Tantalus then sacrificed his son by cutting him up and boiling him in a stew for the gods. When the gods found out what was in the stew, they punished him, as Homer describes:

> Aye, and I saw Tantalus in violent torment, standing in a pool, and the water came nigh unto his chin. He seemed as one athirst but could not take and drink; for as often as that old man stooped down, eager to drink, so often would the water be swallowed up and vanish away, and at his feet the black

Figure 5.2 Johannes Benk, *Fortuna*, Neue Burg, Vienna. Wikimedia Commons.

earth would appear, for some god made all dry. And trees, high and leafy, let stream their fruits above his head, pears, and pomegranates, and apple trees with their bright fruit, and sweet figs, and luxuriant olives. But as often as that old man would reach out toward these, to clutch them with his hands, the wind would toss them to the shadowy clouds. (*Odyssey* 8.582–93)

Tantalus is an anti-ethical figure because he is greedy for both material wealth [Pluto] and immortal life [ambrosia]. His fear of death leads him to steal the precious minerals from the earth (his own grandmother Chthonia) through extraction, and to steal immortal life from the Olympians, which in turn leads him to sacrifice his own son. Tantalus desires what he cannot have (wealth and immortality) as assurance against the contingencies of nature. He wants to escape the ethical condition of vulnerability and relational interdependence through wealth and immortality, even if it means stealing from and killing others.

His punishment is fitting. Because he tried to escape the indeterminacy of death and the vulnerability of life he is forced to live under a hanging rock that might fall and kill him at any moment. Because he stole based on bioethics he is punished with necroethics: to exist as the 'living dead'.[11] Because he tried to stop both pedesis and movement, he is forced to live under a dangling rock whose indeterminate movement will be his death. Because he was greedy to eat and drink the ambrosia and nectar of the gods, he is forced to thirst and hunger forever without satisfaction.

Tantalus is thus the anti-Fortuna. It is perfectly fitting that Homer says that as Tantalus reaches for food a *turbulent* wind blows it away, and as he reaches for a drink it *flows* away. In short, because he spent his life hating the indeterminacy of movement he is forced to live with its fluid dynamics in his death: the flows of water, air, and even minerals tantalise him endlessly (Figs 5.3 and 5.4).

Lucretius is not saying that there is a transcendent punishment for anti-ethical practice, but that there is a real, immanent punishment for anti-ethical practice *in this world*. There are many Tantaluses out there, whose fear of death leads them to steal from and kill people for wealth and power. They are tortured by wanting that which they cannot have (absolute wealth and immortality) and suffer the contingencies of nature as if they could control them.

Tantalus' desire is defined by lack, and therefore he will be condemned to suffer in this life. Socrates thought we needed transcendent punishments after death to prevent us from doing evil on earth, but Lucretius thinks the Socratic hatred of the body and the experience of desire as lack contains already the seeds of its own hell on earth: Tantalus on earth.

Figure 5.3 Tantalus. Wikimedia Commons.

Entropic Ethics: Tityos and Leto

The second aspect of the ethics of motion is that it is entropic or kinetically dissipative: matter flows and continually gives birth to new life while simultaneously destroying the old. There are a multiplicity of desires, but none lives forever nor can desire be satisfied by any external thing (3.984–94).

130   Lucretius II

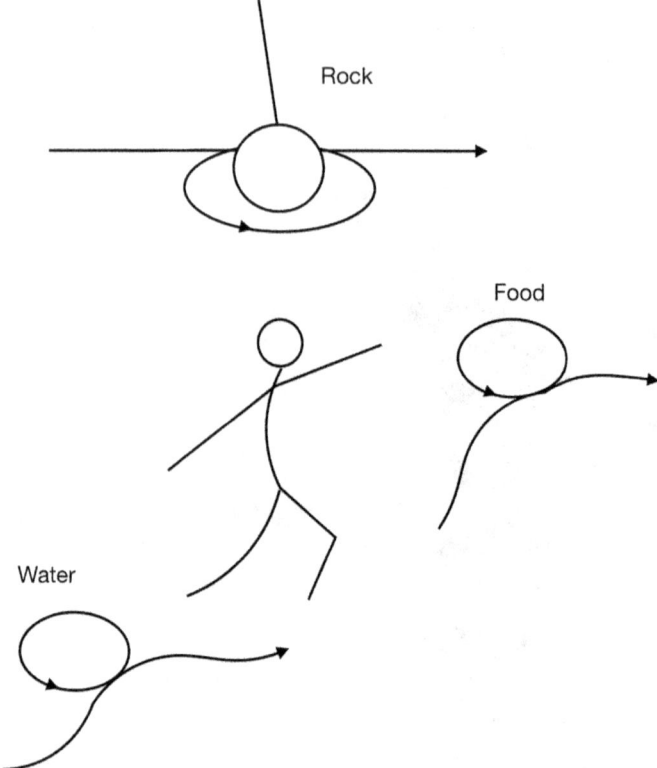

Figure 5.4 Kinetic diagram of Tantalus.

> *nec Tityon volucres ineunt Acherunte iacentem*
> *nec quod sub magno scrutentur pectore quicquam*
> *perpetuam aetatem possunt reperire profecto.*
> *quam libet immani proiectu corporis exstet,*
> *qui non sola novem dispessis iugera membris*
> *optineat, sed qui terrai totius orbem,*
> *non tamen aeternum poterit perferre dolorem*
> *nec praebere cibum proprio de corpore semper.*
> *sed Tityos nobis hic est, in amore iacentem*
> *quem volucres lacerant atque exest anxius angor*
> *aut alia quavis scindunt cuppedine curae.*

Neither is there a Tityos lying in Acheron whom birds root around in, nor at all are they able to keep finding

something pleasurable in his huge chest to probe forever.
However much he stretches out with the vast projection
of his body – say he not only covers nine acres
with his extended limbs but the orb of the entire world –
still he will not be able to endure eternal pain,
nor provide food from his own body forever.
But Tityos is here among us, and winged creatures
tear at him as he lies in love, and anxious anguish consumes him,
or cares carve him up with some other unsatisfied lust.

Ontology. All of nature dies and dissipates. There is no desire or love that lasts forever or that will allow one to live forever. All things [*rerum*] die, but the nature of things is nothing other than the immanent, kinetic process of living and dying itself. Although things appear to be discrete and disconnected at one level, the nature of things or flux of matter is not a continuous or discontinuous thing. It is the process by which matters come to be and pass away.

Ethics. Desire, like life, is not something 'we' have as our property. It is something we share [*usu*] and practise with others and the rest of nature. Desire is something material that moves through us. The desire for something that we do not physically possess is still something positive that we perform and that animates our bodies in pleasure and pain. As many desires as we can have and as many objects for them as we can find will all pass away over time, as will our body. In the face of our ontological situation in which nature is constantly coming into being and passing away, the ethics of motion is not the task of merely affirming all desires (vitalism) or negating them (asceticism). Rather, the ethics of motion is how to let them flow into you, how to circulate them, and how to let them flow out again in a metastable equilibrium of expenditure: the *calathus*. Desire, as a material movement, cannot be stopped and enjoyed forever. Everything must die and every desire for everything must die as well.

Lucretius contrasts Tityos' desire with Leto's. Tityos is a giant, lusting, phallic Titan, and Leto is the Cretan, Greek, and Roman Titan goddess of mothering and nurturing.[12] Both are mytho-poetic figures of desire, but Tityos' desire is one of unrestrained violence, domination, theft, and ultimately lack, while Leto's is one of labour, love, movement, nurturing, and excess. Tityos tries to appropriate Leto through rape in an attempt to obtain his external object of desire: a kidnapped Titan goddess he can have forever. Leto, on the other hand, is a migrant whose creative labours and nurturing support bring new gods into the world.

Leto's ethical practice is a migrant one that desires not only her own enjoyment but the creation of new sources of desire: new gods. She enjoys the creativity but also enjoys the enjoyment of her children. She is not a selfless, sacrificial mother-goddess figure. As the ancient Cretan goddess of childbirth and rearing, she enjoys herself through her children.[13] This is not maternal *sacrifice* or maternal *domination* but a joy *through others*. She enjoys relationally through the flow of her children as they come and go from her home on Delos. The joy of childbirth is both a pleasure and a pain; it comes and goes. In the Homeric hymn to Delian Apollo, many goddesses gather around Leto to support and witness her strength as she births the gods Apollo and Artemis.

Leto, in contrast to the earthbound, vertical phallus Tityos, is a migrant and foreigner in excess of every land (as a result of a curse by Hera for her sleeping with Zeus). Leto thus finds her home on the nonland of the floating rocky island of Delos, a kind of boat island technically detached from the land. Leto does not let go of all desire but rather finds a home for her desire on a mobile island, with crashing waves flowing in and out.

One day, Leto 'threads [διά] her way' from her queenly throne at Delos to Delphi. On the way, Homer says Leto passes by the 'beautiful dancing arenas' [καλλίχορος, *kallichoros*] in the town of Panopeus (*Odyssey* 11.580–1). It is important to note that Leto was worshipped on Delos as the great mother weaver and was often depicted with a spindle, linen clothing, and a woven veil.[14] Given her mythological origins as a Cretan mother goddess, all these images fit together. Leto is another historical incarnation of the Cretan ontology of weaving and unweaving that Lucretius gets from Homer and makes the basis of his theory of the soul-body.

To weave is to move well together. The Cretan labyrinth was a dancing arena or stage where life and death were played out along the lines of the butterfly axe – that other important image of the material and transforming soul. The dancers weave life together in the fertility dance of the labyrinth and then unweave back out again in death, performing and enacting an ethics of motion. The Homeric word *chora* describes well the nature of these beautiful dances [*kallichoros*] woven together in the performance of entropic cycles of life and death. The Homeric Greek word *chora* is the open, undivided space of the pastureland; it was the space created and opened up by the immanent movements within it.

We can now see precisely how Leto functions as the silent ethical figure of motion in Lucretius' example. Leto, the Cretan mother goddess, ties together multiple images of moving well together. Weaving is the collective practice of women that unites knowledge, nurturing, enjoyment, storytelling, and moving well.

Dancing is also a highly relational and entropic form of knowing (life and death) and of moving well together. In the dance an immanent space of desire is made and kept moving precisely by coming together and apart in mutual support. Delos was a sanctuary site for migrants, runaway slaves, foreigners, and others on the move without homes. Delos was the place where strangers moved well together. All of these kinetic practices are linked not to blind lust or the desire for violent appropriation, but rather to moving and desiring well together in practices of ecstatic knowing, oracular speech, and material transformations between life and death. The dead Python rots under Delphi so we may know the death that moves through our bodies and souls. Ancient ecstatic poetry and fertility rituals are not unrestrained expressions of violent desire but collective practices of enjoyment.

Anti-ethics. Tityos is the anti-ethical figure of motion for Lucretius because he cannot control his desires, treats the objects of his desires as purely external (lack), and violently asserts his desires over others in an attempt to satisfy them forever (immortality). Specifically, Tityos tries to kidnap and rape Leto on her way to Delphi. As Homer sings:

> I saw Tityos, too, son of the mighty Goddess Earth – sprawling there on the ground, spread over nine acres – two vultures hunched on either side of him, digging into his liver, beaking deep in the blood-sac, and he with his frantic hands could never beat them off, for he had once dragged off the famous consort of Zeus in all her glory, Leto, threading her way toward Python's ridge over the lovely dancing arenas of Panopeus. (*Odyssey* 11.576–81)

Desire flows through all of nature, but Tityos allows a specific desire to take over all his actions and tries to satisfy it forever at any cost (Figs 5.5 and 5.6). This is not moving well with others. Artemis and Apollo come to the defence of their mother, Leto, and fend off Tityos. The gift of life is thus reciprocated and granted back to the mother. In Tartarus, the gods punish Tityos by having birds feast upon his regenerating liver (the seat of the passions).

Figure 5.5 Attic red-figure amphora depicting Tityos and Leto.

In Lucretius' telling of the myth, he emphasises that all desires are entropically exhausted. There is no way to satisfy or capture desire once and for all in the *calathus* of our bodily souls. Trying to satisfy and thus stop our desires is not only painful and impossible for us, but can also lead to unnecessary suffering for others. 'Nor at all are they able to keep finding something pleasurable in his huge chest to probe forever . . . nor provide food from his own body forever' (3.984–6). For Lucretius, Tityos thus lives on earth in the entropic nature of all desires that cannot be satisfied in the form of external objects.

By contrast, the ethics of motion is neither about the renunciation of desire (since all desires entropically pass away according to their own motions) nor is it about the affirmation of all our desires at the expense of others. Desire is collective and can be enjoyed only by sharing it and passing it on for the enjoyment of others. If the conditions of collective desire are to be reproduced, then they must be shared. Partnership and *pietas* allow desire to circulate and move through our bodily souls and nature entropically and collectively: circulating together. In a

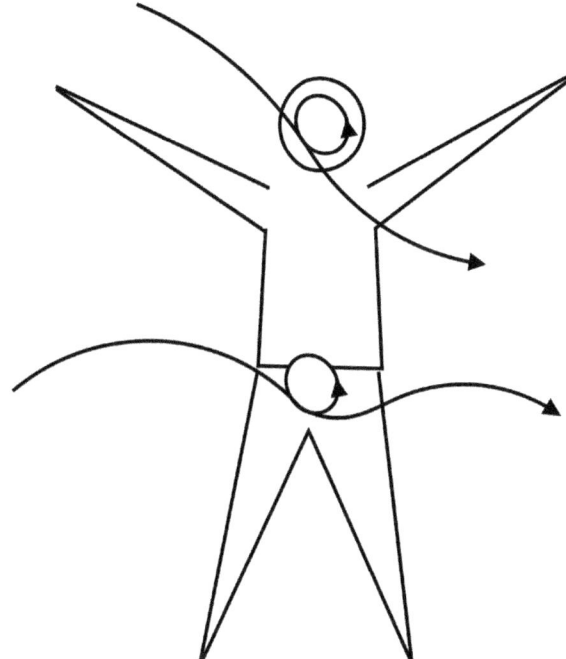

Figure 5.6 Kinetic diagram of Tityos.

strange sense, ethics is a way of living and dying together that secures the future shared life and death of those to come.

Desire is therefore not a lack but a superabundance and expenditure. It cannot be stopped or captured by individuals but must be passed on like a relay (and then, and then, and then . . .). If desire is not shared through consent, it does not pass. The violent assertion of desire against others not only fails to 'satisfy' desire but also disrupts the relay system of shared flows as they pass through one basket into another. Tityos is thus not only made to suffer the constant pain of unsatisfied lust but is also, Lucretius adds, forced to confront the finitude and entropy of bodily desire (without circulation).

Collective Ethics: Sisyphus and Fasces

The third aspect of the ethics of motion is that it is collective. Since matter is always pedetically flowing and entropically swirling, it cannot be dominated once and for all by a single ruler but is always a collective affair (3.995–1002).

Sisyphus in vita quoque nobis ante oculos est,
qui petere a populo fasces saevasque secures
imbibit et semper victus tristisque recedit.
nam petere imperium, quod inanest nec datur umquam,
atque in eo semper durum sufferre laborem,
hoc est adverso nixantem trudere monte
saxum, quod tamen e summo iam vertice rusum
volvitur et plani raptim petit aequora campi.

Sisyphus, too, is here in life before our eyes,
he who savagely thirsts for the rods and awesome axes
from the people and always goes away defeated and dejected.
For to seek power, which is empty and never really attained,
and always to undergo harsh labors in the process,
this is to struggle to push up the face of a mountain
a stone which rolls still yet again from the highest summit
and rapidly seeks the level areas of the even plain.

Relationality. Matter flows pedetically but also collectively. This means that there is simply no single rule or order that can master and control it for all time. The attempt to find such 'laws of nature' or 'laws of politics' is yet another quest for immortality through eternal knowledge. But nothing lasts forever, not even the laws of nature. The flows of matter can be steered like the rudder of Fors Fortuna, but they cannot be combined into a single, homogeneous unity like a giant rock and secured forever at the peak of a 'vertex' [*vertice*] (3.1001).

Pedesis is always relational because the flows of matter are always multiple, singular, and collective. Each flow responds to the others in a metastable equilibrium or 'vortex' [*vertice*] (3.1001). The vertex of social metastability is, in Latin, also a vortex of collective metastable motion. The 'weight' of matter keeps flowing without end. There is no final trick to escape the movement of entropy for us. Matter cannot be dominated; death cannot be cheated.

The fasces. A collective ethics of motion means that people and nature cannot be governed through homogenisation, universalisation, and stasis. Moving well together is both ethical and political insofar as the task is always a collective one, but composed of singularities with their own habitual swerving. Social patterns of motion are like gatherings of heterogeneous sticks from the forest, or *fasces* (3.996). Each stick is singular, and yet when bound together, they produce a metastable vortex or vertex that is stronger than the sum total of their individual strengths. This is why metastable structures such as weather or people [*populo fasces*] (3.996) cannot be well governed by a static set of rules or leaders.

In Lucretius' telling of the myth above, he contrasts Sisyphus, the political ruler, with the collective changing wills of the people defined in the image of an axe surrounded by a bushel of sticks [*petere a populo fasces*] (3.996) – which was the Roman symbol of popular power (Fig. 5.7). This image was passed down to the Romans from the Etruscans and Greeks, and ultimately from the Cretans. The axe, as we have discussed, was not a symbol of warfare but rather the Cretan *labrys* (Greek: λάβρυς, *lábrys*) or double-bladed butterfly soul. The *labrys* is the double-sided soul or movement between life and death. The *labrys* was also the labyrinth of the Cretan mother weaver whose flows twisted and folded like vortical dances. The axe is therefore an image of the bodily soul of a people.

The people are pedetic, singular, and bound in life and death with one another. They are the singular beings who share collectively a process of living and dying with one another. The Romans, and others, carried the *fasces* axe in a political procession because it was an image of the shared political movement. Instead of the Cretan labyrinth dance of life and death, the Romans carried the *fasces* axe in dancing procession. The Romans called the axe *bipennis* or 'two-winged', just like the two wings of the butterfly.

The Latin word *fasces* means 'bundle or band', from proto-Indo-European origins with the same meaning. The *fasces* is an ethical image not of homogeneity but of a group of singular gathered sticks bound together by a band. Since the sticks are merely a bundle and not a totality, they can always be added to or subtracted from and still be 'a bundle'. The size and composition of the bundle depends on what is gathered. So too, ethics is not a question of the unity and strict identity of its material composition but of the contingencies of the collective and their desires. The *fasces* was made from the earth, gathered from the forests, and made of matters that were not quite straight – each a bit twisted or queer.

In short, the ethics of motion, for Lucretius, is fundamentally collective. It is a metastable state or collection of singular material beings whose entropic movements of life and death are brought together in a social circulation or dance: a Cretan *labrys* or collective double-winged *bipennis* butterfly soul. The soul is thus not a merely imagined identity; it is a real, practical identity that gathers all the heterogeneous people into a single process (not state) of living and dying together. The butterfly is

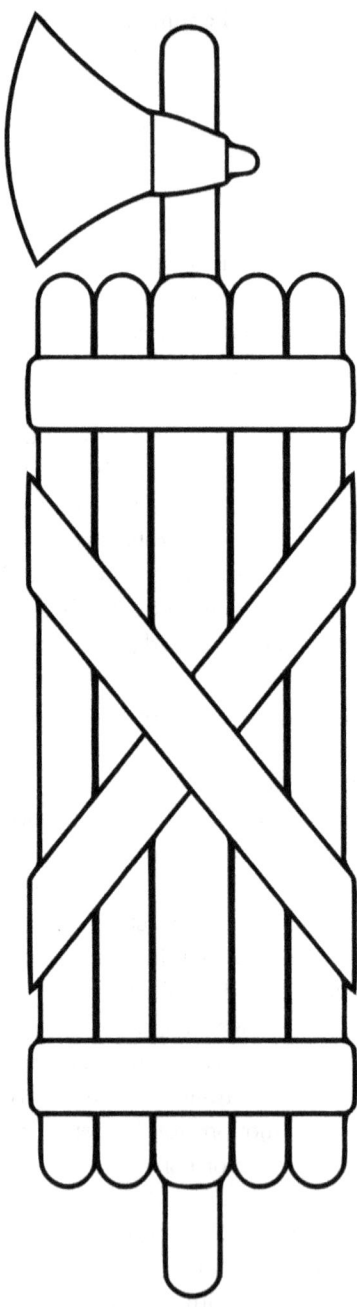

Figure 5.7 Fasces. Wikimedia Commons.

the moving or fluttering soul, just as the people are a moving and circulating, pedetic, social soul.

Sisyphus. Sisyphus is an anti-ethical figure in this myth because he tried to achieve immortality through political domination and evil trickery (Figs 5.8 and 5.9). Sisyphus was a warlord king of Ephyra who

Figure 5.8 Attic black-figure amphora depicting the punishment of Sisyphus in Hades. Wikimedia Commons.

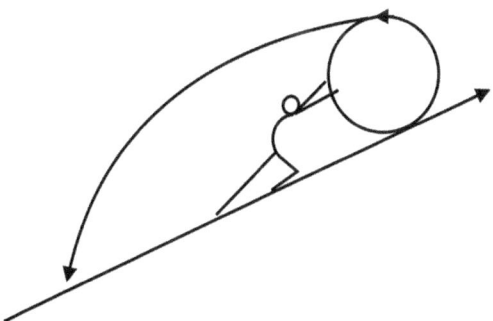

Figure 5.9 Kinetic diagram of Sisyphus.

expanded navigation and commerce through war, theft, and violence. He murdered travellers, migrants, and even guests – a violation of the Greek custom of *xenia*, or hospitality. In short, he was responsible for large-scale primitive accumulation in an attempt to expand his political power and wealth at the expense of others. He even tried to kill his own brother, Salmoneus, by raping Salmoneus' daughter, Tyro, and using her sons to kill Salmoneus – which failed because Tyro discovered the plot and killed the sons.

When Sisyphus died, he even cheated death (Thanatos) by asking him to show him how his chains in Tartarus worked. Sisyphus then locked up Thanatos and escaped. Ares eventually recaptured Sisyphus and returned him to Tartarus, where he was punished by being obliged to roll a heavy rock up a hill, only to have it swerve at the top and roll down again.

In Lucretius' interpretation of this myth, Sisyphus is an anti-ethical figure because he tries to escape death by dominating, accumulating, and murdering others. Sisyphus is the image of ancient political and economic imperialism. Sisyphus believed that if he killed everyone else, or had enough power or wealth, he could escape matter's movement towards death. Furthermore, he believed he could use trickery against the trickery of nature itself to avoid its pedetic and relational swerves. He spent his life tricking others because he thought he could dominate people and nature by doing so.

Sisyphus thus had to spend his death trying to compel a large bundle of matter (the boulder) to move in a straight line up a hill, but at the last minute matter would always trick him and roll back down. As Homer says, 'the weight [of the stone] would turn it back' (*Odyssey* 11.595–600). Immanent to matter is its own inclination, desire, or swerve that cannot be mastered. Politically, the axe-bundle of the people will not be dominated forever. As matter is forced into a single line or set of social laws, or homogeneity, it will erupt in a vortex that will send society back to the level fields of equality [*aequora campi*] (3.1002). The people will always swerve. Ethics is thus a collective practice that responds to the swerves of migrants, foreigners, and guests. There cannot be one set of laws, or even one set of people, forever and all time. Social ethics or politics must respond to the material contingencies of human and non-human matter and work with them. Matter, in all historically racialised, gendered, queer, and economic expressions, resists through swerving, just like Sisyphus' boulder.

We should thus, alongside Lucretius, reject Albert Camus' famous dictum that 'we should imagine Sisyphus happy', and instead 'imagine the boulder happy'! Camus' humanism and anthropocentrism lead us away from the radical naturalism and materialism of Lucretius, for whom nature and matter are in motion and actively desire or incline. Sisyphus was a murderer, a rapist, and an imperialist. We should imagine him *miserable* in his attempts to dominate nature, women, and the colonies, and to attain immortality by a rectilinear fantasy of domination. Existentialism rejected the immortality of the soul but replaced it with the contemplation of a strictly human existence radically different from matter. Sisyphus is and should be miserable, based on matter's more primary swerve in which the boulder turns back *by its own vortical movement*.

Conclusion

In the final lines of Book III, Lucretius builds on his theory of the bodily soul or *calathus* and provides three figures of ethical and anti-ethical practice related directly to his material-kinetic ontology. Our bodily souls are, like the fertile horn of plenty, continually filled up with the seasonal products of the harvest, but these also flow through (via digestion, decomposition, and decay) such that we are never completely filled with the fruits of life (3.1004–7).

> *atque explere bonis rebus satiareque numquam,*
> *quod faciunt nobis annorum tempora, circum*
> *cum redeunt fetusque ferunt variosque lepores,*
> *nec tamen explemur vitai fructibus umquam,*

> to fill it with good things and never satisfy it,
> as the seasons of the year do for us, when they return
> round and bear their produce and various delights,
> and yet we are never filled with the fruits of life,

Matter flows and cycles through us, but like the *calathus*, the cornucopia, and the harvest goddess of pedesis Fors Fortuna, we also transform, share, and excrete these matters. Plato said that the sophists were like 'leaky jars' because the truth always flowed right through them and was not saved and captured into a discrete, eternal form.[15] For Lucretius, however, this the material situation: decay and decomposition, without eternal forms of life. The *calathus* is a metastable equilibrium of flows going in and out in a certain pattern or cycle. The bodily soul is not a state or substance but a kinetic process. Ethics, then, can get off the ground only when it is not crushed by the weight of the Platonic and biopolitical drive to immortality and eternity. Ethics is about how to move well together and is thus stultified by all delusions of transcendence that think only of the agency of human individuals.

This concludes our treatment of Book III, which focused on the place of the human body in nature, and its relation to itself and others. Book IV, however, expands this into a larger environmental or ecological ethics in which the human body is a constant material and haptic relation not just to other humans but to the natural world. Humans and nature share the same ontological fate and thus share a similar ethical starting point for moving well together: mutual decay and decomposition. This will be the expanded topic of Book IV.

Notes

1. See Achille Mbembe, 'Necropolitics', *Public Culture*, 15.1 (2003): 11–40.
2. See Astrida Neimanis, *Bodies of Water: Posthuman Feminist Phenomenology* (London: Bloomsbury, 2017) for a more detailed treatment with respect to gender, class, race, ability, and orientation.
3. See Michel Serres, *The Birth of Physics* (New York: Rowman and Littlefield, 2018), 203.
4. Georges Bataille, *Visions of Excess: Selected Writings, 1927–1939*, trans. Allan Stoekl, Carl R. Lovitt, and D. M. Leslie (Minneapolis: University of Minnesota Press, 2008), 238.
5. Lucretius is not suggesting that those who are in chronic pain should commit suicide. He is asking those who derive *absolutely no* pleasure from the world at all, 'If you hate the body so much why not kill it?' The only people who hate all of matter and the body so profoundly are idealists. The idea that the disabled body is pure suffering is the dominant anti-disability narrative, *contra* the lived experience of disabled lives that include joy and pain. See Carrie Sandahl, 'Black Man, Blind Man: Disability Identity Politics and Performance', *Theatre Journal* 56 (2004): 579–602.
6. See Judith Butler, *Precarious Life: The Powers of Mourning and Violence* (London: Verso, 2006). Butler's description of life is deeply anthropocentric.

7. Karl Marx, *Early Writings* (New York: Penguin, 2005), 351.
8. See Thomas Nail, *Marx: The Birth of Value*, unpublished manuscript, under review with Oxford University Press.
9. 'Fortuna (Fors Fortuna) was probably originally a fertility goddess but became identified with the Greek goddess Tyche.' Lesley Adkins and Roy Adkins, *Handbook to Life in Ancient Rome* (New York: Facts on File, 2009), 290.
10. Joshua Ramey, *Politics of Divination: Neoliberal Endgame and the Religion of Contingency* (London : Rowman and Littlefield, 2016).
11. Mbembe, 'Necropolitics'.
12. Artefacts of Leto have been found on Crete in a hearth temple, and in Phaistos Leto was connected with an initiation cult. Walter Burkert, *Greek Religion* (Cambridge, MA: Harvard University Press, 1985), 365.
13. Over the course of Hellenisation, Leto was identified with the local mother goddess of Anatolian Lycia. T. R. Bryce, 'The Arrival of the Goddess Leto in Lycia', *Historia: Zeitschrift für alte Geschichte*, 321 (1983): 1–13.
14. 'The conception of a goddess enthroned like a queen and equipped with a spindle seems to have originated in Asiatic worship of the Great Mother.' O. Brendel, 'The Corbridge Lanx', *The Journal of Roman Studies*, 31 (1941), 100–27, 113ff. See also Pierre Roussel, *Délos, colonie athénienne* (Paris: Boccard, 1916), 221.
15. See Plato, *Gorgias*, 492e–494a.

Book IV

6. Ethics of the Simulacrum

Book IV of *De Rerum Natura* provides perhaps one of the most radical materialist theories of sensation in the history of philosophy. In Book III, Lucretius gave us an ethical theory based on the kinetic mortality of all living individual bodies. In Book IV, however, Lucretius extends his ethics of motion to *inorganic non-living bodies* as well – or what he calls *simulacra*. Books I and II gave us an ontology of moving and folded matter, and Book III drew on this ontology to show how individual living creatures (*anim-*) emerge as a metastable and entropic process in these flows. Book IV, however, brings all three previous books together to show the full range of entangled living and dying processes that results when inorganic and individual living creatures are considered together as two aspects of the same woven flows of matter. In short, Book IV of *De Rerum Natura* gives us one of the first, if not the very first, 'material ecologies' of nature in the Western tradition.

The argument of this chapter is that Lucretius' ethics of motion does not pertain only to humans or even to living creatures more generally, but provides a fully ecological ethic that takes seriously non-living forms of sensation and affect. Moving well *together* in the face of mutual vulnerability, for Lucretius, is something that includes both living and non-living bodies. This radical thesis contained in Book IV follows as a direct consequence of Book III. If living creatures and their souls are *made from* and *return back to* non-living flows of matter, then moving well together must include an ethics of the non-living flows that are the immanent and constitutive conditions of all individual emergence.

The first major concept in this new naturalistic or 'ecological' ethics is what Lucretius calls *simulacra*, which are the material conditions for all sensation in living and non-living bodies and thus at the core of a truly non-anthropocentric ecological ethics that takes seriously the collective and inorganic nature of movement, desire, and death. The focus of this chapter will be to introduce this first major concept of what we might call Lucretius' 'ecokinetic ethics' through a close reading of the first 200 lines of Book IV. In these beautiful lines, Lucretius provides, among other things, a materialist theory of sensation in which matter is simultaneously *active and passive*, and a performative theory of what I am calling 'ecological' or 'atmospheric' affect. Together these twin insights provide the starting point for building a new ethical naturalism or what today we might call a 'new materialist' ethics.[1] What is so radical about Book IV is that Lucretius' ethical theory is not constrained to the domain of humans or even of living individuals but is *something nature itself does*.

The Language of Flowers

Book IV begins with a proem that repeats almost exactly lines 1.926–50. Before Lucretius introduces the theory of the simulacrum, he reminds us again of the materialist method he is using to derive it. The repetition of these lines, especially in a proem, shows us first of all how important they are as a methodological statement. These are the lines that Lucretius wants us to remember about his work and to keep in mind as the origin of his theory of the simulacra.

Second, these lines are important because they are the only clear place in the whole of *De Rerum Natura* where Lucretius *explicitly* claims to be doing something completely original. The proem of Book III, by contrast, began with a satiric mimicry of Epicurus. Here, in Book IV, however, Lucretius makes clear precisely in what sense his poem is *absolutely irreducible* to Epicurean fundamentalism.

Since these lines are duplicates from Book I, I have already discussed them in *Lucretius I*. However, as the proem of Book IV, these same lines take on further meaning that needs to be discussed with respect to Lucretius' ethico-aesthetic theory of ecological affect developed in Book IV.[2] First of all, it is crucial to remind the reader of the context and importance of the lines immediately preceding these proem lines as they appear in Book I (1.921–6).

nec me animi fallit quam sint obscura; sed acri
percussit thyrso laudis spes magna meum cor
et simul incussit suavem mi in pectus amorem
Musarum, quo nunc instinctus mente vigenti

*avia Pieridum peragro loca nullius ante
trita solo.*

I am very aware how obscure these things are.
But great hope for praise strikes my heart with a sharp *thyrsus*
and at the same time strikes into my breast sweet love
for the Muses. Now roused by this in my lively mind
I am traversing the remote places of the Pierides, untrodden by the
sole of anyone before.

The source of Lucretius' poetic knowledge comes directly from nature *as nature itself*. Lucretius does not learn about nature through detached neutral observation or a series of objective instrumental measures. In other words, Lucretius is not a precursor to the scientific methods found in early modern appropriations of his work by Francis Bacon, René Descartes, and Isaac Newton. Nature's secrets, for example, are not 'tortured' out of her by Lucretius.[3] Instead, Lucretius grounds his poetic knowledge in the sensation of nature, which is, at the same time, *an active performance of nature's own sensation of itself*. Lucretius is therefore also not a precursor to the empiricism of John Locke, George Berkeley, or David Hume. Reason, for Lucretius, likewise does not put nature 'on trial' and sadistically interrogate her, as Kant describes his own method.[4]

In these lines, Lucretius says that he enters into a mutual performative transformation *with and as nature*. Both poet and nature are transformed at the same time because they are the same thing. Lucretius undergoes a kind of geological transformation by performing what nature *already does*. His body becomes the earth, which is invaginated with the seeds of Dionysus' *thyrsus*. So just as the earth gives birth to flowers through seeds, so Lucretius' body gives birth to embodied knowledge. There is a double consequence of this. Flowers have knowledge, and Lucretius himself becomes a flower when he knows.

Through the introduction of matter into the body in the form of such intoxicating or mind–body-altering substances as mead, herbs, fumes, and so on, Lucretius' mind blooms [*mente vigenti*] (1.925) and comes to life. The flower stalk, or *thyrsus*, becomes Lucretius, and Lucretius himself becomes a flowering plant. Rather than presenting himself as something entirely different from nature in order to observe or contemplate it, Lucretius says that his body is animated by and as nature. This is an absolutely crucial and radical comment about the nature of knowledge and sensation. If, in order for Lucretius to know and to sense he must become a flower, then what does this say about flowers? Flowers and nature must already know something that Lucretius can know only by becoming them.

Knowledge is therefore not the mental state of an unnatural and unmoved human mind. If we take Lucretius' claim to originality here seriously, knowledge is an act; it is a movement. Hence, Lucretius becomes a flower and moves through the mountains. New knowledge is tied directly to new places, new flowers, new springs. These lines are a crystal-clear affirmation of Lucretius' connection to the epiphanic and oracular tradition, in which sages and priestesses at Delos, Delphi, Dodona, and countless other sites travelled into the mountains to oracular springs such as Telphusa's, to ingest intoxicating herbs and listen to the earth's volcanic vents, winds, trees, and waters.

In other words, for Lucretius, knowledge is already something nature *does*. Knowledge is not information or ideas *about* nature. The image of the flower contains the basic material structure of what humans call knowledge. The flower lives between worlds. It is buried under the earth in rot, decay, and inorganic death, but then transforms those minerals through a vertical tube structure oriented towards the open sky. Its body feeds from the air and sun and constantly decays and regrows. The flower is a tension between earth and the openness of the sky, death and life, closed and open, down and up.

The flower is the earth made vertical. It is the earth made sacrificial. The flower grows to die and lives on its own death as its lost leaves and flowers return to the soil. The earth thus comes to know the sky and itself through the plant's living and dying. The flower itself is a dramatic expression of the earth's expenditure and excess. The flower is not an eternal truth or immortal beauty, as idealists and philosophers and poets often wax. It is a fleeting moment of joy before death.[5] The flower does not have any representational knowledge about the world, but rather is an immanent and atmospheric performance of nature's knowledge of itself.[6] The flower, like material knowledge, is not a culmination but a sensuous moment, like a poetic idea, in the life of the plant.[7] Why is human difference a more important difference than the difference between earth and sky or flower and stalk?

This is a profoundly important starting point for thinking about the practice of an ethics of motion. Ethics is not deduced from *a priori* principles or something we know *about nature* but rather is something that nature *does* and that *we do with it*. All ethics must be rethought as naturalistic, ecological, and even geological. There is no ethics that is not already entangled in nature's performance. Human animals have adopted the vertical tubular bodies of plants. Our bipedal verticality gives rise to the colourful bloom of the eyes, mouth, ears, and nose: the flower of the sensitive face. This basic natural kinetic structure already existed in plants and flowers. Therefore the flower is not a mere human metaphor for knowledge or beauty. Rather, the flower is already the material constitutive condition for human knowledge and beauty itself (4.1–4).[8]

iuvat integros accedere fontis
atque haurire, iuvatque novos decerpere flores
insignemque meo capiti petere inde coronam,

It is a joy to approach pure springs
and to drink from them, and it is a joy to pick new flowers
and to seek a pre-eminent crown for my head from that place

Lucretius wanders through the mountains, just as Leto and other pilgrims did, to Delphi. He looks for knowledge not in the libraries but in the wilderness. He drinks from wild springs and picks 'new flowers' [*novos flores*] (4.3), like the Delphic bees. Here again Lucretius compares himself to a bee and thus compares poetic sensuous knowledge to flowers to be sampled. From their nectar he ferments his own poetic, sensuous knowledge. He then makes himself a crown of flowers just like the Dionysian revellers.

Here, Lucretius completes the poetic image. Just as the flower already performs the knowledge of the earth, so Lucretius turns himself into a flower. To know nature, one must know nature as nature knows itself. His body becomes the earth, planted with seeds, and his senses blossom. He walks to where the earth touches the sky (the mountains), drinks water, and then crowns his head with flowers. In this way Lucretius tries to know nature not as an ontologically distinct human observer but by becoming the mineral, atmospheric, vegetal, and animal being that he is and that nature has made to know itself.

Lucretius thus speaks to us about nature, sensation, and simulacrum not as a moral theorist telling us what to do; rather he performs for us what flowers already know about ethics. This is a complete inversion of what typically goes by the name of 'environmental' or 'ecological' ethics based on the extension of the idea of 'value' to nature. Rather, for Lucretius, human ethics is already an extension *of nature*.

Process Ethics of the Simulacrum

The *simulacrum* is absolutely central to understanding the ethics of motion. Living creatures have moving and ensouled bodies, as we know from Book III. However, life is only a *metastable state* in a vast natural world of sensuous and affective moving matter. Ethics, therefore, cannot be fully understood epistemologically or individually. Therefore we need not only an ethico-epistemology of motion but also an ethico-aesthetics of motion. The 'we' of moving well 'together' is radically entangled and ecological precisely because of the nature of simulacra. We cannot move well together if the *we* includes only *living* individuals (4.26–32, 4.45–58).

Atque animi quoniam docui natura quid esset
et quibus e rebus cum corpore compta vigeret
quove modo distracta rediret in ordia prima,
nunc agere incipiam tibi, quod vementer ad has res
attinet, esse ea quae rerum simulacra vocamus;
quae, quasi membranae summo de corpore rerum
dereptae, volitant ultroque citroque per auras,

I have further shown how the nature of the mind,
and life is braided together from matter,
and is eventually unraveled back into its first-threads,
now I will begin to treat for you what closely relates
to these things: that there exist what we call *simulacra*,
which, like membranes ripped from the outer surface
of things, fly back and forth through the air.

Sed quoniam docui cunctarum exordia rerum
qualia sint et quam variis distantia formis
sponte sua volitent aeterno percita motu
quoque modo possit res ex his quaeque creari,

I have shown how nature is woven together
through spontaneous flows of endless motion
and through various formative lengths
which measure the creation of things

First, Lucretius provides the context for the appearance of simulacra. In Books I and II, Lucretius showed us how nature is woven [*exordia*] together [*cunctarum*] and into things [*rerum*] through the free swerving of endless kinetic flows. As matter flows, it weaves different lengths and measures that create things, just like the *textum* of lines and metre in poetic performance. In Book III, Lucretius showed us how the living mind was woven from these same flows and becomes unwoven in death. Life and death are nature's poetry in action.

Now, in Book IV, simulacra, he says, are woven from this same material process that the mind is. Lucretius says that simulacra are 'things' [*rerum simulacra*] (4.31), and thus distinct from (although not ontologically different from) the *corpora*, *materies*, or *ordia prima* as described in Books I and II.[9] Simulacra are sensuous things composed of folded and woven first-threads or *ordia prima* (4.28). Simulacra are the folded patterns made by the *corpora*.

Theory of the Simulacrum

The theory of simulacra is perhaps one of Lucretius' most brilliant theories, resonating deeply with contemporary understandings. Unfortunately, it has been largely misinterpreted as 'outdated'. Lucretius, the story goes, thought that we sense things because things emit particles that hit our senses. Today, we know that we see things because light bounces off them and hits our eyes. Lucretius was close, but in the end he missed the mark. In this section I would like to demonstrate that Lucretius' theory of the simulacrum is not only incompatible with classical optics, based on linear causality, but is actually strikingly consistent with contemporary optics.

First of all, Lucretius was physically correct *avant la lettre* that all things continuously shed a material membrane that flies off in all directions through the air. As far as we know now, thanks to the initial discoveries of Ludwig Boltzmann (1844–1906), all matter above absolute zero (i.e. all matter) is continually radiating heat in the form of photons through the air. Even more precisely, we know, thanks to the founding quantum theorist Max Planck (1858–1947), that all matter is emitting electromagnetic radiation in the form of photons at a distinctly measurable lower limit or rate of thermal radiation. Below this level, called Planck's constant, there is an indeterminate movement of matter. Below Planck's constant there is no way to measure the thermal decay rate, not because nothing is happening below this level but because matter is swerving so indeterminately that it cannot be measured in spatio-temporal units or 'quanta'.[10]

Lucretius did not use this terminology or experimentally produce these same results, but his description is not inconsistent with this contemporary understanding. All things *are* continually shedding or radiating membranes or simulacra of photons. Below the level of measurable spatio-temporal things [*rerum*] and simulacra, however, Lucretius says that *corpora* move and continually swerve in '*incerto tempore*' and '*incertisque locis*' [in indeterminate time and space] (2.218–19). For Lucretius, as for quantum physics, entropy and shedding occur precisely because of the non-self-identical or 'swerving' movement of matter. *Corpora* move, but since they do not move uniformly, they do not return merely into themselves but are only partially reabsorbed. The rest is shed like membranes of radiation.

How then does this explain contemporary optics? Lucretius says that the sun is also a body that sheds an incredible amount of extremely fast-moving simulacra. These simulacra, or photons, then hit things on Earth, bounce off, and affect and transform our senses. The optical theory of colour as wavelengths is thus completely consistent with Lucretius' description that all spatio-temporal things shed simulacra which bounce off one another and intermingle as diffracted sensory images.

Diffraction

More specifically, the membranes [*membranae*] (4.31) shed unique simulacra patterns that intersect and transform one another in precise ways. The release of membranes is not just the random radiation of photons. Patterns of moving matter emerge and diffract like waves rippling through the water, meeting and creating something new. This new third diffracted wave is neither the sum of the first plus the second nor an interaction between two distinct waves. Rather the third wave is a new wave or simulacral pattern (Fig. 6.1).

This theory of the simulacrum has profound consequences for ethics, aesthetics, epistemology, and ontology. Ontologically, this theory entails that there simply are no static objects or things. There are only kinetic processes whose continual decay (or entropy) radiates simulacra in all directions. This means that things are fundamentally relational and affected by direct material entanglement. Things really are actively moving together and affecting one another. In strict ontological terms nothing is identical to itself because matter is continually decaying and being affected in a complex knotwork of kinetic patterns.

Epistemologically, the same is true of our minds and bodies. There is

Ethics of the Simulacrum 155

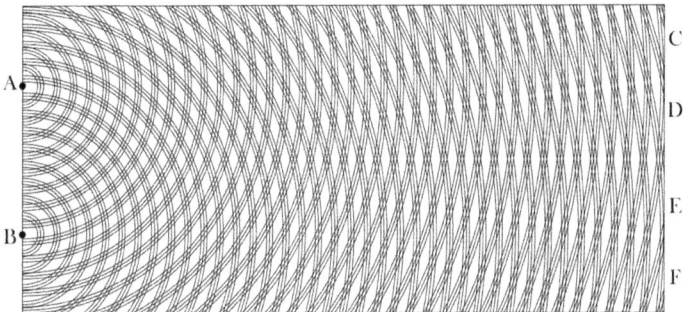

Figure 6.1 Diffraction of light waves. Wikimedia Commons.

thus no such thing as neutral observation, measurement, or contemplation, without transformation. To know is to do, and to do is to move and thus be transformed. The theory of simulacra means that there is no static knower observing a static object. Both observe and affect each other.

Aesthetically then, sensation is never a sensation of something *fully present*. There is no 'thing' that is static or self-identical enough to be present to an observer. Sensation is always an active, moving intertwinement of simulacra as they radiate off other bodies and intermix. This theory of sensation is quite different from the billiard-ball causal theories that were historically inspired by it. This is the case not only because the whole network of interactions is so complex and entangled that one could not possibly calculate the range of interactions, but even more importantly because the *corpora* at the kinetic heart of the process are indeterminately swerving. Thus, indeterminacy and pedesis are built in to the simulacral system. If matter is active, moving, and affective, then any observation or sensation of such things will itself require the use of simulacra to see them. But if the simulacra (photons) are needed to see things, then they also affect things and thus really and physically affect what one is seeing. Again, this is consistent with quantum physics.

For Lucretius, there simply is no static position from which to sense the world that is not already transforming the world. This does not mean that objects 'withdraw' from us and that we only have appearances without reality. It means the opposite: that there are no appearances at all, only real sensation. Things really are throwing themselves into the air and really are affecting us. There is nothing withdrawn or absent about the object because the object also moves and affects itself by shedding. From deep down in the thing up to its surface, simulacra are moving around. Things do not withdraw from nature since material relations are always in flux.

Lucretius' theory of simulacra also has consequences for ethics. First of all it means that there are no static subjects, actions, or objects that define the typical parameters of ethical theory. Subjects, objects, and actions are not fixed things that can be separated from one another and calculated out, but active processes that are continually transforming everything around them and being transformed at the same time. There is no neutral subjective space of ethical contemplation, nor is there any direct consequential control over objects. There is only ongoing ethical practice. Such a practice is not a question of an interaction between subject and object, but rather a mutual transformation or creation of something new which is not reducible to either.

Second, simulacral ethics means that no domain of objects can be legitimately denied ethical consideration. The history of ethics up to the present has been largely defined by the extension of human moral consideration to 'others': to black people, to women, to animals, to the environment, and so on. The problem, for Lucretius, is that this model of 'ethics as extension' has understood the situation completely upside down. Instead of starting with the movement of matter, anthropocentric ethics begins with the stasis and identity of the rational human subject. But as Book III shows, the human body and mind are only a metastable state or product of nature – not the other way around. So why grant ethical action only to humans when the whole of nature has always been relationally intra-active and sensuously affective? Lucretius thus enacts a complete reversal of ethics by starting with entangled bodies in motion and then reposing the question of how to move well together.

The third consequence of simulacra is that ethics is not something that only humans or living beings do. If ethics simply means moving well together, then ecologies are ethical. The truly radical move achieved by the theory of simulacra is that nature and matter are no longer passive objects of so-called ethical consideration, but become active participants in ethical practice. Insofar as nature affects itself it moves with itself in some patterns and not others. Human ethics is therefore a subset of a much larger ethical activity already occurring in nature.

Drawing Figures

There are no things – only processes. Things are always 'drawn out' and continually woven through motion. The theory of simulacra is so radical because it completely destroys the 'essences' of things. Below the manifold and moving simulacra there is no 'real thing' that remains the same despite the peeling away of its membranes. The thing is nothing other than a moving manifold of simulacra. If we took something in our hand and peeled away all its membranes like the layers of an onion, there would be nothing left beneath the layers. Thus simulacra are not at all copies of things – *things are simulacra*. Things have the forms they do because their simulacra move or *draw out their figure* (4.42–3).

> *dico igitur rerum effigias tenuisque figuras*
> *mittier ab rebus summo de corpore eorum;*

> I say, therefore, that forms and fine figures of things
> are sent out from things, from their outer surface

Form is always kinomorphic or figured by strands or string figures of matter.[11] The first-threads, or *primordia*, are the sprouts of things, and like sprouts they shed their outer husk, rind, bark, or shell [*corpore eorum*] (4.43) as they move. So the forms of things are literally drawn out through motion just as one might draw a picture or weave a pattern (4.54–62).

> *Principio quoniam mittunt in rebus apertis*
> *corpora res multae, partim diffusa solute,*
> *robora ceu fumum mittunt ignesque vaporem,*
> *et partim contexta magis condensaque, ut olim*
> *cum teretis ponunt tunicas aestate cicadae,*
> *et vituli cum membranas de corpore summo*
> *nascentes mittunt, et item cum lubrica serpens*
> *exuit in spinis vestem; nam saepe videmus*
> *illorum spoliis vepres volitantibus auctas.*

> First of all, since in the case of visible things
> many things give off *corpora*, in part scattered loosely,
> as wood gives off smoke, and fire heat,
> and in part more closely woven and compacted, just as at times
> when cicadas shed their smoothly rounded clothing in summer,

and when calves while being born give off films
from their outer surface, and likewise when a slippery serpent
sheds its covering on thorns (for we often see
bushes decorated with their fluttering body-armor).

Lucretius is quite explicit about the kinetic nature of things. Matter [*corpora*] (4.55) pours out of things [*diffusa solute*] (4.55) and weaves [*contexta*] (4.57) figures together like fabric, clothing [*tunicas*] (4.58), or armour [*vestem*] (4.61). If these membranes are woven loosely they scatter like smoke. If they are woven more tightly they come off like a whole shell or like a snakeskin. Simulacra are not copies but, like snakeskin or smoke, are completely material and immanent to things. Lucretius thus jettisons the Platonic theory of model and copy, subject and object, nature and culture, and replaces it with a completely materialist theory of active and diffractive simulacra. Sensation is woven together through matter in motion, not neutrally observed.

Swerving Figures

The forms of things are drawn by moving figures, but the flow of the *corpora* is not strictly linear, as we know from Book II. *Corpora* are habitually [*solerent*] swerving (2.221). Thus the string figures that are traced by the flows of matter are not static images flying through empty space. As they move, they diffract with one another and with the air itself. They only preserve their figure when they preserve their order of motion (4.65–71).

> *nam cur illa cadant magis ab rebusque recedant*
> *quam quae tenvia sunt, hiscendist nulla potestas;*
> *praesertim cum sint in summis corpora rebus*
> *multa minuta, iaci quae possint ordine eodem*
> *quo fuerint et formai servare figuram,*
> *et multo citius, quanto minus indupediri*
> *pauca queunt et quae sunt prima fronte locata.*

For why those should fall and separate from things
more than those which are thin; there is no possibility of uttering,
especially since there exist on the outer surface of things *corpora*
which are many and minute, which can be thrown off in the same
order which they had before and preserve the form of the figure,
and much more quickly, being less able to be impeded
in as much as they are few and are located right up front.

Matter is continually falling [*cadant*] (4.65) off things [*recedant*] (4.65), but when it is thrown [*iaci*] (4.68) off in the same kinetic order or pattern [*ordine eodem*] (4.68), its form is preserved by its kinetic figure [*formai servare figuram*] (4.69). In other words, matter is active in the shapes that it traces out in space. Objects have no static form or essence. Objects, as their Latin root suggests, are what are 'thrown off', *iaci*, '-jected'. But beneath this *ob-jection* is not something other than the objecting process. There is only the objecting process of simulacra flying off things in ways that more or less preserve their figure in mid-air.

It is a terrible lapse of Western metaphysics to have preserved the idea that objects are 'out there' distinct from one another and from human perceivers. For Lucretius, the object is all over the place. It spreads its agency across an entire field of action. The object is not 'over there' but rather actively constituting a positive space-time made *through* its simulacral movement. The Greeks had a wonderful name for a space made through movement: *chora*. From this Greek word Lucretius uses the derived Latin word *locus*, referring to the same kinetic distribution of space. When we 'see' an object, we are actively helping to make a continuous process of vibrating strings [*ordia*] that weaves us at the same time as our bodies are weaving it. A single object wraps up a whole room.

Lucretius thus offers us a radical new theory of the object. The object is not passive but lavishly and excessively throwing itself away [*iacere ac largiri multa videmus*] (4.72). The object's expenditure creates itself through destruction. Its immolation is its fertility. What a mistake to have ever talked about static forms and passive objects when the whole world is tearing itself apart before our eyes. We die for objects as they die for us. This is the real 'natural contract'.

Material Ecology and Environmental Affect

Lucretius' theory of simulacra means that there are no discrete subjects and objects – only affective ecologies. The whole environment is not just something to be passively 'considered' but something that plays an active role in constituting an entire atmosphere or situation. To illustrate this, Lucretius describes the beautiful way in which atmospheric colour and light transform and shape the movement of things (4.81–3).

> *et quanto circum mage sunt inclusa theatri*
> *moenia, tam magis haec intus perfusa lepore*
> *omnia conrident correpta luce diei.*

> And the more the walls of the theater encircle and enclose,
> the more all these things within are soaked
> with splendor and laugh when the light of day is diminished.

Early Roman theatres were sunken pits filled with seats and covered with a purple cloth to keep the sun off the viewers. This poetic image could not be more fitting for the point Lucretius wants to make: matter is performative. The environment is not an empty space filled with discrete objects but something much more like a woven cloth rippling in the wind that throws off pattern, colour, and movement everywhere lavishly. The cloth-wrapped performative space is a space made by woven motion.

Things, Lucretius says, are soaked [*perfusa*] with splendour and begin to move and laugh in response to the undulations of colour and light as the sun goes down. Shadows begin to ripple across things and through the air, showing the entanglement of everything in the theatre. The laughter [*conrident*] of things is not metaphorical. Nature really is undulating pleasantly in the wind. Matter shakes without breaking or coming completely apart. Pleasant movement without complete destruction (i.e. not *ataraxia*) is a recurring ethical image for Lucretius, found in the laughter of Venus or in the springtime winds of Favonius. Lucretius' theatre thus becomes the 'other' of Plato's cave. It is precisely the play of light, shadow, and sensation that reveals the nature of things instead of obscuring the true forms of being.

This theatrical scene shows dramatically what is otherwise happening all the time. Matter is flowing off itself and diffracting with other matters in a complex and kinetic ecology. Ecology is not something that only happens out in the woods. Nor is it merely the passive stage that actors play on. *Contra* Shakespeare, all the world is *not a stage*, and all the men and women are *not* the only players.[12] Humans do not play on the static stage of nature. The whole stage, the actors, the audience, and the whole theatre are soaked through with material ecological affects that ripple across them like water or like bees into a beehive [*caveai*], as Lucretius describes it (4.78). The ecological theatre is a buzzing beehive made by the movement of matter through it. The form of the honeycomb is an emergent pattern or figure traced by, drawn out, and woven by kinetic habits. Ecological affects such as temperature are connected with the increased oscillation of matter and with emotion.[13] But if emotion is not merely mental representation, then nature too has emotion.

Water and food shortages are related to fluctuations in the climate and increase the likelihood of social conflict.[14] Wearing or seeing certain colours also has proven effects on human behaviour.[15] Even just looking at or walking around living plants and forests can significantly change the chemical composition of the human body, altering mood, blood pressure, and stress hormones.[16] This is all to say that Lucretius' theory of simulacra is strikingly prescient about what we are only recently discovering scientifically about the entangled relationship of ecological affects.[17]

Given Lucretius' description of this simulacral ecology, and what we know from contemporary studies on ecological affect, an ethics based on individuals is completely misguided. Ethics is nothing if not ecological and simulacral. If the entire world is in motion, radiating, intertwining, and diffracting itself, then the ethics of moving well together must take these movements seriously. Ignoring them and treating ethics as a strictly anthropocentric project (as if ecology played no role in actively shaping ethical landscapes and human beings themselves) is partly to blame for global pollution and the feedback loops of toxic particles (dioxins, phthalates, glysophates, etc.) now coursing through our bodies. If we think ethics is something only humans do, then we are more likely to forget that the rest of nature not only plays an active role in producing human bodies, but is identical with humanity itself. We live and move in affective tangles because of the nature of simulacral matter.

Weaving String Figures

It is absolutely crucial to remember that simulacra, for Lucretius, are not discrete particles or representations.[18] We should not imagine that simulacra are like individual photos on film images that peel off things one by one in discontinuous succession. As collective and intertwined ecological processes they cannot be isolated. Lucretius is extremely clear about this in lines 4.87–9.

> *sunt igitur iam formarum vestigia certa,*
> *quae volgo volitant subtili praedita filo*
> *nec singillatim possunt secreta videri.*

> There are therefore then figurative traces
> which freely fly around composed of subtle threads
> and which are not able to be seen singly or separately.

Sensation is fundamentally atmospheric and ecological. Simulacra are composed of flows or material threads [*filo*] (4.88) that move all around through the air, drawing out [*formarum*] (4.87) tracks, traces, or footprints [*vestigia*] (4.87). Since these movements are collective processes, they are not reducible to the 'things' [*rerum*] or the simulacra they produce. Simulacra are composite things woven together through a vast ecological network of diffracting flows of matter [*corpora*]. It is therefore fundamentally impossible to separate out 'one' simulacrum [*nec singillatim*] because simulacra are multiplicities in process.

What we sense when we sense the world, or when the world senses itself, is nothing but simulacra, all the way down. But simulacra are nothing but moving woven patterns of subtle flows of matter streaming out together, folding and unfolding continually before our eyes. If they are folded tightly enough they appear stable, if they are folded loosely they appear unstable (smoking, bleeding, liquid, and so on). It is all a question of weaving.

Lucretius says that these threads of matter literally pour, leak, or flow out [*diffusae*] (4.91) of things [*rerum*], and that their artful twisting, winding, and curving [*flexum*] (4.93) draws out the shape of things and the shape of the simulacra that flow out of things. In other words, because the flow of matter is always swerving inside and outside things, there is simply no original thing of which simulacra are faithful or unfaithful copies. There are only continually woven processes, all the way down to the swerving flows of matter themselves. Flows of matter that are thrown off mirrors, water, and shiny surfaces look similar [*simili specie*] because the path of woven matters is less bent or curved than others (4.100).

Matter flows, but simulacra are sensed when the flows of matter fold back over themselves and tangle with one another in a continuous pattern of repulsion, rhythm, and return that allows matter to affect itself and produce sensation (4.104–9).

> *sunt igitur tenues formarum illis similesque*
> *effigiae, singillatim quas cernere nemo*
> *cum possit, tamen adsiduo crebroque repulsu*
> *reiectae reddunt speculorum ex aequore visum,*

> There are thus thin kinetic patterns of similar
> images, which though no one is able to see discretely,
> nevertheless by continuous and frequent repulsion they rebuff
> and return a visible figure from the surface of mirrors.

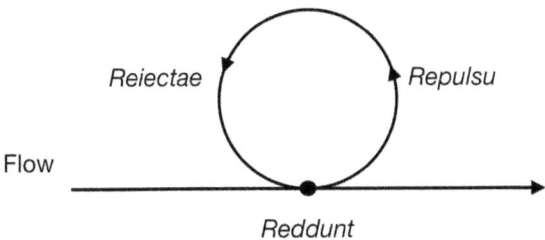

Figure 6.2 Flow, rejecta, reddunt.

All of nature is composed of a continuous movement of weaving matter which 'reverberates, throws back, and restores things' [*repulsu reiectae reddunt*] through folding (Fig. 6.2). Simulacra do not just move between things. Things are nothing but simulacra, which are themselves nothing but flows or threads of matter [*primordia*] (4.111) continually folded and woven together [*exordia rerum cunctarum*] (4.114–15), and constantly reverberating off one another in various sonic, visual, olfactory, and haptic patterns.

This is why images appear not just near the surface of things but in mid-air through diffraction (4.129–40). Just as we see giant faces, mountains, or monsters in the clouds, so too do we see diffracted images patterns in mid-air. Clouds, like simulacral diffractions, are liquid [*liquentia*] (4.141) and perpetually fluid [*perpetuoque fluant*] (4.144) kinomophic assemblages. Clouds are certainly more fluid than most simulacra around us on the surface of earth, but the basic structure is the same. Nature is one big entangled parallax of shifting flows.

We know this because whenever we take out a mirror, Lucretius says, it immediately starts reflecting simulacra around without perceptible delay. This means that the flow of matter must be occurring everywhere all the time at very high speeds (4.155–8).

et quamvis subito quovis in tempore quamque
rem contra speculum ponas, apparet imago;
perpetuo fluere ut noscas e corpore summo
texturas rerum tenuis tenuisque figuras.

And however suddenly, at whatever time you place a mirror
in front of each thing, an image appears,
so that you may realize that constantly flowing from the outer surface
of things are thin woven webs and thin figures.

Just like the high speed and constant flow [*perpetuo fluere*] (4.157) of photons (and their quantum fields), matter [*corpore*] (4.157), according to Lucretius, is constantly 'weaving things' together [*texturas rerum*] by drawing out their figures [*figuras*] (4.158). Simulacra do not fly through empty space. Space, as we know from Books I and II, is made by matter in motion. Space, *locus*, for Lucretius, is porous and folded. Wherever it seems empty, we need only hold up a mirror to see it shot through with tangled webs of simulacra.

Brevi spatio, temporis in puncto

Matter makes space by moving. This is a radical thesis even by today's standards. As matter flows and unfolds from things, it weaves figures or patterns called simulacra, which are metastable and entangled things [*simulacra rerum*] and are thus relatively discrete and spatio-temporal.

In the final lines of Lucretius' description of simulacra he puts forward perhaps the most revolutionary physical thesis of Book IV, and perhaps in all of *De Rerum Natura*: that the origin of the emergence of simulacra occurs in '*brevi spatio, temporis in puncto*', echoing the indeterminate space-time of the swerving of the first-threads in Book II, '*incerto tempore, incertisque loci*' (4.159–60, 4.163–4).

> *ergo multa brevi spatio simulacra genuntur,*
> *ut merito celer his rebus dicatur origo.*
>
> Therefore many images are produced in a brief space,
> so that deservedly the birth of these things is said to be quick.
>
> *necessest*
> *temporis in puncto rerum simulacra ferantur*
>
> it is necessary that images
> be carried off from things in a point of time,

Simulacra are things [*simulacra rerum*], and things are by definition spatio-temporal and relatively discrete – as Lucretius described in great detail in Books I and II.[19] Therefore simulacra are produced [*genuntur*] or thrown off from larger composite things in the fastest possible space-time. If they were not, then there would be some thing between them, which there is not, according to Lucretius. This is the explicit point of these lines.

However, the implicit question being asked is, 'What is between spatio-temporal simulacra?' Or even more dramatically stated, 'What is the origin of space-time itself?' In effect, Lucretius has already given us the answer to this question in Book IV: the *primordia* or first-threads of matter. Just as the flows of matter weave things through folding, so space-time itself emerges from the indeterminate movement of matter.

Lucretius here temporalises space '*brief* space' and spatialises time '*point* of time'. Discrete space-times are, like simulacra, folds in the flows or threads of matter. Furthermore, since we know from Book II that matter flows by habitually swerving '*incerto tempore, incertisque loci*', then we reach the radical conclusion that determinate space-time emerges from indeterminate fluctuations of matter. This sounds incredible, but it is, like most theses in Lucretius, strikingly contemporary (Fig. 6.3).

Lucretius is essentially describing what we now call quantum gravity. Most theoretical physicists today agree that space-time is not an *a priori* or metaphysical given but rather an emergent property of our quantum universe. More specifically, the emergence of space-time is a quantum effect of the flux of indeterminately high energies at work below the level of measurably discrete space-time fluctuations. Below the lowest theoretically measurable limit of reality or the Planck limit are energies that are so indeterminately high that they produce black holes that do not let light escape.[20]

Lucretius suggests that simulacra move at the speed of light when he says that simulacra flow off things as fast as light from the sun travels to earth (4.161–2). 'Don't you see then how in an instant of time an image falls from the shores of heaven to the shores of earth?' The speed of light is one of the constants used to determine the Planck limit, below which matter moves so quickly and so indeterminately (*incerto tempore*) that even

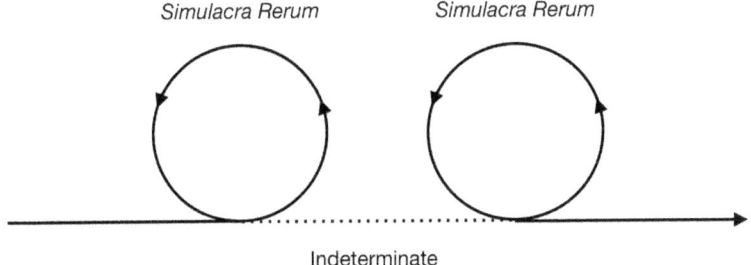

Figure 6.3 Indeterminate conjunction.

photons are not yet determinately discrete. Spatio-temporal discreteness is something that emerges from a more fundamentally indeterminate flux or inclination of energy/matter.

Lucretius was thus perhaps the first to pose a version of quantum-gravity theory *avant la lettre*. Even more surprising is that his answer is not inconsistent with what we currently know about the nature of the indeterminately high vacuum fluctuations that lurk beneath the fabric of space-time itself.

Conclusion

What does the theory of simulacra mean for ethics? First of all, it means that if the movement of matter [*primordia*] is fundamentally *indeterminate*, then ethics, at its deepest ontological level, is not contemplation, *ataraxia*, or normative. Ethics is something that must be done in motion. There is no 'natural state' of things and certainly no universal normative principles for right action. Ethics cannot be universally normative, by virtue of the '*brevi spatio, temporis in puncto*' of matter's fundamental indeterminacy.

Second, since *simulacra rerum* are folded and woven from threads [*filo*] or flows [*flux*] of this indeterminate matter, this means that all of nature is moving and co-affecting itself in a constant set of diffraction patterns. This means that Lucretius' kinetic ethics of moving well together cannot be limited to the living individuals described in Book III. Kinetic ethics must be fundamentally collective, ecological, and process-oriented.

However, the theory of simulacra is only the starting point of Lucretius' ecological ethics. In the next chapters, I would like to show that Lucretius puts this method to the test to see how this new ethical perspective can help us move well together in a number of concrete situations.

Notes

1. For an introduction to new materialism, see Stacy Alaimo and Susan J. Hekman, *Material Feminisms* (Bloomington: Indiana University Press, 2008); Vicki Kirby, *What If Culture Was Nature All Along?* (Edinburgh: Edinburgh University Press, 2018); Rick Dolphijn and Iris Tuin, *New Materialism: Interviews and Cartographies* (Ann Arbor: Open Humanities Press, 2012); and Chris Gamble, Josh Hanan, and Thomas Nail, 'What is New Materialism?' (under review).

Ethics of the Simulacrum   167

2. I have already said how important these lines are for Lucretius' materialist philosophical method in Thomas Nail, *Lucretius I: An Ontology of Motion* (Edinburgh: Edinburgh University Press, 2018).
3. Francis Bacon, *The New Organon* (Cambridge: Cambridge University Press, 2000), 36, Book I, Aphorism XIX. See also Thomas Nail, *Theory of the Object*, unpublished manuscript, under review with Oxford University Press, ch. 11.
4. Immanuel Kant, *Critique of Pure Reason*, trans. Werner S. Pluhar (Indianapolis: Hackett Publishing, 1997), 19, 'a judge who compels a witness'.
5. Georges Bataille, *Visions of Excess: Selected Writings, 1927–1939*, trans. Allan Stoekl, Carl R. Lovitt, and D. M. Leslie (Minneapolis: University of Minnesota Press, 2008), 235.
6. Emanuele Coccia, *The Life of Plants: A Metaphysics of Mixture*, trans. Dylan J. Montanari (Cambridge: Polity, 2019).
7. Bataille, *Visions of Excess*, 10.
8. Bataille, *Visions of Excess*, 79.
9. See Nail, *Lucretius I*.
10. Max Planck calculated black body radiation at 'thermodynamic equilibrium', which is purely hypothetical. There is no absolute equilibrium. So his measurements assumed a background space-time and were not quantum-gravitational but are now used as the basis to measure the effects of quantum gravity.
11. Donna Haraway, *Staying with the Trouble: Making Kin in the Chthulucene* (Durham, NC: Duke University Press, 2016).
12. William Shakespeare, *As You Like It*, Act II, scene vii.
13. Thalma Lobel, *Sensation: The New Science of Physical Intelligence* (New York: Atria Books, 2016).
14. David Agren, 'The Unseen Driver behind the Migrant Caravan: Climate Change', *The Guardian*, 30 October 2018, https://www.theguardian.com/world/2018/oct/30/migrant-caravan-causes-climate-change-central-america?fbclid=IwAR2rkDDWxkUjrDOLmQFg-c82WMasutlJ08aqrTJjpz7pIo--rcBXjNQW8iM (accessed 11 September 2019).
15. See Lobel, *Sensation*, chs 4, 5, 6 on colour and light and dark.
16. Florence Williams, *The Nature Fix: Why Nature Makes Us Happier, Healthier, and More Creative* (New York: Norton, 2018).
17. See Benjamin Lieberman and Elizabeth Gordon, *Climate Change in Human History: Prehistory to the Present* (London: Bloomsbury, 2018), and

Nigel Clark, *Inhuman Nature: Sociable Life on a Dynamic Planet* (Thousand Oaks: Sage, 2011).
18. For a related treatment of string figures, see Haraway, *Staying with the Trouble*, 10: 'Playing games of string figures is about giving and receiving patterns, dropping threads and failing but sometimes finding something that works, something consequential and maybe even beautiful, that wasn't there before, of relaying connections that matter, of telling stories in hand upon hand, digit upon digit, attachment site upon attachment site, to craft conditions for finite flourishing on terra, on earth.'
19. See Nail, *Lucretius I*.
20. Nail, *Theory of the Object*, ch. 11.

7. All Perceptions are True

One of the most significant barriers to the ethics of moving well together, according to Lucretius, is what he calls 'twisted reasoning' [*perversa ... ratione*] (4.833), which acts *as if* the mind were something above and beyond nature and sensation. Ethical practice, however, like movement, *does not* originate in the mind but in nature and in the body. Nature, body, and mind, as we have seen, are completely continuous with one another – without any ontological division in the movement of matter. The mind and body are metastable formations in the flows of matter.

Twisted reasoning posits a dualistic division between mind and the rest of nature, including the body – as if the mind were something that came from but ultimately broke with nature. By using this twisted reasoning, according to Lucretius, the mind is prone to a number of errors of 'self-deception' (4.817) that entangle us in all kinds of mental delusions that undermine the task of ethics. The real ground of ethics lies in sensuous perception. This is what Lucretius shows us in lines 4.216–822.

In these lines Lucretius puts forward one of the most radical and heretical arguments in the history of Western philosophy and against all forms of idealism. Lucretius argues the thesis that *all perceptions are true*. This thesis seems counter-intuitive at first, because the ontological division between nature, body, and mind is so ingrained in Western thought. However, if we do not accept a division between epistemology and ontology, then Lucretius' thesis follows directly: if the mind is something natural, then nature is something minded. If perception is something nature does to itself, then it cannot be false. The mind is also a perceptual organ whose actions of thought are onto-epistemologically true as well.

The error of self-delusion occurs, however, when we act *as if* nature, body, or mind were *false*. This, for Lucretius, is a direct contradiction and impossibility. The idea that there could be 'false being' is possible only if one accepts an ontological dualism between God and nature, or mind and body. If nature is a *multiplicity* of flows or processes, there is no *one* absolute truth nor are there *many* false positions. The whole distinction between true and false is uprooted at its dualistic core. The question of ethics, then, is not a question of good and evil, or true and false, but of how to move and distribute things well with others.

Humans do not 'construct ideas *about* nature' with their minds or cultures and thus remain cut off from the nature of things – nature really constructs itself *through* human actions. Thus ethics is not just something humans do to one another or to nature but something nature does to itself.

The Flow of Things

Things flow without cease. This is an absolutely essential starting point for overcoming the division between mind and nature and the twisted idealism of ethical theory. 'Matter' [*corpora*] (4.217) 'flows continuously' [*perpetuoque fluunt*] (4.218) 'without any delay, division, or discrete break in the flow' [*nec mora nec requies interdatur ulla fluendi*] (4.227). Since there is no division in the continuous flux of matter, the division between mind and nature is ontologically impossible. All things are in flux, radiating simulacra in all directions and diffracting with one another. The threads of matter [*primordia*] weave together the flow of simulacral bodies.

These material flows weave patterns that can be touched, seen, tasted, smelled, felt, and thought together as different 'co-moving' [*commovet*] simulacral dimensions (4.235). There is no action at a distance in sensation. All sensation is true precisely because there is *no distance*, 'delay, division, or discrete break in the flow' of matter. Distance and division are the precondition for the division between true and false. Performatively speaking, however, no performance can be false in what it *does* if it is a kinetically continuous region of nature.

For example, it seems obvious to say that the movement of a river is not true or false. If we direct it one way to irrigate crops, this is not true or false; the redirecting simply has a range of ecological and agricultural effects that we can describe and prefer or not prefer. The human utterance 'This is not a river' is a true performative speech-act. However, when one says 'This is not a river' and points to a river this becomes a 'false' statement. But if such speech habits and kinetic coordinations of sound and action are not universal but historical patterns of action, then they cannot be absolutely true or false either. Performative speech-acts then reveal themselves as continuous with nature as real patterns and habits, and thus as part of a fundamentally ethical practice to prefer some sounds ('This is a river') to others ('This is not a river'). What we call a true statement is just a coordinated habit. When the habit of sound and action is broken we call this 'false'.

Poetry, then, is the act of making new sounds/action patterns. Ethics is the collective practice of following some patterns and not others. In this sense, Lucretius does not and cannot accept the historical divisions between ethics, politics, aesthetics, epistemology, and ontology. Each is only a dimension or region of a single, continuously moving reality. We can focus on what it means to move well together just as one can take a walk down one trail or another of the same forest (Fig. 7.1).

Interweaving Sensation

Sensation, for Lucretius, is a mutual and reciprocal process. This point follows from the continuous fluctuating of things in which there is no

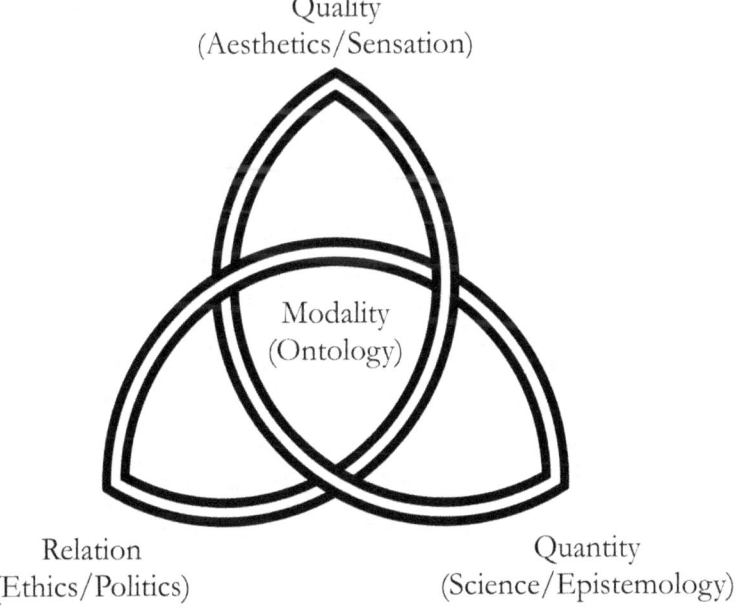

Figure 7.1 Quality, quantity, relation, modality.

delay or discrete division in nature. There is no action at a distance because nature is not made of discrete particles or atoms. Lucretius is quite clear about this when he writes that 'wherever we turn our sight, all things there strike it directly with their shape and color' [*propterea fit uti, speciem quo vertimus, omnes res ibi eam contra feriant forma atque colore*] (4.242–3). Vision is thus not a merely passive or neutral reception of sense data. This is not only because all of nature flows and releases simulacra but also because vision is something actively directed or turned [*vertimus*] in the world. Vision is something that is actively performed and even something that actively transforms what it sees, insofar as it is in a position that reflects and emits light. What we see is not there passively but is an actively diffracted simulacral image of the meeting between the movement of the body, head, eye, and other aspects of nature. The *where* of moving bodies is something we actively *do* and is thus part of the *what* that is seen.

The French philosopher Maurice Merleau-Ponty expresses this Lucretian insight quite well when he says,

> We see only what we look at. What would vision be without eye movement? And how could the movement of the eyes bring things together if the movement were blind? If it were only a reflex? If it did not have its antennae, its clairvoyance? If vision were not prefigured in it?[1]

'Vision', Merleau-Ponty says, 'is a *palpation with the look*, it must also be inscribed in the order of being that it discloses to us; he who looks must not himself be foreign to the world that he looks at.'[2] This is a crucial insight already developed more radically by Lucretius: if nature is not ontologically divided from itself, then vision is already nature responding to itself in the active movement of the searching eye and moving body that responds pre-subjectively and affectively to the world. Vision, as Merleau-Ponty says, 'is not a decision made by the mind, an absolute doing which would decree, from the depths of a subjective retreat'.[3] For Lucretius, vision is already nature responding to itself. Vision is not two separate parts interacting but is one continuous flux of transformation. Merleau-Ponty focuses on *human* vision, but the same is true of nature's own vision of us. Nature palpates us with *its own look*. Merleau-Ponty was close but still got things 'twisted': nature is not 'flesh' (which is still too closely modelled on the anthropocentric and biocentric idea of 'living flesh'), but everything is a *material* and simulacral fabric.

This is an absolutely radical claim. If there is no action at a distance, then vision does not merely tell us something about the object being perceived, it expresses a transformation of the whole situation. Our eyes are just one region of this transformation responding to a mutual palpation of eye and nature. Lucretius thus says that 'the image *produces vision* and supports an *inter-knowledge*' [*internoscere*] (4.245) of the between, or becoming, of the situation. Light physically touches and palpates our eyes, and our eyes physically move and palpate the light back. Vision and knowledge are thus not universal but situated and positional.

How or in what manner [*quam*] a quantity [*quanto*] of air is agitated [*aëris ante agitatur*] and for what duration [*perterget longior*] from our body determines how far away things will look (4.250–4). The object, the air, and the eye thus play simultaneously active roles in the creation of vision. Instead of an action at a distance, there is a continuous transformation of the whole. Different lengths of air vibrate [*perterget longior, aëris ante agitatur*] at different frequencies depending on colour, shape, and distance from our moving head. This is how the perception of distance works in a world without any ontological division: different degrees and frequencies of flux. For Lucretius, there are no static essences, objects, or 'immortal *eidos*'.[4] There are only flows of phantasmal, decaying processes whose metastable and intertwined patterns are the real world without essence.

In *Lucretius I*, I used the phrase 'we know now' in a strictly and positional historical sense. Given where, when, and how we are, this is the real performative structure of knowledge we have regarding quantum theory. Here, then, we can see explicitly that the use of scientific knowledge, including my own in *Lucretius I*, is fundamentally situated and historical – not absolute. We always return to Lucretius from where we are: the present. But this does not make his resonance with contemporary physics any less real. There is a real diffraction of contemporary quantum physics with Lucretius' texts.

Any theory of observation that does not take quantum/simulacral entanglement into account is not consistent with the ethico-aesthetics developed by Lucretius in Books III and IV. Some of the most important methodological insights of twentieth-century physics have still not been taken seriously by most twenty-first-century physicists. Werner Heisenberg's 'complementarity', Niels Bohr's 'indeterminacy', and John Bell's 'inequality and entanglement' are experimental and contemporary ideas that are consistent with Lucretius' theory of simulacral diffraction.[5] If Heisenberg, Bohr, and Bell were right that there is no ontological division between observer and observed, then Lucretius' thesis that 'all perceptions are true' also follows directly. Science is nature observing itself.[6]

We do not see things bit by bit, Lucretius says, 'but rather the *whole all at once*' (4.262). However, the whole is not the interaction of all its discrete parts. Simulacra are not discrete. Rather, we sense the whole diffractive pattern at once. Henri Bergson draws similarly on Lucretius' theory of images in *Matter and Memory* when he writes that 'we grasp, in perception, *at one and the same time*, a state of our consciousness and a reality independent of ourselves', and not 'atoms or whatnot – which interpose their solidity between the movement itself'.[7]

Mathesis naturalis

Nature is mathematical not because we humans have discovered transcendent, ahistorical formalisms or universal laws above nature (*mathesis universalis*), but because nature itself actually *does* mathematics. This is yet another radical conclusion of Lucretius' thesis that there is no delay or discontinuity in the flow of simulacra between humans and nature (4.227). First of all, if humans are not separate from nature, then nature *does* mathematics *through* human bodies. But even more generally, because nature 'flows continuously' [*perpetuoque fluunt*] (4.218) and diffracts itself into 'orders, patterns, structures, and logical relationships'[8] via simulacra, then nature actively produces the differential and fractal geometry that humans study and call 'mathematics'.

Lucretius' famous example of this is that square towers look round from a distance, 'because every angle looks blunt at a distance, or rather it is not discerned and its blow perishes' (4.355–6) before it hits our eyes. There are no eternal, unchanging forms in nature or in the mind, because the mind is continuous with nature and the mind knows nothing beyond natural sensuousness. Form, including mathematical form, is the product of a kinetic process of simulacra that blunt themselves through diffraction patterns [*hebescere*] (4.359). Just as in calculus the method of exhaustion draws an infinite number of flows running tangential to a curve, so there are an infinite sum of real simulacra actively flowing through all natural curves and forms.[9] Nature is the performance of a real differential geometry that calculus can approach only by trying to do what nature already does in the method that is called 'exhaustion'.

Nature is mathematical process. However, there are no 'ones' or unities in nature, only a 'process of unification', infinitely approaching but not reaching our perceptual limits. From a distance, the tower appears to have one side, but closer up it appears to have four, and even closer it has a multiplicity of sides following the unique micro-curvatures of each brick, crack, and hole in the walls. The consequence of Lucretius' example opens the door to an anti-Platonic, kinetic mathematics of flows. Mathematical unity is not a mental discovery of pure forms but is rather an *effect of sensuous perception at a distance*. As perception approaches the object closer and closer, the moving multiplicity of nature emerges. Unity and dimensionality is not an *a priori* form but something produced and continually reproduced in nature.

Lucretius compares the production of form to an object being shaped by a moving lathe. Geometrical angles continually flee their form and our perception [*suffugit sensum simul angulus omnis*] (4.360). Form is the result of a mutual shaping or interweaving between body, eye, mind, and object as a continuously moving and open whole. Lucretius uses yet another weaving image to describe the way simulacra flow off objects as wool is spun into a fibre [*lana trahatur*] (4.376).

The Fault of the Mind

All our perceptions are true, and all error is the fault of the mind, which tries to deduce universal attributes from the singularities of sensation. 'Nor yet do we admit that the eyes are at all deceived in this . . . Thus do not falsely attribute this fault [*adfingere*] of the mind to the eyes' (4.379–85). The Latin word *fingere* means 'to form, fashion, devise, make, or add on to'. For Lucretius, the movements of the mind do not *re-present* reality but rather are added on to other perceptions. The mind, like the other senses, cannot doubt another sense but is merely added to the others. Together, the senses produce a heterogeneous composite of sensation. Error arises when the creative movements of the mind are privileged or used to judge the other senses and attribute universal unities, fixities, and identities to the processes and movements of nature beyond what is actually sensed.

However, the eyes alone are not 'able to know the nature of things' because the nature of things is not reducibly visual, nor oral, nor audible, nor mental. The senses do not know anything *about* the nature of things because they *are the nature of things*. The nature of things, as discussed in Books I and II, is the immanent material condition of things. The nature of things [*natura rerum*] is not reducible to sensuous *rerum* in the same way that the flow of a river eddy is not reducible to the eddy itself, which is continually replenished. The senses are always true because they always perform the nature of things without representing them. The nature of things is not something that Lucretius knows about with his mind alone. That is Epicurean rationalism.

The nature of things is something that Lucretius immanently performs in the poetic act itself. Again, if there is no delay or discreteness between simulacra or humans and nature, there is no such thing as representation. The nature of things is continuous with the performative *textum* of the poem itself as it is sung or read. This is why weaving is the central poetic image of *De Rerum Natura*. Nature and poetry are both weaving performances (*textum/nexus/plexus/flexus*). Poetry is not *like* the weaving of nature; it *is* nature weaving itself in song. Nature is poetic.

How can one know the kinetic process that one enacts in the very performance of the act or practice of knowing? This is why epistemology is always ethical. It is practice; something *done*. However, if knowledge is something done, then by definition its sensuous act cannot be universal – since an act is always singular, positional, and sensuous. This is precisely the danger of reading Lucretius as an Epicurean rationalist/fundamentalist putting forward philosophical propositions in accordance with the master. This kind of reading misses the central paradox of kinetic materialism: knowing the moving nature that one is. Lucretius thus performs *avant la lettre* a Kantian immanent critique, but of the *material* conditions of *nature*, not the *ideal* conditions of the *mind*. The nature of things is knowing only *through* the fully sensuous *performance* of all the senses together as nature's own performance of itself through the poetic act (4.380–3).

> *nam quo cumque loco sit lux atque umbra tueri*
> *illorum est; eadem vero sint lumina necne,*
> *umbraque quae fuit hic eadem nunc transeat illuc,*
> *an potius fiat paulo quod diximus ante,*

> For it belongs to them (the eyes) to see at whatever point there is light and shadow. But whether the lights are the same or not,
>   or whether it is the same shadow which was here and now moves over there,
> or whether it rather happens as we said a little before,

All Perceptions are True   177

The eyes see and immanently perform light and shadow in their palpating dilation and movement, but the mind adds something unseen: spatio-temporal unity and difference. The mental actions of unity and difference are sensuous things added to our perception of things. The performative act of adding ideas to things is true as a performative act of nature sensing itself, but false as an attribute of substance. Nature is not a substance but the process itself of sensuous addition, which the mind also performs.

Perceptual 'illusions', such as bent sticks in water, the feeling of stability on a moving boat, the meeting of parallel columns at a distance, the sun touching the mountains, and so on, are not false but are rather expressions of a real kinetic process of the body with and as nature. Nature tells us something about our own body and its movements and position through simulacra. The senses in turn tell us something about the natural world of which they are continuous.

The lessons of the senses tell us about the intertwining of nature with itself, but the mind acts as if the continuous transformation of the sensuous whole is an 'illusion' (4.462–8).

Cetera de genere hoc mirande multa videmus,
quae violare fidem quasi sensibus omnia quaerunt,
ne quiquam, quoniam pars horum maxima fallit
propter opinatus animi, quos addimus ipsi,
pro visis ut sint quae non sunt sensibus visa;
nam nihil aegrius est quam res secernere apertas
ab dubiis, animus quas ab se protinus addit.

We see an amazing number of other things of this type,
all of which seek to shatter one's trust, so to speak, in the senses
but in vain, since by far the largest part of these deceive
because of the inferences of the mind, which we ourselves contribute
so that things not seen by the senses are taken as things seen.
For nothing is more difficult than to distinguish clear things
from doubtful ones which the mind adds immediately on its own.

For Lucretius, the mind does not represent or judge [*opinatus*] sensation or nature, but rather 'adds' [*addimus/addit*] mental sensations or ideas of its own to the whole sensuous assemblage. Stasis, for example, is not something our senses ever *do* because they are always actively responding to their milieu. The idea of stasis is a cognitive activity added to things by our minds. But the addition itself *is a kinetic act*. Ideas are something we *do*, not something we *have*.

Simulacra do not represent one another. They are not models of originals. They are the kinetic performance of nature itself, more primary and immanent than any division between true and false, model and copy, nature and human, and so on. The mind, as Lucretius says in Book III, is an organ like our others and interwoven with the whole body. This is the basis for Lucretius' complete rejection of scepticism.

Against Scepticism: Against Idealism

The most extreme idealist and unethical position is that of scepticism. Not only does scepticism assume that the mind is radically different from nature and the body such that it can doubt them, but it then assumes an absolute form of ideal mental knowledge in the form of the certainty of its own doubt. This was Descartes' logic. Lucretius, however, sings this critique in two beautiful lines of hexameter (4.469–70):

> *Denique nil sciri siquis putat, id quoque nescit*
> *an sciri possit, quoniam nil scire fatetur.*

> Next, if anyone thinks that nothing is known, he also doesn't
> know whether this can be known, since he admits he knows nothing.

Scepticism is a 'twisted reasoning' because it doubts or treats as false its own immanent performativity. It acts as if it has not acted. It thinks as if it is not thinking and knows as if it knows nothing. The sceptic, Lucretius says, has 'stuck his head under his feet', as if thought comes first and supports the senses and all of nature. Marx, following Lucretius, makes a very similar statement about Hegel in the postface to the second edition of *Capital*.

> The mystification which the dialectic suffers in Hegel's hands by no means prevents him from being the first to present its general forms of motion in a comprehensive and conscious manner. With him it is standing on its head. It must be inverted, in order to discover the rational kernel within the mystical shell.[10]

The twisted reasoning of all idealism is to move, act, and know while *denying* its very own act of knowing as a material practice or performance continuous with sensuous nature itself. Lucretius was one of the first in the Western tradition to fully invert this twisted reasoning and place nature and sensation at the foundations of philosophy (4.474–7).

> *quaeram, cum in rebus veri nil viderit ante,*
> *unde sciat quid sit scire et nescire vicissim,*
> *notitiam veri quae res falsique crearit*
> *et dubium certo quae res differre probarit.*

> I will ask: Since he has never found any truth in things before,
> from where does he know what it is to know and not know in turn,
> what thing created the concept of true and false,
> and what thing has demonstrated that the doubtful differs from the sure.

Knowledge, for Lucretius, comes from *somewhere* [*unde*] (4.475). It is geographically, materially, and historically situated. We can now see in these lines that, for Lucretius, the thesis that 'all perceptions are *true*' means something more radical than we first thought. All perceptions are *true* not in the sense in which they are the opposite of what is *false*, but rather in the most profound sense of the term: that they are the real, immanent, material conditions that produce the division between true and false in the first place.

The radical nature of this point cannot be understated. The distinction between true and false is an emergent property of nature itself. In other words, humans are not the origin of the division between true and false, but the apparent division is already something produced by a more radical material movement of nature. Nature, therefore, cannot be said to lack knowledge of the true but is actually the true producer of the knowledge – that is, of truth and falsity itself (4.478–9).

> *invenies primis ab sensibus esse creatam*
> *notitiem veri neque sensus posse refelli.*

> You will find that the concept of truth is created first of all
> from the senses and that the senses cannot be refuted.

Humans are not freaks of nature.[11] We cannot 'explain human existence in terms of an *immaculate conception*, where human species-being is exceptional because it breaks with all precedent'.[12] The concepts of true and false are born from the senses, thus *the senses themselves cannot be reduced to true and false*. Ethical and moral theories of goodness/truth and evil/falsity are predicated on the immaculate conception of humans cut off from nature. A radical and materialist naturalism must therefore reject the division and thus the traditional categories of ethical thought.

The senses are radically and performatively true. Since nature is not a substance but a process, it has no static or fixed state that can be called true or false. A discrete and binary division cannot be applied to that which is neither true nor false but which is the condition of knowledge itself. Sensation does not abide the law of non-contradiction;[13] 'unless they [the senses] are true, reason too becomes completely false' (4.485). Nature and sensation are the material conditions of contradiction and division as such. Without the senses, reason and the mind become completely empty and meaningless. How can reason possibly come from nature and yet be radically different from nature?

No sense can refute another because each is true in a qualitatively unique way, according to Lucretius. This includes thought. Thought cannot refute or represent the senses, just as the senses cannot refute one another. Also, 'They [the senses] cannot refute themselves, since equal trust must always be granted them' (4.497–8). 'Accordingly, that which has appeared to the senses on each occasion is true' (4.499–500). In fact, Lucretius says, it would be better to give purely sensuous descriptions of events as processes, even if their cause was not known, because at least then we would not err by doubting the senses.

All reasoning that begins with the division between true and false, between nature and culture, and mind and nature, for Lucretius, is fundamentally 'warped' from the beginning. Once a dualism is posited, we never get the two back together again. 'Truth' then should be understood as what nature *does* and 'false' as that which performatively doubts the continuous flow of nature and simulacra that it is.

The Diffractive Harmony of the Senses

The senses do not represent one another, nor do they have any ability to refute one another (4.522–3).

> *Nunc alii sensus quo pacto quisque suam rem*
> *sentiat, haud quaquam ratio scruposa relicta est.*

> Now understanding how the other senses sew together their
> own things requires no rocky road of reasoning.

This is an absolutely radical rejection of representation in all its forms. The Latin is tricky to translate concisely, though. The senses (other than thought) form a kind of 'performative agreement' [*pacto*] (4.522) among themselves about how things [*rem*] (4.522) are 'sewn' up [*suam*] (4.523). One reads *suam* at first as coming from the possessive pronoun *suus* ('its own'), but the root *su-* in Latin also suggests 'to sew'. In other words, what things are is precisely the processes that iterate, sew, and stabilise them as such. The implication here is that the senses do not merely represent things but rather form a kind of diffractive relationship with them that transforms them – just as two pieces of cloth are sewn together. The relationship is transformative.

The senses sense their object, but in sensing their object are also sensing themselves *through* the object. Even more important, however, the senses and object are collectively transformed in the same act of weaving and entanglement. Representation is therefore out of the question. There is only transformation. The five senses, if it makes sense to limit sensation to five, do not represent one another or even fit together like pieces of a puzzle, but diffract with one another and their objects of sensation. The result is a continuously transforming knotwork of woven and unwoven fabrics, not a representational hierarchy.

Flows of sound (sound waves), for example, are material and can physically scratch the throat (4.525–32) and are shaped by the tongue as they flow out of the body (4.550–5). Loud sounds can damage our ears, bright lights can damage our eyes and so on, because sensation is affective. We only tend to think about this mutual affecting when it hurts us, but such transformations are always occurring. The senses do not merely receive but participate in the world because they are the world as well. Our sense organs dilate and palpate in a diffractive harmony with the world.

The Language of the World

The flow and diffraction of simulacra is the way the world talks to itself and senses itself. Language, for Lucretius, is not representational but more like a system of relays. In this broader definition, language is not the sole property of humans. Lucretius gives the beautiful example of the play of sonic simulacra through the mountains and their relation to oracular knowledge (4.580–9).

haec loca capripedes Satyros Nymphasque tenere
finitimi fingunt et Faunos esse locuntur,
quorum noctivago strepitu ludoque iocanti
adfirmant volgo taciturna silentia rumpi
chordarumque sonos fieri dulcisque querellas,
tibia quas fundit digitis pulsata canentum,
et genus agricolum late sentiscere, quom Pan
pinea semiferi capitis velamina quassans
unco saepe labro calamos percurrit hiantis,
fistula silvestrem ne cesset fundere musam.

Locals imagine that goat-footed satyrs and nymphs
inhabit these places, and say that there are fauns.
It is by their night-wandering shriek and playful trickery,
they commonly say, that the still silence is broken
and the sounds of strings arise and the sweet complaints
which the flute pours forth pressed by the fingers of the players.
In addition, they say, the country-dwelling sort commonly senses it
when Pan, shaking the covering of pine on his half-civilized head,
often with his curving lip runs over the open reeds,
so that his pipes may not stop issuing their sylvan muse.

In the mountains nature becomes an instrument (Fig. 7.2). The curvature of the mountains forms a resonance chamber in which the sounds and movements of plants, animals, winds, and falling rocks in the valley echo around like the air inside a flute, drum, or lyre box. The first instrument was nature's own bodily resonance chamber.[14]

This is an important and revealing example in the context of Lucretius' theory of sensation. Sensation is weaving. Sensation, like sewing, is a reciprocal transformation and affecting since the two pieces of fabric fold together and become something new. Sensation is the sense of one's self as an other because self-sensation always occurs through another. It is an echo. The Latin word *imago* means 'image' or 'phantasm', but also *echo*.[15] Lucretius moves his discussion of simulacra from human sensation to non-human sensation in the sonic form of the echo. Echoes are a great poetic image of the simulacra precisely because they are non-representational. Waves of sound flow out and return in a precise pattern and duration that is no mere representation but a creative transformation of the initial sound diffracted through the world. In echoes, flows of sound go out and 'record' the history of their

Figure 7.2 Pan and Daphnis. Wikimedia Commons.

diffractions as they move through the world. When they return, they return transformed.

The sensation of bats, dolphins, and other echolocating beings is based precisely on the differential iteration of simulacral flows. It is the difference between the initial sound and the returning sound that makes perception possible. Perception is fundamentally differential and not representational. Representations are tautological, self-identical, and empty. They tell us nothing about the world. Echoes, like simulacra, however, are creative, responsive, and are the world's sensation of itself.

Mountain music and speech is historically associated with the satyrs, fauns, nymphs, and Dionysus, who were also figures of fertility, prophecy, knowledge, and music. These are precisely the figures Lucretius most frequently connects with the poetic philosophical tradition. For Lucretius, however, these woodland gods are not transcendent but immanent to nature itself. Knowledge and poetry are something nature itself already does in the mountains (4.590).

cetera de genere hoc monstra ac portenta loquontur,

They tell of other odd creatures and portents of this sort.

The Latin word *portenta* comes from the proto-Indo-European root *ten- ('to stretch, draw'). 'To portend' means 'to move' or 'stretch onward and further along'. A portent is not a prediction about an abstract future yet to come but a practical act that stretches or prolongs itself *into* the future. As such, oracular knowledge and epiphany are not speculative and metaphysical but immanent material acts that lead, draw, or figure the future. Echoes are portents insofar as they literally stretch out ahead beyond their source and then return transformed to tell the listener something about the path ahead. Portents are not speculative but performative and transformative. The future is not temporal but kinographical. Portents, just like simulacra, 'draw out' and 'figure' form through motion. Simulacra and echoes move forward and draw out the forms of sensation.

Nature speaks. Birds sing, wind whispers, air smells, clouds draw patterns in the sky, and so on. All these are portents, simulacral signs, diffracting echoes, or relays that connect with one another in certain patterns that tell us and nature *how things are folding and unfolding up ahead*. Language *as simulacral relays* is something nature did well before humans arrived. Humans received and shed their own simulacra flows and carefully observed and manipulated the diffraction patterns already found in nature.[16]

The source of the animist belief in the language, song, and oracular speech of nature (shared by Greeks, Romans, and many indigenous peoples around the world)[17] is the real active material flows of nature. This is not anthromorphism. Nature was already speaking before humans discovered that nature speaks and portends in various patterns. In short, speech and language, for Lucretius, is fully material, kinetic, and simulacral because it operates by relay, diffraction, and echo – not by representation.

The system of habituated material relays feels magical in the way it can reliably tell us about near future events. For example, the shape of clouds tells us about the weather. The movement inland of certain birds indicates that something, such as bad weather or an invading armada of ships (4.592–4), has disturbed them upon the water.

ideo iactant miracula dictis
aut aliqua ratione alia ducuntur, ut omne
humanum genus est avidum nimis auricularum.

Thus with words
they boast of wonders or they are led on by some other reason,
since the entire human race is exceedingly eager of ears.

Humans are literally 'led on' [*ducuntur*] (4.593), 'conducted, drawn forward, escorted', by the flows and figures of simulacra into common patterns of movement. This is possible because humans listen with desire to the portents, relays, and echoes of nature. Lucretius here, as throughout, offers a materialist explanation for what is often taken to be a metaphysical belief in transcendent, fate-controlling gods.

There are no gods, but if we listen carefully enough, we can hear that nature does speak and lead us ahead with common patterns. If language is nothing other than a pattern of signs relaying with one another, then nature is already linguistic.[18] Language and so-called symbolic representation act *as if* language refers to a non-existent temporal 'future', when in fact their speech performance is completely immanent to the existing world. What seems like 'reference to something else' is nothing other than a kinetic habit in a relay system.

Language does not speak about things. It is a material process that coordinates patterns of sounds with movements. 'Meaning' is the immanent anticipation of the pattern that typically follows by habit. There are no pre-existing 'wholes' or abstract 'general' ideas or 'forms', only simulacral diffraction patterns that tend to diffract in a similar way each time. Forms, as Lucretius has argued throughout *De Rerum Natura*, are drawn and iterated by flows of matter. One sign is not 'about' another sign. Rather, like a line of upright dominoes, one sign tends to knock into another in a predictable chain reaction. Instead of forms, generalities, or wholes, there are 'kinetic patterns'.

Lucretius is extremely clear about this. No sense can 'judge' [*opinatus*] another but is rather added [*addimus/addit*] to it. This means necessarily that language cannot be *about* anything at all. Language is not symbolic representation. Since this is what many people claim makes humans radically distinct from nature, we must conclude, with Lucretius, that there is no ontological division between nature and humans. His theory of language thus consistently follows from his rejection of such a division.

Ethically speaking, this is also why, to move well together, we must let nature speak and we must listen to what it says. If nature *cannot* speak, then we must *represent* it in the so-called 'parliament of things'.[19] But if nature *can* speak, then representation is fundamentally anthropocentric and guilty of the very division it is attempting to overcome. Lucretius thus gives us a superior starting point for an ecokinetic ethics.

The Ecokinetic Imagination

The mind, for Lucretius, is a sense organ like any other. It does not represent nature but is a relay that is *affected* by the flows of simulacra and *affects* them in turn. Matter from the world flows and diffracts in every direction. Some of these flows (light, sound, temperature, and so on) affect the body, of which the mind is an immanent part. Simulacra thus *directly* affect the mind because the mind is not separate from the body. The mind, for Lucretius, is bodily. Therefore 'things move the mind' [*moveant animum res accipe*] (4.722). The flows, however, that affect the mind are so fine that we do not have any direct sensation of them (4.728–31).

> *quippe etenim multo magis haec sunt tenvia textu*
> *quam quae percipiunt oculos visumque lacessunt,*
> *corporis haec quoniam penetrant per rara cientque*
> *tenvem animi naturam intus sensumque lacessunt.*

> For indeed these images are much more fine in texture
> than those which take hold of the eyes and strike the faculty of sight,
> since these pass through the pores of the body and stir
> the fine nature of the mind within and provoke sensation.

Matter from the environment affects our mind. However, affect (in contrast to empirical sensuous emotion) is not something that can be directly sensed. For example, small changes in temperature, slow or subtle shifts in lighting, the shape and size of a room, and ambient smells all have an effect on our thinking and feeling even if, and perhaps because, we do not directly sense or realise they are affecting our bodies in these ways.[20] Simulacra of all kinds weave together affects that move our bodies and minds in extremely subtle ways that contemporary neuroscience, physiology, and ecopsychology are only just beginning to study. Lucretius was well aware of these subtly woven [*textu*] (4.728) patterns of affect that occur below the level of conscious sensation and feeling.

For example, when our minds are moved, we imagine all kinds of things. We can think of things that do not exist, such as centaurs and Cerberus, and we can 'feel' happy or sad. What is the origin of these ideas and feelings? We tend to have 'new ideas' in the shower or on long walks, for example, in part because of the release of dopamine and other chemical transformations that we do not directly sense. Moving around literally changes our minds because our bodies are changing as well. Certain sounds, such as wind and water, can relax our bodies and make our minds more creative. The physical act of breathing increases oxygen and blood-flow to the body and brain and can create a feeling of well-being and literal inspiration, historically associated with the Muses. In short, material flows pass into and through our bodies in the form of physical, chemical, hormonal, molecular, and electrical affects that also move our minds.

The imagination, for Lucretius, comes from nature in motion. The imagination is not just a 'mental synthesis' of two parts of the brain that have coordinated their neuronal firings to produce novel combinations.[21] This only raises the question of how and why such coordinations emerged in the first place. For Lucretius, this question is answered ecologically. Our imaginations and the movements of our minds are nature itself and are coordinated with other natural patterns. For example, when the narrator of *In Search of Lost Time* tastes a madeleine, it triggers his involuntary memory of his home in Combray. His brain and body then enter into a feedback loop from this initial sensation. The patterns of the body and mind do not transcend their material and ecological conditions, but are rather feedback loops directly entrained with them. The question of how 'we' imagine and move well together should thus be understood as an ecological 'we' that is doing the imagining. Human ethics and mind are not extended to nature but rather habituated and coordinated enfoldings of nature itself.

We see dead people and phantasms [*simulacra*] for precisely this reason. The neurons that fire together wire together. The more our bodies are in the habit of acting in certain ways and our brains are in the habit of firing in certain ways, the more likely we are to feel, see, and imagine people who we saw or interacted with many times (4.757–62). Our bodies and minds are being affected in an incredible number of ways at once. However, Lucretius says, we only sense some and not others because of habits by 'which the mind has prepared itself'. Thought and imagination are not *ex nihilo* products of an internal mind. They are kinetic patterns of action directly and physically shaped and habituated by nature.

As such, ethics is not alien to nature, nor are its ideas 'about' nature. Aristotle was right to emphasise habit and practice as requisites of ethical life, but he was wrong to limit these practices to formal normative 'virtues' (bravery, truth, temperance, and so on) and to limit habit to human habits alone. Habits, for Lucretius, are ecological, physiological, architectural, and atmospheric as well. Human habits of thinking and moving well are continuous with larger ambient patterns of motion in which they are enfolded. Therefore, ethics is not only about moving well together and not fearing/hating death but also about habituating oneself and/as the world at the same time. We move well together in reciprocal patterns.[22] Moving well is thinking well.

Conclusion

All perceptions are true because perception is continuous with nature. Only if we assume a discontinuity between mind and nature or between mind and the other senses (representation) do we pose the unresolvable problem of a disconnected mind and ethics. In order to move well together we need to avoid using 'twisted reasoning' (4.832–5). In the next chapter, Lucretius deals with several major ethical consequences of this position.

Notes

1. Maurice Merleau-Ponty, *The Primacy of Perception*, trans. James M. Edie (Evanston: Northwestern University Press, 1964), 162.
2. Maurice Merleau-Ponty, *The Visible and the Invisible*, ed. Claude Lefort, trans. Alphonso Lingis (Evanston: Northwestern University Press, 1992), 134.
3. Merleau-Ponty, *The Primacy of Perception*, 162.

4. 'The immortal *eidos*, unvarying and true, becomes, for him, error, and the lying *eidolon*, phantasmal and dead, becomes truth, tranquil appearance in a real world.' Michel Serres, *The Birth of Physics*, trans. Jack Hawkes (Manchester: Clinamen Press, 2000), 105.
5. See Karen Barad, *Meeting the Universe Halfway* (Durham, NC: Duke University Press, 2007), and Thomas Nail, *Theory of the Object*, unpublished manuscript, under review with Oxford University Press, ch. 16.
6. Nail, *Theory of the Object*.
7. Henri Bergson, *Matter and Memory* (New York: Zone Books, 2005), 203.
8. Keith Devlin, *The Maths Gene* (London: Weidenfeld and Nicolson, 2000), 73. See also Vicki Kirby, *Quantum Anthropologies: Life at Large* (Durham, NC: Duke University Press, 2011).
9. Michel Serres, *The Birth of Physics*, trans. David Webb and William Ross (New York: Rowman and Littlefield, 2018), 125–30.
10. Karl Marx, *Capital Volume 1* (New York: Penguin, 1976), 103.
11. 'Man is born as a freak of nature, being within nature and yet transcending it. He has to find principles of action and decision-making which replace the principles of instincts. He has to have a frame of orientation which permits him to organize a consistent picture of the world as a condition for consistent actions. He has to fight not only against the dangers of dying, starving, and being hurt, but also against another danger which is specifically human: that of becoming insane. In other words, he has to protect himself not only against the danger of losing his life but also against the danger of losing his mind.' Erich Fromm, *The Revolution of Hope: Toward a Humanized Technology* (New York: Harper and Row, 1968), 61.
12. 'If we return to Descartes and humanism we see a man of his times who relied heavily upon the existence of God to validate the terms of his inquiry. But do we covertly recuperate this divine "backstop" in a godless universe when we explain human existence in terms of an immaculate conception, where human species being is exceptional because it breaks with all precedent, all natural and (therefore) instinctual or programmatic processes? Can antihumanism justify its faith in the subject who appears as First and Final Cause of his own ability to self-author, a subject whose unique capacity to make moral and ethical judgments, however misguided, forms the basis of both secular and theological interpretations of what it means to be human.' Vicki Kirby, 'Originary Humanicity: Locating Anthropos', *philoSOPHIA*, 8.1 (2018), 43–60, 52.

13. See Nail, *Theory of the Object*, ch. 17.
14. See Thomas Nail, *Theory of the Earth*, unpublished manuscript, under review with Oxford University Press. See also the cultural and geophysical language of Silbo, a whistle-based language used on the Canary Islands, https://www.youtube.com/watch?v=PgEmSb0cKBg (accessed 12 September 2019).
15. For a list of Latin usages of the term *imago* as 'echo', see Lewis and Short, *Oxford Latin Dictionary*, http://www.perseus.tufts.edu/hopper/morph?l=imago&la=la#lexicon (accessed 12 September 2019).
16. See Thomas Nail, *Being and Motion* (Oxford: Oxford University Press, 2018), 177–93, for a more developed kinetic theory of language.
17. See Eduardo Kohn, *How Forests Think: Toward an Anthropology Beyond the Human* (Berkeley: University of California Press, 2015), and Robin Kimmerer, *Braiding Sweetgrass: Indigenous Wisdom, Scientific Knowledge and the Teachings of Plants* (Minneapolis: Milkweed Editions, 2015).
18. 'Or more instantiations of a language whose "langue" involves the Earth itself? What subject speaks these messages? Who authors and reads them? How, or why, should we censor these questions from their *natural* extension? For if humanity is not the origin of re-presentation, if the Earth re-presents itself to itself, then repetition must be domiciled with/in Presence.' Kirby, *Quantum Anthropologies*, 41.
19. See A. F. Conty, 'The Politics of Nature: New Materialist Responses to the Anthropocene', *Theory, Culture & Society*, 35.7–8 (2018): 73–96.
20. Thalma Lobel, *Sensation: The New Science of Physical Intelligence* (New York: Atria Books, 2016), and Brian Massumi, *Parables for the Virtual: Movement, Affect, Sensation* (Durham, NC: Duke University Press, 2002).
21. Jean-Paul Sartre, *The Psychology of the Imagination* (London: Routledge, 2016), 4.
22. For some some excellent examples of this kind of ecological ethical symbiosis, see Kimmerer, *Braiding Sweetgrass*.

8. The Material Unconscious

There is nothing in the mind that has not first been in the senses and nothing in the senses that has not already been in nature. This is the bold argument at the heart of Lucretius' radical naturalism. The consequences of this simple idea are profound and have several ethical implications.

The argument of this chapter is that one of the main consequences of Lucretius' naturalism is a materialist theory of the unconscious. This chapter unpacks this interesting theory through a close reading of lines 4.823–1057. The aim of the reading will be to show that when Lucretius flips 'upside-down reasoning' right-side up, it results in a completely transformed relationship between mind and nature. This is what I am calling the 'material unconscious'.

More specifically, I would like to show the reader that this entails a unique theory of knowledge not exclusive to humans and a convincing rejection of utilitarian ethics. The main consequence of the material unconscious for ethics is that it redefines ethics as composed of practical and unconscious habits of motion – not conscious maxims, rational laws, virtues, or pleasure-seeking utilities.

Against Utilitarianism

If there is matter before there is mind (or body), historically speaking, then matter *cannot be* something useful to the mind. Rather, it means that the mind is already something material, natural, and thus ordered and reproduced in certain ways that shape the structure of utility, pleasure, and pain in ways that precede the mind's desires (4.832–5).

> *cetera de genere hoc inter quae cumque pretantur,*
> *omnia perversa praepostera sunt ratione,*

nil ideo quoniam natumst in corpore ut uti
possemus, sed quod natumst id procreat usum.

Other things of this sort that people expound
are all backwards, the product of upside-down reasoning,
since nothing arises in the body so that we might make use of it,
but that which arises in the body creates its own use.

The mind does not demand that the body act in useful ways, but rather the body already provides the immanent conditions of useful action in the first place. We could say the same of nature. Things do not emerge in nature to be useful to us, but rather nature creates its own uses – of which human uses are only a tiny subset. Nature uses itself *through* humans.

One of the reasons for our current ecological crisis is precisely the use of upside-down reasoning. Humans have treated their own bodies and nature as means to the ends of their minds – when the situation is precisely the inverse. If only we had taken Lucretius and pre-Western oral traditions seriously on this crucial point much earlier in the Western tradition, perhaps things might have turned out differently.

Seeing did not exist before light. Words did not exist before tongues. The body did not evolve for the sake of using its limbs, but rather the limbs and body are the material unconscious through which we exist in the first place (4.835–42). For example, food and water were not created to be useful for us. We only exist because there is food and water. Because food and water are structured the way they are, we, humans and animals, could come into existence in the first place.

It is completely inverted to place our desire for pleasure as a uniquely human or even ethical priority. Pleasure exists before humans. Humans only exist because there is pleasure in nature. We desire food and drink not despite entropy but precisely because of entropy. The very idea of food and drink is by definition dependent on entropic exhaustion, decay, and death, which precede us. We live not despite death but because there is already death. Only because other beings died can we live and desire food. Lucretius gives numerous examples that follow out the logic of this basic material priority (4.855–65).

One of the most ethically important products of this upside-down reasoning is the fear of death. However, far from being the end, death is actually the prior and immanent condition of being. We feel that death is a lack or an end only relative to a tiny portion of the universe. But our life is the result of death. Our desires exist only because of entropy and decay. What a strange thing to fear ourselves and our own moving materiality. Desire, by definition, cannot lack anything because the material conditions of our desire are already defined by an excessive movement of nature actively consuming itself.

When we think that things (our arms, for example) are 'useful' or 'pleasurable' for us, this is absolutely ridiculous, Lucretius says (4.855–65). Our arms are already the biological conditions of our body from which 'we' are not distinct. To say something is pleasurable or useful is already to pretend that 'we' is some inner mental voice separate from the body, such that even our own arms are 'useful to us'. Who is this 'us' that is not the arms? Who is this us that is not already nature?

Nature's Mind

Perhaps the most radical consequence of Lucretius' inversion of this upside-down reasoning is that nature itself has 'will' [*voluntas*] *and* mind. Lucretius is explicit about this first point and only implicit about the second. The second simply takes Lucretius' logic to its ultimate conclusion regarding the evolutionary origins of the senses. His argument is that what humans sense both precedes and produces human sensation in the first place. Since mind is a type of sense organ, this means that what the mind senses (namely thought) must have already preceded the human mind and helped shape it, just as light shaped the human eye. The inverse of this, that thought and mind emerge dramatically *ex nihilo*, would be a direct contradiction of Lucretius' arguments against *ex nihilo* creation and against the primacy of sense before sense organs. There can be novel patterns of motion, but ontologically speaking there can be no dualism or division between mind and nature. This follows implicitly from Lucretius' argument.

Explicitly, however, Lucretius is also quite clear that the movement of matter directly produces the *will* of the mind (4.881–4).

dico animo nostro primum simulacra meandi
accidere atque animum pulsare, ut diximus ante.
inde voluntas fit; neque enim facere incipit ullam
rem quisquam, quam mens providit quid velit ante.

I say that first moving images fall upon
our mind and strike the mind, as we have said before.

Thence the will is produced; for no one begins to do
anything before the mind prepares in advance.

Simulacra flow, fall, and swerve [*accidere*] (4.882) into the mind and literally 'produce its will' [*voluntas fit*] (4.883). Lucretius could not be more clear: the supposedly unique human mental features of will and freedom are 'products' of matter in motion. It is only because matter flows and swerves freely that the human mind and its will can even exist and have will in the first place.

Matter is pedetic and indeterminate, as Book II showed in detail. Lucretius calls the minimal swerve of matter its *voluntas*. From within the infinite chain of interconnected and continuous *minima*, the will [*voluntas*], inclination, or desire [*voluptas*] is the name of the kinetic novelty of matter. The swerve does not break the continuous chain of movement [*motu conectitur*], but responds to what came before in a novel way that is irreducible to any mechanistic laws (2.251–60). The human mind is also part of this same kinetic continuum and is literally produced by the free movement of matter.

Cicero and Plutarch completely misinterpreted Lucretius' swerve as the *product of human freedom*, when the material and historical situation is *precisely the inverse* for Lucretius. Humans have will and freedom only because matter does. This does not mean that human agency is determined by matter but that both matter and human minds, bodies, and souls are all free because they are all material. They all swerve pedetically. There is no ontological division whatsoever.

Lucretius says that the mind 'prepares itself in advance', but this 'will' is already 'produced' *by and as* material nature in the first place. The mind is therefore habituated through nature's own habituations. The mind prepares itself because it has already been pre-prepared by the flows of simulacra affecting it from outside and inside. The whole division between outside and inside is thus completely overturned in Lucretius' account. The preparation of the mind is what neuroscientists today call 'background brain activity' – the coordinated neurological activity in the brain and body that precedes a so-called 'conscious' thought. Although the brain is highly active, neuroscientists tend to 'average out', as they say, the background in order to isolate and abstract the moment of conscious brain activity.[1] Quantum-field theorists do the same thing when they 'renormalise' the indeterminacy of background 'vacuum fluctuations' in order to foreground discrete quanta of energy.[2]

Even quantum-gravity theorists do this when they bracket out energies below the Planck unit and inside black holes.³ What all three contemporary sciences share is an active elimination of indeterminate movement, that is, a movement that is so entangled that it cannot be predicted at all (not even probabilistically). This indeterminacy is what Lucretius calls pedesis, or the *clinamen*.

For example, Lucretius' explanation of how we walk involves several coordinating movements. The body, mind, and soul are all affected by simulacral flows from outside the body, but they are also each affected by others in turn, as he showed in Book III. This is well beyond mere 'embodied cognition'.⁴ Nature affects the mind, which affects the soul, which affects the body (4.886–9), but they *all affect one another*. Therefore the simple act of walking, for Lucretius, involves a real co-movement of the whole. This also means that any simply extensive movement from point A to point B also involves a real material transformation of the whole nature–mind–soul–body assemblage.

Again, Lucretius uses the image of the rudder to describe agency [*gubernaculum*] (4.904). This is in contrast to Plato, who uses the image of the captain as the mind, the ship as the body, and the ocean as nature. For Lucretius the materialist, agency is distributed throughout the whole ocean–ship complex. There is no captain who sits above the ship and commands it autonomously (4.895–905). This is precisely why Lucretius asks the listener of his poem to give their ears and mind to the poet, so that the 'true words' do not re-echo off their target (4.912–15). Knowledge is not about rational understanding, but rather it requires a material and practical transformation and orientation of the body. Lucretius thus uses the image of the diffractive simulacra and sonic echoes to describe the materiality of poetic knowledge itself. The poet emits sounds at various patterned intervals and waves in the hope of physically affecting the listener's mind, body, and soul. Knowledge is not something known only through the mind but also through natural and bodily orientations. This is a clear divergence from Epicurean method and much closer to rhetoric and poetry than to philosophy.

Knowledge and Dreams

Knowledge, for Lucretius, is a performative act that changes us. Simulacra flow through us according to iterative patterns or material habits. This is not inconsistent with what contemporary neuroscientists call 'engrams', or biochemical patterns of neuronal firing. The more the simulacral flows of neurological electricity move in a certain pattern, the easier it is to fire them again – like channels of water.

For Lucretius, memories are not stored in our brains like files in a filing cabinet. Knowledge and memory are continuous processes [*constat*] (4.885) that move through us and prepare [*providit*] (4.884) the mind to receive and repeat certain material habits. Accordingly, this is not unrelated to the ethics of motion. Knowledge is always already an ethical act, and ethics as a practice cannot be separated from knowing.

Lucretius says that even when we sleep, our bodies and brains are actively iterating various motions and forming patterned habits that shape us. He even goes as far as to say that he himself dreams of the nature of things, records them in Latin, and then shares them with the listener (4.970). The implications of this example have potentially radical consequences that build on but diverge from Epicureanism, as we shall explore in a moment. But first, Lucretius gives a strikingly contemporary-sounding account of why we sleep and what our bodies and minds do when we sleep. This material explanation leads him to suggest, quite radically, that the poetry and knowledge we are hearing in his song came from his material unconscious.

According to Lucretius, we sleep because our minds, bodies, and souls are, following Book III, *metastable processes* that require them to 'work' or 'labor' [*opera*] (4.920) to sustain the habitual patterns of motion (electrical, chemical, etc.) that reproduce and form us. Just like simulacra, human and animal bodies are diffractive patterns iterated over and over again. They are formed through figuration. We sleep when the metastable labours that sustain us become too disordered, entropic, or turbulent [*conturbantur*] (4.943). We sleep not because we are out of energy, but because the mind and body need time to organise the iterative patterns of motion in the body and mind.

In contrast to Plato, who thought that the body could be reordered by the contemplation of perfect geometrical forms,[5] Lucretius' explanation is actually consistent with much of what we currently know about brain science. The body and mind are material processes that order, disorder, and reorder themselves. There are no forms that matter in motion does not create through habituated flows of simulacra.

Contemporary neuroscientists do not know for sure why we sleep or what happens while we sleep. However, most believe that during the night our brains 'consolidate' neuronal patterns or engrams into 'memories'. Numerous studies show that people retain memories better after sleeping.[6] Lucretius was, in general, not wrong about this. This is why he says that when we sleep, we often dream of the ordered patterns of motion that we frequently perform (4.962–5).

Et quo quisque fere studio devinctus adhaeret
aut quibus in rebus multum sumus ante morati
atque in ea ratione fuit contenta magis mens,
in somnis eadem plerumque videmur obire:

And usually to whatever pursuit a person is devoted and persistently clings,
and in whatever things we have been engaged in before
and on which our mind has been more intent,
in dreams we often seem to engage in the same things.

In dreams the mind reiterates common kinetic patterns that our bodies and minds often produce and even mixes and combines them. Flows of simulacra from outside (temperature, light, sound, etc.) also affect us while we sleep.

Additionally, Lucretius says, this material disturbance [*conturbantur*] (4.943) occurs in our minds and bodies because the flows of air moving around cause damage outside and inside our bodies that needs to be repaired during sleep (4.932–43). This, too, is consistent with what neuroscientists know about sleep. While we are awake, our metabolism generates 'reactive oxygen species' or 'metabolic wastes' that damage our cells.[7] In sleep our metabolism decreases and the body creates antioxidant molecules that combat these free radicals.[8]

Finally, Lucretius describes the material conditions of his own knowledge (and our own): the material unconscious (4.969–70).

nos agere hoc autem et naturam quaerere rerum
semper et inventam patriis exponere chartis.

and I perform my task and seek the nature of things
constantly and, finding it, set it out in our native pages.

Why is Lucretius, the good Epicurean fundamentalist, dreaming about the nature of things and not staying up all night reading Epicurus? This method is completely contrary to Epicurus' own writings about dreams, in which they have no divine or prophetic meaning but are merely stray images hitting our minds from outside.

Fragment 24: Dreams have no divine nature [*physin*] nor any prophetic force, but they originate from the influx of images.

For Lucretius, however, all perceptions are true, *even dreams*. The material unconscious, for Lucretius, is not a privileged realm where truth or our deepest desires necessarily come from (following Plato, the Stoics, and eventually Freud). Nor, however, is it merely a random influx of images without meaning (following Epicurus).[9] Dreams, like thought, are a true performance without symbolic representation. Dreams are real material entanglements with nature that simply continue on as we sleep. They iterate and diffract habits of waking life and therefore are not reducible to representations *of something else*.

For example, Lucretius does not say that his dreams are sent to him as prophecies by gods, but nor does he say that they are lacking in 'natural force' or divine import. In this passage we therefore have a clear consolidation of two main features that define the originality of Lucretius' philosophical and poetic method: the Latin language and a naturalistic interest in oracular knowledge. For Lucretius, knowledge of the nature of things does not come from rational thought or argumentative writing alone.[10] The knowledge of nature is nothing other than nature itself knowing itself. Therefore, knowledge is performative. If we want to know, we must also *act*, and attend to the nature of that acting. Since the body and mind keep acting in sleep, there is no reason why the knowledge of nature cannot also be found there.

Just as our minds and bodies are not ours alone but are caught up in a whole ecological knotwork of diffracted flows, so our unconscious is not ours alone, either. Nature speaks through our dreams just as it does in our senses and minds in waking life. The only difference is that our limbs are limp.

This makes Epicurus' fetish of rational thought crystal clear. Knowledge of the nature of things cannot come from dreams because dreams are merely sensuous images without reason. Epicurus therefore lacks a genuinely practical ethics for this same reason. He cannot imagine ethics or knowledge without conscious contemplation. Lucretius, by contrast, connects his ethico-epistemology with the material and even unconscious transformation of our bodies as natural bodies. There is nothing to know *about* nature. There are no static Epicurean gods to contemplate – only matter in motion.

Libido

Not only does our will [*voluntas*] and knowledge come from the flows of matter [*semina rerum*], but so do our desires [*libido*] (4.1045). The flows of matter have their own *voluntas* and their own desire or libido. Just as our agency or will is the product of matter's agency, so our desire is also the product of matter's desire. As material bodies, our will to know and desire to move well with others is completely continuous with the nature and the desires of our own bodies.

In short, the deep currents of a material unconscious are flowing through our bodies. Libido, for Lucretius, is the real material movement that joins, weaves, and binds matters together. This occurs at the most general level between the seeds of things that flow, fold, and weave together [*semina rerum*], described in Book II, but also at the level of all living creatures, including humans. Human libido, for Lucretius, is merely one regional expression of a much larger material process of entanglement and composition. Human libido is neither reducible to other libidos, nor does it transcend them. We should recall here the opening lines of Book I, '*hominum divomque voluptas, alma Venus*' (1.1–2), Venus is the immanent desire of gods and men. *Venus voluptas* is the transversal movement through which all of matter composes and decomposes itself (4.1039).

> *namque alias aliud res commovet atque lacessit;*
>
> For different objects move and arouse different things

Nature enjoys itself. Different matters move together or arouse one another [*commovet*] differently. Libido is therefore not unique to life and certainly not to humans. Life gets its libido from the flows of matter in the first place. If desire did not already come from matter, then we risk positing an *ex nihilo* emergence of desire.

The seeds of things are flows or threads of matter that stir up, move, and agitate [*sollicitatur*] the 'beginnings of desire' [*semen*] in humans and animals (4.1037–8). Today, we call these 'hormones and neurological impulses'. Lucretius is only making the general point that material flows or 'the beginnings or seeds of desire' [*semen*] literally move though our body. In other words, libido does not come from the gods and it is not caused by mere mental action. It is an affective or unconscious movement of matter that is the source of our desire (4.1045–6).

*inritata tument loca semine fitque voluntas
eicere id quo se contendit dira lubido,*

The places are excited and swell with the beginnings of desire
to send it forth to where the portentous libido stretches,

For Lucretius, our *libido* and *voluntas* is fully material. As material it is also pedetic and without absolute beginning or end. That is, libido and the beginnings of desire [*semine voluntas*], like the seeds of things [*semina rerum*] themselves, can be directed in all kinds of ways 'into whatever body' [*in corpora quaeque*] (4.1065). The material libido is polymorphous and not sexually normative. Nature has a multiplicity of differently sexed bodies that move and arouse one another in different ways. They do not even have to be the same species – as the recurring example of the bees shows.

Reproduction, for Lucretius, is not the goal or end of nature. *Contra* Plato, libido is not a desire for immortality achieved through heterosexual reproduction. Following Empedocles, Lucretius defines love much more broadly as the drive for co-movement, attraction, and composition. For Empedocles, nature *loves* itself as it congeals, and *struggles against* itself when it breaks apart. Sexual reproduction is not the aim of nature or even of living creatures but rather something that happens as an outcome of a more primary, cosmic, libidinal movement.

The libido also presents a danger: that these material intertwinings will become exclusive and all-consuming habits to the detriment of other patterns of motion. Libido is not good or bad in itself, for Lucretius. It simply raises again the question of moving well. How does one circulate libidinal movements, and where? What Plato takes to be the ultimate goal of intellectual love of the eternal, Lucretius takes to be an impossible attempt to arrest the flow of libidinal energies.

The Wound of Love

The 'beginning seeds of desire' [*semina voluntas*] strike and flow through the body, opening it up like a wound [*cadunt in vulnus*] (4.1049). The aleatory and pedetic nature of matter means that the movement of the seeds of desire is also subject to swerving. The Latin word *cadunt* means both 'fall' and 'accident', because again desire is not biologically reductionistic. For Lucretius, biology is not destiny. There is no destiny, no telos. The seeds of desire swerve and can be put into *any* body whatsoever.

The wound is the material site where that which is inside flows out and that which is outside flows in, in 'mutual pleasure' [*communis voluptas*] (4.1207). Venus and Mars flow into and out of each other in a continuous circulation of pleasure through their open wounds [*vulnere amoris*] (1.33–4).

The wound is a fold in the flows of matter. But every fold, like every wound, leaks. The wound is a fold where inside and outside are opened to each other and leak blood or sexual fluids. Desire and love bring things and people together but only through mutual vulnerability. Their union might lead to the exclusion of others or might dissolve or destroy the composite. Lucretius thus uses the poetic image of the wound in these lines to indicate the ambivalent nature of love to bring both pain and pleasure.

For this reason Lucretius also says that it is also acceptable to 'flee the images and to drive off from yourself what nourishes love and to turn your mind elsewhere' (4.1063–4). In other words, the libido can be redirected through the body or the mind. We should therefore not read these passages as merely being about sexual desire aimed at intercourse and/or reproduction. If, according to Lucretius, the libido can be redirected by the mind, this means that libido is material, mental, and sexual at the same time. There is no division.

This further complicates the role played by what I am calling the material unconscious in *De Rerum Natura*. Lucretius frequently sings of his *desire* to know the nature of things, or his *desire* to tell his listeners about something, or his ecstatic pleasure in thinking about nature.[11] Just as Lucretius says he discovers the nature of things in dreams, so he is implicitly here suggesting that all his own desires to learn and share the nature of things are also an expression of this natural libido that flows through our bodies.

Instead of, or perhaps in addition to, sexual intercourse, Lucretius directs his libido towards the nature of things and poetry. This point could not diverge more from Epicureanism. Epicurus and his followers did not encourage us to direct our libidinal desires but rather to quiet and still them. We are not supposed to desire knowledge but simply to have knowledge through logic, reason, and calm contemplation of the gods.

What appears to be a simple gesture that knowledge is material and bodily ends up having enormous consequences for later thinkers and traditions: naturalism/ecology, Marxism, feminism, queer theory, critical race theory, and disability studies, to name a few major ones. Marx, Nietzsche, and Freud each took up this call in their own ways.

However, just because Lucretius redirects his libido into poetry on this occasion does not mean that he thinks sexual intercourse is 'bad'. This is the case first of all because all matter is sexual in the general sense in which Empedocles defines love. Second, Lucretius encourages us to be careful about where this libido is directed. His worry is not that people will have sexual intercourse for pleasure but that they will let this pleasure completely destroy their lives.

Lucretius never says love is bad but just that we should consider the various possibilities for libidinal circulation, or what I am calling 'moving well together'. We can redirect our libido into a vast array of sexual activities that have nothing to do with monogamous reproduction or even human love. Lucretius thinks that the demand that all sexual activity be teleologically aimed at love is unfounded in nature. Nature copulates with itself in many ways simply for the sake of enjoyment. The animal world, for example, is filled with non-reproductive sexual activities of all kinds (4.1073–4).[12]

Nec Veneris fructu caret is qui vitat amorem,
sed potius quae sunt sine poena commoda sumit;

Nor does the one who shuns love lack the enjoyment
of Venus, but rather receives the enjoyment without the penalty.

Lucretius is extremely clear that *enjoyment* [*fructu*] (4.1073) is natural and shared by all of nature [*alma Venus*] (1.2). Matter, recall, *inclines* and *desires* itself through the swerve (2.251–60).[13] This is completely *contra* Epicurus, who clearly rejected such pleasures and explicitly condemned sexual intercourse, saying, 'Sexual intercourse has never done a man good, and he is lucky if it has not harmed him.' Not only does Lucretius diverge from this, but he even expands the definition of sexual intercourse, following Empedocles, to the whole of nature. Rather than the tranquil contemplation of gods, Lucretius affirms the becoming of death through sex and sex through death. Each provides the conditions of the other, just as Empedocles says in *The Alternation of Becoming*. There Empedocles describes love as 'joy' and 'Aphrodite' and 'limbs that the body has received in the flower of blooming life'.[14] Lucretius continually uses the Latin 'Venus' to describe the acts of love in these lines and even uses the same turn of phrase about copulation: 'with limbs intertwined they enjoy the flower of their age' (4.1105–6). The influence of Empedocles is thus clear in Lucretius' theory of libido.

The Knots of Love

The flows of matter weave into things, and things weave into our bodies, souls, and minds. The flows of simulacra (chemical, kinetic, sonic, and electromagnetic) stimulate our body's own internal energies. This is desire. Human desire, like the will, Lucretius says, is a product of a more primary process that exceeds but does not transcend the human.

The danger, according to Lucretius, is that our libidinal flows will become exclusive, self-enclosed, all-consuming, and cause us to abandon the ethical practice of moving well together with the wider world of material relations that compose us. Nature weaves and unweaves itself with all kinds of beings in an open, metastable process, but obsessive love ties up and inhibits this wider weaving. It captures [*captum*] (4.1147) the couple in a 'net' [*plagas*] (4.1146) [*retibus*] (4.1147) that binds them in knots [*nodos*] (4.1148), which folds them up [*implicitus*] (4.1149) in constricting tangles [*adstrictosque*] (4.1187). This kind of obsessive, 'closed-in' love seeks in vain for a static resolution and eternal satisfaction of desire (4.1101–4).

> *sic in amore Venus simulacris ludit amantis,*
> *nec satiare queunt spectando corpora coram*
> *nec manibus quicquam teneris abradere membris*
> *possunt errantes incerti corpore toto.*

> so in a love affair Venus teases the lovers with images
> nor are they able to be satisfied by gazing at the bodies before them
> nor with their hands can they rub off anything from the soft
> limbs as they wander without direction over the whole body.

Obsessed lovers are like those who try to drink from a rushing stream in vain. They are like Tantalus, who treats desire as a lack that can be satisfied by something if only he could have it. Lucretius, as we have already seen, believes that this idea of desire as property, possession, and thus lack is simply not the way nature works. Desire is not a lack that is satisfied. It is a real material flow that, like the river, keeps flowing.

Sexual desire is thought to be a lack only from the limited perspective of the human body. From the point of view of nature, however, it is a pure excess, expenditure, or 'overflowing' [*abundans*] (4.1199), as Lucretius says. *Voluntas* and *libido*, remember, are 'products' for Lucretius, not *ex nihilo* drives that lack objects. Unsatisfied love is yet another expression of the fear of death, the hatred of matter and movement, and the quest for static, self-satisfied desire. The flow of libidinal pleasure is not enough for the love-knotted couple; they want final satisfaction and thus stasis.

Feminine Desire

For Lucretius, libido is a material movement common to all nature and thus precedes human sexuated desire. Sexual difference is thus fully material but not biologically reductionistic. Desire does not come preformed. *Contra* Freud, for example, desire is not organised according to a heteronormative Oedipal structure. Nor is desire and sexual difference something *merely constructed* by humans, for Lucretius. Humans can certainly direct their desires in various ways, but there is no proper telos or form for their direction. The desire that moves through bodies is a real and material process that affects all creatures and sexes.

Lucretius thus explicitly rejects the idea put forward by many philosophers before and after him that women are merely passive and lack desire altogether (4.1192–3).

> *Nec mulier semper ficto suspirat amore,*
> *quae conplexa viri corpus cum corpore iungit*
>
> Nor does a woman always sigh with feigned passion
> when, embracing a man, she joins body together with body

Feminine desire in its 'own nature, [is] overflowing' [*ardet abundans natura*] (4.1199–200). 'Wherefore again and again, I say, pleasure is shared' [*communis voluptas*] (4.1207). This is a complete rejection of both Platonic and Aristotelian theories of femininity and the whole metaphysical, ethical, and epistemological systems that support their androcentric philosophies.[15] Aristotle wrote in the *Politics* that 'as regards the sexes, the male is by nature superior and the female inferior, the male ruler and the female subject',[16] and in the *Generation of Animals* that 'we should look upon the female state as being as it were a deformity [*anapērian*], though one which occurs in the ordinary course of nature [*phusikēn*]'.[17] Even when Freud finally grants women desire, it is a pre-castrated desire in the form of 'penis envy'. Feminine desire is thus modelled on male desire as an expression of biological and natural lack for Freud.

At this point it is no surprise that Lucretius' rejection of formalism in favour of pedetic materialism means that no such formal castration of feminine desire is possible *a priori*. A cosmos without beginning or end, overflowing with swerving matters and emergent metastable forms, cannot justify any natural, ontological, ethical, or fixed biological hierarchy of men over women. There is in Lucretius therefore a kind of materialist 'aleatory feminism'.

> The theme of a Venusian maternal-feminine fecundity infuses the entirety of Lucretius' poem; indeed it begins with an extended invocation of Venus' many wondrous qualities and delights. Matter, in its new philosophical manifestation in the Latin language now appearing as *materia* rather than *hulē*, is of course directly related to *mater* (mother). The centrality of this feminine principle in Lucretius' work cannot be overestimated. By elevating maternal and earthly fecundity and establishing an unequivocally feminine principle at the root of all existing things, and in foregrounding the originary role of chance in the form of the *clinamen*, the uncaused swerve that ensures the collision of atoms, Lucretius is thus the mirror image of Aristotle. The aleatory feminine appears in this remarkable text no longer as a symptom of a patriarchal metaphysics but as the plural and generative origin of the entire cosmos.[18]

After all, Lucretius attributes all generative life, decay, and death to the movement of female desire: Venus. The human experience of Venus is nothing other than the same *communis voluptas* (4.1207) shared by all of nature, through human bodies and practices of performative sexuation.

Maternal Seeds

One important consequence of the materiality of desire, and of feminine desire in particular, is that Lucretius ends up making a strikingly contemporary insight about sexual reproduction: that it is the result of a mutual activity of male and female matters. Historically, the Western tradition has tended to associate seeds with semen. In Lucretius, however, this is explicitly not the case. The *semina rerum* or *materies* that are the material 'nature of things' cannot, by definition, be sexuated, since they are themselves not alive. Matter [*mater*], recall, is not strictly identical with things [*rerum*]. Matter is not reducible to things either alive or dead and thus cannot be sexuated in any meaningful way. Rather, sexual differentiation is itself a real process immanent to female and male sexes – because it is their immanent condition of emergence and trans-sexual *trans-formation*. Matter is first and foremost trans-sexual because it is immanent to all discrete sexuated forms.

This is precisely why Lucretius associates the *semina rerum* with female and male sexual desire. Lucretius directly equates *semina* with *materies* (1.53–61),[19] and *materies* with the etymologically related *mater* (mother) and *mater materque* (great mother) (2.599–623), which includes Venus and all the other generative feminine goddesses of *De Rerum Natura*.[20] It is therefore not surprising to read in lines 4.1209–10 that women also have '*semine forte virilem femina*' or 'virile feminine seeds' that mix together with male seeds. 'For an offspring is always the product of twofold seed' [*semper enim partus duplici de semine constat*] (4.1229). Lucretius also connects the seeds of things with masculine figures, such as Ouranos' severed seed [*genitabilis*] (1.11), which rains down from the sky to co-create Venus (1.2–5), father Epicurus' seeds of reason [*disserere*] (1.54), and, of course, the semen-stained [*semen*] sheets of young boys (4.1030–6).

Seeds are not discrete atomic pellets with a single sex. They are flows of sexually reproductive fluids that congeal into male and female things. Plant ovules are the products of seeds that have grown into plants, and seeds are the products of plant ovules that will in turn produce more seeds. Nature thus transforms itself back and forth between male and female sexes. What we typically call 'natural sexual division or desire' is based on a complete misunderstanding of how queer and *trans-sexual* nature really is. Sex and gender are products of material processes that trans-form and traverse all sexes and genders.

Again, if we think that Lucretius is talking about atoms and that these atoms are like seeds, then the poetic image of the 'twofold seed' [*duplici de semine*] makes no sense whatsoever. Two seeds cannot 'fold' into each other unless we are talking about more *thread-like* flows being woven together like strands of genetic material intertwining themselves.

Lucretius, again, seems well ahead of his time on this point. Up through the seventeenth century, philosophers and scientists still believed in homunculus sperm-preformation theories, in which God pre-created all human generations inside women's bodies. Even twentieth-century theories of macho sperm competing to fertilise an egg hold to the same androcentric story of active male seeds implanting a passive female body. Actually, the most recent science on human reproduction is much closer to Lucretius' theory. Male and female fluids are mixed together [*commiscendo*] (4.1209) into a single, folded-up fluid that is stored in side channels and slowly directed towards the egg.[21] The movement of sperm is not strong enough to travel to the egg – it requires the co-movement [*comoventi*] of fluids and eventually the intertwining of genetic flows.

The reduction of women to a place of biological 'natural' inferiority and mere passivity in history has been one of the most unethical errors of the Western tradition. This is inseparable from the broader hatred of matter and passivity that Lucretius criticises in Book III as the 'fear of death'.[22] It has also been used as a justification for excluding women and femininity in all its guises from the 'together' of 'moving well together'. For Lucretius, however, *desire matters*.

Semele and Dionysus

Dionysus appears again. The folding, mixing, and co-moving occurs, according to Lucretius, because of the Venusian stimulation [*Veneris stimulis*] of a mutual [*mutuus*] passion [*ardor*] (4.1215–16). *Stimula* was the Roman name of the Greek bull priestess Semele, the mother of Dionysus. As she was sacrificing a bull at the altar of Zeus, Zeus came to her and she became pregnant with Dionysus. From the death of the bull came the life of Dionysus.

When Hera found out about the affair, she came to Semele in the guise of an old woman and convinced Semele to admit the affair. When Semele confessed, Hera convinced her that Zeus should show himself in his full god-like appearance – as he appears to Hera – to prove his true identity. Out of jealousy and distrust, and against Zeus's warnings, Semele demanded that Zeus show himself as a god. When he did, Semele was immolated – since no mortal can see a god in their pure form. Before she died, however, Zeus put Dionysus in his thigh or groin and gave birth to him. From the death of Semele came the life of Dionysus.

Lucretius invokes a naturalised mythological connection between Venus and *Stimula* to show the interconnected process of life and death, masculinity and femininity. Fertility from sacrifice, sacrifice from fertility. Nature is an indeterminate process producing, traversing, and transforming female and male bodies, making men into women (Zeus into a mother) and women into men (Semele into Dionysus). Semele Thyone became her name after Dionysus brought her back from Hades to live among the immortals. Semele is also the figure of feminine desire that seizes female devotees of Dionysus during his revels – traversing their bodies.

The importance of feminine desire reappears for Lucretius as a crucial part of what desire is more broadly. Since both men and women engage in a mutual *Veneris stimulis*, both are part of the same overflowing material desire. Lucretius quite literally refers to the sexual fluids, blood, and saliva as the materiality of desire. This pleasure is neither good nor bad in itself: all love comes with the risk of distrust, jealousy, and romantic idealism.

Conclusion

Lucretius is one of the first philosophers, if not the first, to have taken seriously the material unconscious. Simulacra, sleep, dreams, desire, and sex are not inseparable from ethical practice and the nature of things. Far from being 'digressions', as some scholars have called them, the final sections of Book IV on love and sex are integral to aesthetics, epistemology, and ethics.

Far from being mere appearance or errors, as they are for Epicureans, all perceptions, conscious and unconscious, are true and real performances of nature. To desire well is to know that the desiring libido is continuous with death and decay, without any trace or hope of immortality. There is no escape from death because desire and will are material flows continuous with nature. To live well is to die well is to *move well together*.

Notes

1. 'Deconstructing Brain Waves: Background, Cue, and Response', *PLoS Biol*, 2.6 (2004): e180, https://doi.org/10.1371/journal.pbio.0020180 (accessed 12 September 2019).
2. See Thomas Nail, *Theory of the Object*, unpublished manuscript, under review with Oxford University Press, ch. 16.
3. See Nail, *Theory of the Object*, ch. 16.
4. Francisco Varela, Evan Thompson, and Eleanor Rosch, *The Embodied Mind: Cognitive Science and Human Experience* (Cambridge, MA: MIT Press, 1995).
5. See Plato, *Timaeus*, trans. Peter Kalkavage (Newburyport, MA: Focus Publishing, 2001).

6. Jérôme Daltrozzo, Léa Claude, Barbara Tillmann, Hélène Bastuji, and Fabien Perrin, 'Working Memory is Partially Preserved during Sleep', *PLOS One*, 7.12 (2012): e50997, https://www.ncbi.nlm.nih.gov/pmc/articles/PMC3517624/ (accessed 12 September 2019).
7. Lulu Xie, Hongyi Kang, Qiwu Xu, Michael J. Chen, Yonghong Liao, Meenakshisundaram Thiyagarajan, John O'Donne, Daniel J. Christensen, Charles Nicholson, Jeffrey J. Iliff, Takahiro Takano, Rashid Deane, and Maiken Nedergaard, 'Sleep Drives Metabolite Clearance from the Adult Brain', *Science*, 342.6156 (2013): 373–7, https://science.sciencemag.org/content/342/6156/373 (accessed 12 September 2019).
8. E. Reimund, 'The Free Radical Flux Theory of Sleep', *Medical Hypotheses*, 43.4 (1994): 231–3.
9. Diskin Clay, 'An Epicurean Interpretation of Dreams', *The American Journal of Philology*, 101.3 (1980): 342–65
10. The epistemological importance of dreaming is also attested to in numerous oral traditions. See Eduardo Kohn, *How Forests Think: Toward an Anthropology Beyond the Human* (Berkeley: University of California Press, 2013).
11. See Thomas Nail, *Lucretius I: An Ontology of Motion* (Edinburgh: Edinburgh University Press, 2018), ch. 1.
12. See Catriona Mortimer-Sandilands and Bruce Erickson (eds), *Queer Ecologies: Sex, Nature, Politics, Desire* (Bloomington: Indiana University Press, 2010).
13. See Nail, *Lucretius I*, ch. 10.
14. Empedocles, 'On Nature', in *Early Greek Philosophy Part 2*, ed. and trans. André Laks and Glenn W. Most (Cambridge, MA: Harvard University Press, 2016), 415, 421.
15. See Emanuela Bianchi, *The Feminine Symptom: Aleatory Matter in the Aristotelian Cosmos* (New York: Fordham University Press, 2014).
16. Aristotle, *Politics*, 1254b13–14.
17. Aristotle, *Generation of Animals*, IV.6, 775a15–16.
18. Bianchi, *The Feminine Symptom*, 232.
19. Nail, *Lucretius I*, 52–4.
20. See Nail, *Lucretius I*.
21. See Emily Martin, 'The Egg and the Sperm: How Science has Constructed a Romance Based on Stereotypical Male/Female Roles', *Signs: Journal of Women in Culture and Society*, 16 (1990/1), and Robert D. Martin, 'The Macho Sperm Myth', *Aeon*, 23 August 2018, https://

aeon.co/essays/the-idea-that-sperm-race-to-the-egg-is-just-another-macho-myth (accessed 12 September 2019).
22. 'What happens if nature is neither lacking nor primordial, but rather a plenitude of possibilities, a cacophony of convers(at)ion? Indeed, what if it is that same force field of articulation, reinvention, and frisson that we are used to calling – "Culture"? Should feminism reject the conflation of "woman" with "Nature," or instead, take it as an opportunity to consider the question of origins and identity more rigorously?' Vicki Kirby, *Quantum Anthropologies: Life at Large* (Durham, NC: Duke University Press, 2011), 88. See also Stacy Alaimo, 'Eluding Capture: The Science, Culture, and Pleasure of "Queer"', in Catriona Mortimer-Sandilands and Bruce Erickson (eds), *Queer Ecologies: Sex, Nature, Politics, Desire* (Bloomington: Indiana University Press, 2010).

Conclusion

We are witnessing a return to Lucretius. What felt like early shoots in 2014 are now starting to bear fruit in numerous recent books that break with received tradition. This book is part of a handful of recent works offering new interpretations of Lucretius. The authors of this return offer different perspectives but also share a common belief that something is missing from our current reception of Lucretius, and that certain problems in contemporary life might find their surprising solutions in the work of this ancient poet. Just like the moderns and the Romantics before us, we are just now beginning to rediscover a Lucretius for *our* time.

Since the introduction to this book has already provided a short summary of the main theses of Lucretius' ethics of motion, the conclusion will instead provide the larger historical context for the present intervention, the motivation for undertaking the *Lucretius* project, and aspirations for the future.

The New Lucretius

The new Lucretius has an old lineage that traces its roots back to the German philosopher Karl Marx's 1841 dissertation on 'The Difference Between the Democritean and Epicurean Philosophy of Nature'. There Marx gave one of the most radical and heterodox interpretations of Epicurus and Lucretius that the world never saw. The complete work was not even available in German until 1927, and not in English until 1975 in his expensive collected works. It is no wonder that it remains one of the most neglected of all Marx's books. However, in his dissertation, Marx was the first to argue not only that Epicurus had a distinct philosophy different from Democritus', but that the core concepts of atomism (atom, void, fall, swerve, repulsion) were all actually continuous dimensions of the *same flow of matter*.

This radical idea was virtually left for dead until the French philosopher Gilles Deleuze miraculously picked it up in 1962 in his book *Nietzsche and Philosophy*. There, Deleuze credited Marx's brilliant discovery, but argued instead that the swerve was the result of a vital 'force' immanent to matter. Later Deleuze developed this reading into a new 'immanent' interpretation of Epicurus and Lucretius that appeared as an appendix to his 1969 *Logic of Sense*.

From there, the French philosopher Michel Serres explicitly adopted the idea of a vital and unpredictable force immanent to matter and developed it into the first truly pathbreaking, book-length treatment of a new, turbulent Lucretius consistent with the early chaos theory of the day, *The Birth of Physics in the Text of Lucretius* (1977). Unfortunately, Serres's book was not translated into English until 2000, after which it quickly went out of print.[1]

Beginning in 2016 an unusual burst of new books was published, tracing their lineage back to this tradition and overturning the old orthodox reception of Lucretius. In 2016 a wonderful collection of essays offering contemporary reassessments and reinterpretations of Lucretius that drew on the 'immanent' tradition was edited by Jacques Lezra and Liza Blake and published as *Lucretius and Modernity*. In the next year Ryan Johnson published *The Deleuze–Lucretius Encounter*, and in the autumn of 2017 Pierre Vesperini published a devastating critique of the 'myth of Lucretius' in his *Lucrèce: Archéologie d'un classique européen*. Among other things, Vesperini argued convincingly against every single major point that Stephen Greenblatt made in his error-filled narrative history of the discovery of *De Rerum Natura*, *The Swerve* (2011). Vesperini argued that Lucretius was not a faithful Epicurean; that Lucretius was not an unknown radical of his day; and that Lucretius did not provide a 'complete kit for modernity', but was historically appropriated by mechanistic modernists and then retroactively lionised by the Romantics.

The apotheosis of this burst came in January 2018, when Serres's *The Birth of Physics* was retranslated and republished with a blurb by Claire Colebrook explicitly acknowledging the timely importance of reintroducing this book for its contributions to twenty-first-century *new materialism*. Two months later saw the publication of my first book, *Lucretius I: An Ontology of Motion*, and Lezra's book *On the Nature of Marx's Things*. There has been an absolutely unprecedented explosion in heterodox readings of Lucretius. In just the past eight years, there has also been a notable return of Lucretius to the footnotes of books on new materialism.[2] I

Conclusion   213

think the time is right now for a full return to Lucretius, materialism, and radical naturalism.[3]

The Kinetic Lucretius

My books on Lucretius are part of this tradition, but also diverge from it in important ways worth mentioning. I diverge from Marx's reading insofar as Marx treats Epicurus and Lucretius as identical and I do not. The difference between Epicurus and Lucretius is one of the most important contributions of my books.

The kinetic Lucretius I develop also diverges from Deleuze's vitalist reading. Deleuze, following Marx, reads Lucretius and Epicurus as identical, but breaks from Marx in arguing that the swerve is identical with Spinoza's and Nietzsche's concept of *conatus*, 'vital striving', 'force', or 'power'. What I have tried to show in my book is that this kind of neo-vitalist reading is textually unsupportable. Matter is, above all, in motion, and motion is not about life. It is just as much about death, decay, and decomposition. It is purely arbitrary to privilege one side of this ontological binary, life versus death, and claim that everything is life, or alive, or vital power. Vitalism in all its old and new forms is just another way of explaining the movement of matter with recourse to something else: life. At its worst, it falls prey to the fear of death that Lucretius locates as the locus of unethical action. The ontologisation of life is yet another way to escape death, to hate matter and motion.

This book even diverges from the great Michel Serres's *The Birth of Physics*. Serres, like Marx and Deleuze, equated Epicurus and Lucretius. He also accepted the existence of Lucretian atoms, despite their absence from *De Rerum Natura*. Serres showed how Lucretius prefigured chaos theory's understanding of turbulence, entropy, and far-from-equilibrium states. However, in addition to these insights, my *Lucretius* books have tried to argue that Lucretius also prefigured quantum theory's understanding of entanglement and indeterminacy.

Motivations and Aspirations

But why return to Lucretius today? To overcome our present. In the 1960s Michel Foucault said that he and Deleuze had returned to Nietzsche to overcome their philosophical milieu.[4] They used Nietzsche's historical method to overcome the ahistoricism in the prevailing paradigm of phenomenology, and they used his theory of desire to overcome the dehumanised formalism of the equally dominant French structuralism.

Today, I would like to make a similar gesture with my books on Lucretius. After all, Nietzsche got much of his Nietzscheanism from Lucretius in the first place. In brief, I would like to use Lucretius' naturalism and materialism to overcome the anthropocentrism and constructivist anti-realism of contemporary poststructuralism. The result, I hope, will be a *kinetic new materialism*, distinct from current vitalist new materialisms, object-oriented ontologies, and speculative realisms.

Mechanistic materialism has been thoroughly criticised across the humanities and sciences, but I think we have been too quick to throw out the baby of materialism with the mechanistic bathwater. Lucretius is such a wonderful figure to return to today because he embodies the diffractive relations we need to rediscover between the arts, sciences, and humanities for a new posthumanities and a new materialism. Lucretius was a scientist and philosophical poet. Knowledge today, however, has been so compartmentalised that thinkers like Lucretius are extremely rare. This is a profound loss for universities.

However, if we are going to address contemporary ethical practice at the global level seriously, we no longer can be merely scientists, philosophers, or poets. It is no longer enough to be merely the scholars of such and such a figure or topic; the humanities and sciences need to come back together again. The study of nature unites all theoretical practice. Globalisation and climate change demand that we see the big picture – that human activity is completely continuous with natural processes. Humans are geological actors, and the Earth is not a passive stage for our performances. The disconnect between the humanities and natural sciences is part of the same disconnect between humans and nature. We have divided up our knowledges as we have divided up our world, and the consequences have been disastrous. We can no longer study nature as if our acts of inquiry were not already ethical and transformative practices of nature itself.

There will be no resolution to the deepest problems of our times until the Lucretian unity of humans, nature, and art (the humanities, sciences, and arts) are brought back together again in collective ethical practice.

Notes

1 There were numerous and widely differing interpretations of Lucretius through the nineteenth and twentieth centuries, but here I am highlighting the 'immanent' interpretation with which my own reading is connected.
2 Jane Bennett, *Vibrant Matter: A Political Ecology of Things* (Durham, NC: Duke University Press, 2010); William Connolly, *World of Becoming* (Durham, NC: Duke University Press, 2010); Levi Bryant, *The Democracy of Objects* (Ann Arbor: Open Humanities Press, 2011); Peter Merriman, *Mobility, Space and Culture* (London: Routledge, 2013), 3–5; Ilya Prigogine and Isabelle Stengers, 'Postface: Dynamics from Leibniz to Lucretius', in Michel Serres, *Hermes: Literature, Science, Philosophy* (Baltimore: Johns Hopkins University Press, 1982), 135–58; Tim Cresswell and Craig Martin, 'On Turbulence: Entanglements of Disorder and Order on a Devon Beach', *Tijdschrift Voor Economische en Sociale Geografie*, 103.5 (2012): 516–29.
3 It is time to tear down the whole anthropocentric project of Western metaphysics, with its wretched hatred of death, matter, the labouring classes, women, racialised colonies, queer desire, and nature in general.
4 Michel Foucault, 'Structuralism and Poststructuralism', in *Aesthetics, Method, and Epistemology* (New York: The New Press, 1999), 433–58.

Index

Note: Page numbers in *italics* indicate figures. Page numbers flowed by an n refer to end-of-chapter notes.

abstraction, ethical, 115–16
accumulation, primitive, 54–6
Achilles, 80
action, ethical, 89, 96
aesthetics, 155; *see also* ethico-aesthetics
affect, 186–7
affect theory, 75–7
affective ecologies, 159–64
affective theory of emotion, 71–5, 76–7
agency, 8, 71, 95, 194, 195
air, 66
aleatory feminism, 205
Amalthea, 25–6
anger, 92–3, 94
anima (body, mind, soul)
  life and death, 97–100
  scatology of spirit, 106–7
  as woven vessel, 101–4, 117
animals, 21–2, 55, 58, 93, 121, 156
  bees, 30–3, 151
  goats, 24–30
  swallows, 21, 22–4
animus (breath; wind; life), 37, 65–6
anti-ethics, 126–8, 133–5, 139–41
anxiety *see* fear
Aphrodite, 32, 202
Apollo, 42n, 132, 133
argumentative theses, 10
Aristotle, 54, 55, 188, 204
Artemis, 101, 132, 133
asceticism, 3, 5, 57, 119, 131
ataraxía, 3, 4, 24, 35
atomic reason, critique of, 78–82
atomism, 91, 211

atoms, 26, 89, 97
augury, 22–3, *23*
awareness, 72, 73

background brain activity, 194
Bataille, Georges, 86, 118
becomings, 26
bees, 30–3, 151
'Bees of Malia', *34*
Bergson, Henri, 174
bioethics, 112, 113, 119, 121, 128
biopolitics, 64, 112, 113, 120–1, 122
Birth of Physics in the Text of Lucretius, The (Serres), 212, 213
birth of spring, 35–7
blind desire [*caeca cupido*], 52, 53
body
  affect theory, 75–6
  affective theory of emotion, 73–4, *74*
  discordant harmony of the soul, 70–1
  dualism, 169–70
  fear of death (necrophobia), 48
  harmonic theory of the soul, 69
  hatred of, 57–8, 69–70, 115
  life and death, 97–9
  as part of a woven vessel [*calathus*], 101–4, 117
  scatology of spirit, 106–7
body temperature, 93
Boltzmann, Ludwig, 153
brain, 194, 196–7
breath / breathing, 18, 36–7, 50, 65–6, 86, 187

Index 217

butterflies, 65–6, 70, 137–9
butterfly axe, 60, *66*, 80, 132, 137

calathus (woven vessel), 101–4, *102*, 141–2
  Fors Fortuna, 126
  kinetic ethics, 116–20, *118*
Camus, Albert, 141
Capital (Marx), 178
capitalism, 6–7
Ceres, 101
chance, 125
chaos theory, 125, 213
Charon, ferry man of Hell, *47*
chora (space made through movement), 25, 132–3, 159
Cicero, 95, 194
circulation, 117–18, *118*, 120
classism, 54, 55, 58
climate change, 2, 7, 36, 122
clinamen see pedesis
close reading, 8–9
clouds, 163
coldness, 92, 93
collective desire, 134–5
collective ethical life [*pietas evertere*], 58–60, 116, 120, 134–5
collective ethics, 17, 135–41, 171
colour, 159–60
coniuncta (conjunction), 72
consciousness, 49, 73
contemplation, 38
copia (source material), 19
corpora, 9, 33, 153, 154, 155, 157–8; *see also* matter
Crete, 28, 33, 49, 65–6, 78, 132, 137
critique of atomic reason, 78–82
critique of kinetic reason, 64–83
  critique of harmonic reason, 68–71
  critique of pure emotion, 71–7, *74*
  material conditions of reason, 64–8
  soul as weaving, 77–82
Critique of Pure Reason (Kant), 64–5
Curetes, 28, 30, 33

Damasio, Antonio, 75, 76
dancing, 132–3
De Rerum Natura, The Swerve (Greenblatt), 212

death, 85–6, 108–9
  as anti-value, 113–14
  fear of death (necrophobia), 6, 7, 44, 46–7, 115, 192–3: collective ethics, 58–60; harmonic theory of the soul, 68, 69–70; hatred of the body, 57–8; liquid desire, 48–9; mask of materialism, 50–2; practical ethics, 49–50; primary consequences, 123; primitive accumulation, 54–6; statism, 52–3; statues, 56; Tantalus, 128
  and life, 97–100, 112, 120, 192
  migrant nature, 107–8
  in motion, 46–8
  movement of, 100–4
  river of death, 50, 126
  scatology of spirit, 104–7
  and sex, 202
  soul, 96–7
Deleuze, Gilles, 44, 75, 103, 110n, 212, 213
Delos, 132–3
Delphic bees, 33
Demeter, 101
Descartes, René, 178
desire, 19–20, 50, 116, 193
  affective theory of emotion, 74
  bees, 31, 33
  birth of spring, 36
  blind desire [*caeca cupido*], 52, 53
  collective, 134–5
  divine, 38
  feminine, 204–5, 207–8
  goats, 25–6
  libido, 199–200, 201–4
  liquid, 48–9
  perversion, 58
  swallows, 23–4
  Tityos, 131–2, 133–5
  wound of love, 200–1
Diana, 49
dice games, 125
'Difference Between the Democritean and Epicurean Philosophy of Nature, The' (Marx), 211, 213
diffraction, 154–6, *155*, 163
diffractive harmony of the senses, 180–1
digestion, 104–7

Dionysus, 25, 26, 28, 33, 49, 207–8
disability, 119, 121, 142n
discordant harmony of the soul, 70–1
divine desire, 38
dreams, 196, 197–8
dualism, 169–70
duty ethics, 5

echoes, 182–3, 184
ecokinetic imagination, 186–8
ecological affect, 159–64
ecological ethics, 150–1, 161
economics, 6–7
ecstasy of the sensuous, 37–9
ecstatic knowledge, 31
elected office [*honorum*], 52
elemental soul, 87
embodied knowledge, 149–51
emotion
   affect theory, 75–7
   affective theory of, 71–5, 76–7
   critique of pure emotion, 71–7
   in nature, 161
   thermodynamics of, 92–3
Empedocles, 18, 87, 200, 202
energetic expenditure, 94
entropic ethics, 129–35
entropy, 50, 100, 154
environmental affect, 159–64
epic poetic tradition, 18, 52
Epicurean rationalism, 176
Epicurus
   critique of religion, 16–17
   death, 114
   desire, 201, 202
   ethics, 3
   gods, 59
   as horse, 24, 25
   Lucretius as a follower of, 17–19, 20
   Lucretius' critique of, 21
   as Lucretius' father, 28, 30, 32
   Plato, 68
   soul, 87
   as swan, 21
epistemology, 64, 89, 154–5, 176
equivalence, 6–7
eternity, 104
ethical abstraction, 115–16
ethical action, 89, 96
ethical freedom, 60–1

ethical indeterminacy of matter, 87–90
ethical practice, 108–9, 113, 120
ethical strength [*virtus*], 125
ethical theory, 39
ethical values *see* values
ethico-aesthetics, 9, 152, 173
ethics
   collective, 17, 135–41, 171; *see also*
     collective ethical life [*pietas evertere*]
   ecological, 150–1, 161
   entropic, 129–35
   Epicurean, 3
   geological, 36, 151
   Lucretian, 3–6; *see also* ethics: of
     motion
   material unconscious, 191
   materialist, 21–2
   and materialist physics, 57–8
   of motion, 2–3, 61–2, 107, 125,
     131–3, 134: woven vessel [*calathus*],
     116–20, *118*; *see also* ethics: pedetic
   and ontology, 90–1
   pedetic, 20–35, 124–8: bees, 30–3;
     goats, 24–30; swallows, 21, 22–4
   practical, 49–50
   process-based, 123, 152–3
   simulacra, 152–3, 156, 166
   thermodynamic, 93–6, 121–2
   see also anti-ethics; bioethics;
     necroethics
existentialism, 141
exordium, 87
expers (having no part in), 88, 116
eyes, 17, 175, 177; *see also* vision

faculties, harmony of, 70
fasces (heterogenous sticks), 136–41, *138*
fear, 92, 93, 94
fear of death (necrophobia), 6, 7, 44,
   46–7, 115, 192–3
   collective ethics, 58–60
   harmonic theory of the soul, 68,
     69–70
   hatred of the body, 57–8
   liquid desire, 48–9
   mask of materialism, 50–2
   practical ethics, 49–50
   primary consequences, 123
   primitive accumulation, 54–6
   statism, 52–3

statues, 56
Tantalus, 128
fear of matter (hylephobia), 44, 55
fear of motion (kinophobia), 44, 51, 55, 119
feeling, 76; *see also* emotion
feminine desire, 204–5, 207–8
ficta (feign; falsify), 18–19
first-threads [*primordia*], 9, 87, 157, 165
flow of things, 170–1
flowers, 30
　language of, 148–51
flows of matter, 38, 89, 99, 117, *118*, 136, 162, 170
flows of sound, 181
folded matter, 86–7
food digestion, 104–7
form, 157, 158, 174, 175, 185
Fors Fortuna, 125–6, *127*
Foucault, Michel, 213
fourth nature of the soul, 85, 87–9, 91, *92*
freedom, ethical, 60–1
Freud, Sigmund, 204–5

gender, 32, 206
geological ethics, 36, 151
glory [*kleos*], 52
goats, 24–30
gods, 4, 59, 185
gold Minoan labrys (double axe), *66*
goodness, 35–6
Greenblatt, Stephen, 110n, 212

habits, 188
harmonic reason, critique of, 68–71
harmony of the faculties, 70
heat, 92, 93
hedonism, 3, 5
Hegel, Georg W.F., 178
Hera, *80*, 207
heroism [*kleos*], 52
historical ontology, 8
Homer
　Illiad, 80
　Odyssey, 24, 35, 36, 88, 101, 102–3, 126–7, 132, 133, 140
Homeric tradition, 28, 65–6
honey, 30–1, 78

honorum (elected office), 52
horses, 24, 25
hylephobia (fear of matter), 44, 55
hyperkinetic modernity, 1

idealism, 119, 178–80
　transcendental, 60
Iliad (Homer), 80
illusions, 177
imagination, ecokinetic, 186–8
imitari (imitate), 19
immanent values, 60
immobility, 55, 64, 69
immortality
　fear of death (necrophobia), 51
　hatred of the body, 57
　impossibility of, 45, 99, 100
　individualism, 58–9
　Platonic theory of the soul, 69–70
　statism, 53, 55, 56
indeterminate conjunction, *165*
individualism of the soul, 58–9
inorganic non-living bodies *see simulacra*
iuncta (join; connection), 72

James, William, 75, 76
joy before death, 48

Kant, Immanuel, 64–5, 70
katastematic pleasures, 3, 24, 56
kinetic ethics *see* ethics: of motion
kinetic pleasures, 3, 4, 37
kinetic theory of memory, 114–15
kinetic theory of mind, 64–83, *74*
　critique of harmonic reason, 68–71
　critique of pure emotion, 71–7
　material conditions of reason, 64–8
　soul as weaving, 77–82
kinophobia (fear of motion), 44, 51, 55, 119
knowledge, 98, 176
　and dreams, 195–8
　ecstatic, 31
　nature, 89, 149–51, 179–80, 184
　oracular, 181–2, 184, 198
　performative, 31
　poetic, 31, 149, 151, 195
　scientific, 173
　transformative, 31

labouring classes, 54, 55, 58
labrys (double-sided soul), 137
language, 90, 148–51, 181–6
Leto, 131–3, *134*
libido (desires), 199–200, 201–4
life, 65
   collective ethical life [*pietas evertere*], 58–60, 116, 120, 134–5
   and death, 97–100, 112, 120, 192
   hatred of, 57
   as process, 122–3
   as property, 120–2
light, 17, 153, 159–60, 172, 173
   speed of, 165
light waves, *155*
liquid desire, 48–9
love, 200–4, 208
Lucrèce: Archéologie d'un classique européen (Vesperini), 212
Lucretian ethics, 3–6; *see also* ethics of motion

Mars, 53, 201
Marx, Karl
   capitalism, 7
   decay, 86
   'The Difference Between the Democritean and Epicurean Philosophy of Nature', 211, 213
   Georg W.F. Hegel, 178
   philosophy, 38, 39, 40n
   primitive accumulation, 54, 55–6
   private property, 123
Massumi, Brian, 75, 76
material conditions, 60–1
   of reason, 64–8
material ecology, 147, 159–64
material soul, 86
material unconscious, 191–208
   desires [*libido*], 199–200
   feminine desire, 204–5
   knowledge and dreams, 195–8
   love, 200–4
   maternal seeds, 205–7
   nature's mind, 193–5
   Semele and Dionysus, 207–8
   utilitarianism, 191–3
materialism
   mask of, 50–2

   metaphysical, 60
   transcendental, 60–1
materialist ethics, 21–2
materialist physics, 57–8
maternal seeds, 205–7
mathematics, 174–5
matter, 9
   ethical indeterminacy of, 87–90
   fear of matter (hylephobia), 44, 55
   flows of, 38, 89, 99, 117, *118*, 136, 162, 170
   folded, 86–7
   swerving, 18, 46, 95, 124, 153, 154
   see also corpora
Matter and Memory (Bergson), 174
Memmius, 19, 40n, 56
memory, 114–15, 196, 197
mental tranquillity, 71
Merleau-Ponty, Maurice, 172
metallurgy, 30
metaphysical materialism, 60
metaphysics, 159
methodological axes, 8–10
migrant nature, 107–8
mind, 37
   affect, 186–8
   dualism, 169–70
   fault of, 175–8
   fear of death (necrophobia), 48
   life and death, 97–8
   materiality, 86
   of nature, 193–5
   as part of a woven vessel [*calathus*], 101–4
   scatology of spirit, 106–7
   Spinoza's theory of, 75–6
   utilitarianism, 191–2
   see also kinetic theory of mind; soul
Minoan, 41n
Minoan 'snake goddess', *105*
Minoan stone bull's head, *29*
mobility, 1, 55; *see also* immobility
moral duty, 5
morality, 49, 57
motion, 1
   death, 46–8
   ethics of, 2–3, 61–2, 107, 125, 131–2, 134: *calathus* (woven vessel), 116–20, *118*; *see also* pedetic ethics

fear of motion (kinophobia), 44, 51, 55, 119
  ontology of, 45–6, 124–5, 131, 154
  see also movement; swerving
Mount Olympus, 35, 36
movement, 18, 65
  death, 100–4
  desire, 19–20
  emotion, 73, 75
  see also motion; swerving

natura rerum (nature of things), 175–6, 198, 201
nature, 32
  emotion, 161
  energetic expenditure, 48
  geological ethics, 36
  hatred of, 58
  imagination, 187
  kinetic iteration, 60
  knowledge, 89, 149–51, 179–80, 184
  language, 184, 185, 186
  as mathematical process, 174–5
  as matter in motion, 45, 46, 90–1
  migrant, 107–8
  mind of, 193–5
nature of things [*natura rerum*], 175–6, 198, 201
necroethics, 128
necrophobia (fear of death), 6, 7, 44, 46–7, 115, 192–3
  collective ethics, 58–60
  harmonic theory of the soul, 68, 69–70
  hatred of the body, 57–8
  liquid desire, 48–9
  mask of materialism, 50–2
  practical ethics, 49–50
  primary consequences, 123
  primitive accumulation, 54–6
  statism, 52–3
  statues, 56
  Tantalus, 128
necropolitics, 113, 120
neoliberal capitalism, 6
nervous system, 72, 77, 82
neuroscience, 194, 195–6, 196–7
nexus (tying or binding together), 72
Nietzsche, Friedrich, 49, 57, 213–14
Nietzsche and Philosophy (Deleuze), 212

nominis (name; knowledge), 88
non-living bodies *see simulacra*

objects, 159, 181; *see also* things
observation, 173–4
Odysseus, 88, 102
Odysseus and Penelope (Tischbein), 103
Odyssey (Homer), 24, 35, 36, 88, 101–3, 126–7, 132, 133, 140
Olympus, 35, 36
omnino (everything; entirely), 88
ontology, 89
  and ethics, 90–1
  historical, 8
  of motion, 45–6, 124–5, 131, 154
opes (property; wealth), 53
optics, 153
oracular knowledge, 181–2, 184, 198
othering, 121
Ouroboros, *104*
ownership *see* property

Pan and Daphnis, *183*
path of truth, 18
pedesis, 22, 25, 32–3, 95–6, 124, 136, 155, 195
pedetic ethics, 20–35, 124–8
  bees, 30–3
  goats, 24–30
  swallows, 21, 22–4
Penelope, 102, *103*
perception, 169, 174, 175, 179, 183, 188; *see also* sensation; vision
perceptual illusions, 177
performative knowledge, 31
performative speech-acts, 170–1
Persephone, 102
perversion, 58
Phaedo (Plato), 68–9
Philodemus, 18, 40n
philosophy, 38, 39, 40n
photons, 153, 154
physics, 57–8, 153, 173
pietas evertere (collective ethical life), 58–60, 116, 120, 134–5
Planck, Max, 153
Planck's constant, 153, 165, 167n
Plato, 68, 103, 141, 195, 196, 200
Platonic theory of the soul, 69–70, 78, 84n

pleasure / pleasures, 5, 19, 81, 116, 192, 193
  collective ways of pleasurable life [*commoda vitae*], 17
  katastematic, 3, 24, 56
  kinetic, 3, 4, 37
Plutarch, 95, 194
Pluto, 126, 128
poetic knowledge, 31, 149, 151, 195
poetry
  as act of weaving, 78–80, 81–2, 176
  epic poetic tradition, 18, 52
  libido, 201, 202
  nature, 184
  Philodemus, 40n
  Rainer Maria Rilke, 50
  sounds, 171
political power, 52, 54–6
Polyphemus, 102–3
poppy goddess, *79*
poppyseeds, 78
portenta (to stretch; to draw), 184
power, 52, 54–6
practical ethics, 49–50
primitive accumulation, 54–6
primordia (first-threads), 9, 87, 157, 165
process ethics, 123, 152–3
processes, 89, 91, 100, 157–8
property, 53, 120–3
psyché (breath, life, thought), 65–6, 70
Pythagorean mathematical ratios, 69

quantum field theory, 194
quantum gravity, 165–6, 195
quantum physics, 154, 173
quantum theory, 213

radiation, 153–4
ratios, 69
reason, 149
  critique of atomic reason, 78–82
  critique of harmonic reason, 68–71
  material conditions of, 64–8
  see also critique of kinetic reason
reasoning, twisted, 169, 178–9
relationality, 136
religion, 15–17, 40n
reproduction, 200, 205–7
Rhea and the infant Jupiter, *27*

Rilke, Rainer Maria, 50
river of death, 50, 126

Sarcophagus of Agia Triada, *67*
satyrs, 25, 26
scarcity, 7
scatology of spirit, 104–7
scepticism, 178–80
Science journal, 93
scientific knowledge, 149
seeds, maternal, 205–7
Semele, 207–8
sensation, 38, 65, 170, 179, 180, 182
  hatred of, 57
  as reciprocal process, 171–4
  see also perception; *simulacra*
senses, 175–7
  diffractive harmony, 180–1
  evolutionary origins, 193
sensuous vision, 37–9
Serres, Michel, 98, 212, 213
sex, 32, 33, 200, 202, 206
sexual reproduction, 200, 205–7
Silenus, 26, 69
silver drachma, *80*
Simmias, 68–9
simulacra, 147–8, 178
  form, 174
  language, 181–2
  material ecology and environmental affect, 159–64
  process ethics, 152–3
  processes, 157–8
  space-time, 164–6
  swerving, 158–9
  theory of, 153–6
simulacral ethics, 152–3, 156, 166
Sisyphus, 136, 137, 139–41, *139*
slaves, 55, 121
sleep, 196–7
snakes, 104
Socrates, 69–70, 128
song, 24, 28, 30, 33
soul, 37, 65, 66
  affective theory of emotion, 72
  collective ethics, 137, 139
  death, 96–7, 97–100
  discordant harmony, 70–1
  harmonic theory, 68–9
  individualism, 58–9

Index   223

kinetic theory of mind, *74*
materiality, 86
as part of a woven vessel [*calathus*], 101–4, 117
Platonic theory, 69–70, 78, 84n
scatology of spirit, 104–7
weaving, 77–82, 86: fourth nature, 85, 87–9, 91, *92*
see also mind
sound, 171, 181
space, 164
  chora (space made through movement), 25, 132–3, 159
space-time, 164–6
speed of light, 165
Spinoza, Benedictus, 44, 75–6, 95
spirit, scatology of, 104–7
spring, birth of, 35–7
springtime, 22
stasis, 24, 51, 56, 177–8
statism, 52–3
and primitive accumulation, 54–6
statues, 56
status, 56
Stimula, 207
substances, 89
suicide, 119, 142n
superstition, 40n
swallows, 21, 22–4
swans, 21
swerving, 155, 194, 212, 213
  corpora, 158–9
  matter, 18, 46, 95, 124, 153, 154

Tantalus, 124–8, *129*, *130*, 203
Tartara (river of death), 50
theatre, 160
theory of mind, Benedictus Spinoza, 75–6; *see also* kinetic theory of mind
thermodynamic ethics, 93–6, 121–2
thermodynamics of emotion, 92–3
things, 157
  flow of, 170–1
  nature of [*natura rerum*], 175–6, 198, 201
  see also objects
thought, 38
Tityos, 130–1, 133–5, *134*, *135*
Tomkins, Silvan, 75

Tong, David, 95
tranquillity, 71, 94
transcendent values, 4–8, 16, 61, 62
transcendental idealism, 60
transcendental materialism, 60–1
transformation, 181
transformative knowledge, 31
translation, 9–10
truth, 18, 19, 38
twisted reasoning, 169, 178–9
Tyche, 125

University of Colorado, 93
usufruct [*usu*] (use; practice; employ), 122
utilitarianism, 5, 191–3

values, 81, 113
  anti-value, 113–14
  immanent, 60
  transcendent, 4–8, 16, 61, 62
Venus, 4, 38, 53, 199, 201, 202, 205
vertere, 10
Vesperini, Pierre, 212
Virgil, 33
virtues, 4–5
virtus (ethical strength), 125
vision, 37–9, 172–3; *see also* eyes
vitalism, 103–4, 107, 108, 110n, 213
voluntas (will), 74, 193–4, 199, 200, 204
voluptas (desire) *see* desire

walking, 18, 108, 195
wealth [*opes*], 53
weaving, 45–6
  and dying, 96–7
  Leto, 132–3
  poetry, 78–0, 81–2, 176
  scatology of spirit, 106–7
  sensation, 182
  simulacra, 152–3, 158, 161–4
  soul, 77–82, 86: fourth nature, 85, 87–9, 91, *92*
  woven vessel [*calathus*], 101–4, *102*, 141–2: Fors Fortuna, 126; kinetic ethics, 116–20, *118*
will [*voluntas*], 74, 193–4, 199, 200, 204
wisdom, 22–3, 33
women, 21–2, 54, 55, 58, 121, 133, 156
  feminine desire, 204–5, 207–8
  maternal seeds, 205–7

Woolf, Virginia, 47
working classes, 54, 55, 58
wound of love, 53, 200–4
woven vessel [*calathus*], 101–4, *102*, 141–2
    Fors Fortuna, 126
    kinetic ethics, 116–20, *118*

Zeus, 21, 24, 25–6, 28, 33, 126, 207

EU representative:
Easy Access System Europe
Mustamäe tee 50, 10621 Tallinn, Estonia
Gpsr.requests@easproject.com

www.ingramcontent.com/pod-product-compliance
Lightning Source LLC
Chambersburg PA
CBHW071113160426
43196CB00013B/2556